# URBAN AFFAIRS

*Best Wishes*
*Elaine Viets*

# URBAN AFFAIRS
## Elaine Viets

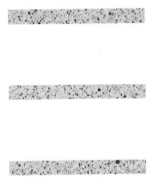

*Tales from the Heart of the City*

*The Patrice Press / St. Louis, Missouri*

Library of Congress
Cataloging-In-Publication Data

Viets, Elaine, 1950-
    Urban affairs: tales from the heart of the city / Elaine Viets.
    p.    cm.
    ISBN 0-935284-65-6: $17.95
    1. Saint Louis (Mo.)—Social life and customs—Anecdotes.
I. Title.
F474.S25V54 1988
977.8'66—dc19                                                    88-39857
                                                                      CIP


The Patrice Press
1701 S. Eighth Street
St. Louis MO 63104

Printed in the United States of America

To my beloved Don H. Crinklaw, who helped me with this book,
To W.A.K., who listened,
And to Alana Perez, the world's best agent.

# Acknowledgments

I wish to thank . . .

Paul Dickson, author of ''Family Words,'' who urged me to put together this book.

Don Crinklaw, my husband, who lets me steal his jokes.

Alana Perez, my long-suffering agent.

David Lipman, managing editor of the *St. Louis Post-Dispatch,* for his help and advice.

The late William C. Fogarty, who copyedited many of these columns. His sharp eyes are much missed.

Dick Richmond, Mike Gold and Ann DeLarye-Gold, who gave me valuable advice.

The Olympia Broadcasting Networks.

Glen E. Holt, executive director, Anne Watts, access and information services, and the staff of the St. Louis Public Library for their help, research and great ideas. They are fun to work with.

And the people this book owes its look to:

Artist R. J. Shay,

Michael Feher of Feher Photography,

Photographer Tony Schanuel,

Michael Kilfoy of Kilfoy Design Associates,

Jacque Hicks, cover photo cosmetic stylist, The Delcia Agency,

Donald G. Young, cover photo hair stylist.

Thanks also to my always reliable sources: Janet Smith, Rich Hinds and my City Hall, police and other sources who must remain anonymous.

And finally, to my readers, who call me with ideas, questions and critiques.

# Contents

# URBAN AFFAIRS

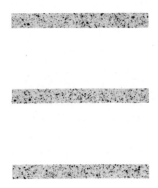

## *Why I Live in the City*

I was born in the city. What I remember best about it were the sounds of my neighborhood: The siren song of the police cars. The sharp quick "Hot Tamales!" cry of the Tamale Man. And the high-pitched, churchlike chant of the newspaper sellers as their carts rumbled down the street on Saturday night: "Post Pay-pers."

Then one day the sirens got a little louder. There was a police shootout on my street and a stray bullet went through my parents' window.

The neighborhood was going bad. There was tension, uneasiness and frightening encounters. And no one knew how to fight it. All you could do was take your kids and move to a safer place.

And so my parents, like so many others in the '50s, moved to the suburbs and to silence. I did not hear the police sirens any more. Not in a nice neighborhood. I didn't hear the chant of the paper sellers, either. We bought the paper after church on Sunday. We got our tamales in the cold quiet of the frozen food case at the supermarket.

Everything was quiet. Even the drone of the lawn mower on Saturday morning.

To my parents' generation, the city was for old people and criminals. When we drove through a dilapidated city neighborhood, they warned us to "Lock your doors." And asked us, "Aren't you glad you don't live in a place like that?"

We lived in a fresh new subdivision in a white house with black shutters. We had a barbecue grill and a station wagon. We had the good life.

If you asked me, it was a little too good. The suburbs didn't have alleys, or taverns on the corner, or strippers like Evelyn West. I still remember her ads in the newspaper: "Evelyn West, the biggest and the best, and her $50,000 treasure chest—insured by Lloyd's of London."

I could hardly wait to grow up and get insured.

I could hardly wait to grow up and go back to the sounds of the city. I missed the neighborhood. I missed the shops where the owners would gossip with you, and complain about business. I missed being able to walk to the library and my friends' houses. In the suburbs everything was miles away, and you were dependent on the bus or the parental taxi service. Both were cranky and unreliable.

I moved back to the city in 1974. I bought a rundown two-family flat and tried to renovate it. The family did not approve.

"It took us three generations to get out of the slums, and you're back in," thundered one relative.

But I wasn't slumming. I was living on the South Side, the old German neighborhood where my grandparents once lived. Its faults are the same as its virtues: The people are hard-working, hardheaded and independent. That's what you say when you like them. Otherwise, they're stodgy, stubborn workaholics.

They make Garrison Keillor's Lake Wobegon look like a zingy little commune in Marin County, California. And the South Siders are real. You couldn't make them up.

Almost every big city, and most small ones, has its own South Side. Chicago has a version. So does Boston. See if you recognize them in your area.

They live in neat brick bungalows with small scraps of green lawn. All the concrete steps are painted gray, all the trim is painted forest green, and everything else that doesn't move is painted white.

And every inch is cleaned. South Siders are fanatically neat. Their friends call them Scrubby Dutch. So do their enemies.

There's a woman on my street who gets up early every morning to pick the leaves that fell on her lawn during the night. She uses a scissors to cut any grass blades that grow too tall between mowings.

Her grass is Zoysia, the official grass of the South Side. It is the closest thing in nature to AstroTurf.

The only acceptable lawn ornaments are concrete birdbaths and Blessed Virgins, concrete swans painted white and filled with petunias or geraniums, and yellow plastic sunflowers that twirl in the wind.

And yet, underneath this sameness is a wonderful wacky streak. Only the South Side has the man who concreted his lawn and painted it green. And the woman who wires silk roses on a dead bush. There's the bar that sells brain sandwiches so tasty, people come from Alaska and Florida when they get a craving.

My neighborhood has splendid alleys with sneaky stray cats. The back fences are draped with red climber roses. There are sunflowers growing back by the ashpits. Old houses with strange curlicues along the roofs.

And paper sellers, with their old wooden carts of Sunday papers.

The first night I moved back to the city, I heard the rumble of their metal-wheeled carts. Then the paper boy's high, sad chant came drifting down the street like an enchanted fog: "Post PAY-per."

I knew I was home again.

## St. Louis Has Brains, a Celebration of the City Sandwich

Brain sandwiches are the haute cuisine of the tavern: brown and crispy on the outside, white and cloud-soft on the inside. They are the saloon souffle, the only art form that combines grease with class.

Brains are a city specialty. Our brains should be a source of civic pride. Yet, St. Louis faces a brain drain so severe, we could wind up without a single sandwich.

People think they're disgusting. "Ugh," they say, as if they'd been invited to an autopsy. "Who eats brains?"

These are the same folks who let snails slither down their throats and smear fish eggs on crackers. They refuse to complain when their steak tartare turns up raw.

Judy N. believes brains suffer from a public relations problem. "Other squishy foods have euphemisms," Judy said. "No one says, 'Could I offer you a little ox stomach?' It's tripe. Sushi is raw fish. Sweetbreads are such a successful euphemism, nobody knows what they are."

OK, brains are disgusting. But that shouldn't be a drawback. Most things in a tavern are disgusting, including the customers.

Good brains are also difficult to make. They're not fast food. They take at least 20 minutes to cook. Brains are difficult to store. And brain preparation resembles a freshman biology experiment.

Take my word for it. The secret is NOT in the sauce.

"It's the cleaning," said a brain cook. "This is time-consuming, but it must be done well if you want the best results. Brains have a thin membrane which must be thoroughly removed. We soak the brains in ice-

cold salt water . . .''

Further details belong in a horror story. Here's a little hint you'll never find in Heloise: Blood left in the brain gives it an unpleasant bitter taste.

But brains have a certain wacky style. No other food could have created a scene like this. A gentleman ordered brains in the Majestic Restaurant.

''I'll see if we still have them,'' said the waitress. She yelled back to the kitchen, ''Hey, you got any brains?''

''If I did,'' said the cook, ''would I be working here?''

But the restaurants and taverns that sell brains are dying out. So I asked readers to locate places that served the succulent sandwiches. They sent in some 31 names. Each said their favorite had ''The Best Brains in St. Louis.''

This was a serious claim. Something only other brain lovers could determine. So I asked them to vote for their favorites. The five restaurants with the most votes became the finalists for the *St. Louis Post-Dispatch* Best Brains in St. Louis Contest.

At last, an election based on brains.

My favorite finalist was Grandma Dot's, a restaurant across the river from St. Louis in Belleville, Ill. At first I was worried about Grandma. She sent a sweet little note offering to fix me ''two brain sandwiches, bread pudding and coffee.'' It was signed ''Yours in Christ.''

I figured Grandma didn't have a chance. But on the last day of the balloting, two fat envelopes arrived stuffed with 40 ballots. Each one was a vote for Grandma Dot's. The return address on the envelopes was the same as Grandma's place. Grandma had the instincts of a Chicago precinct captain.

Grandma became one of our four finalists. The others were Pirone's Bar & Deli, Ferguson's Pub, The Haven, and Dieckmeyer's Restaurant & Tavern.

Now that we had the finalists, we needed the judges. Our Brain Trust included the cigar-chomping Alderman Red Villa. Villa is known for his brains—he's the smartest politician in St. Louis.

For good taste, nobody could beat our second judge, Vince Bommarito. Vince runs Tony's, the city's classiest restaurant.

The third judge was Michael Porter, the Bard of the Brain. Michael thrilled readers with his explanation for why he ate brains.

''We like to smother them in ketchup, then eat them with a knife and fork,'' he wrote. ''And that, my sweet, makes us hoosiers feel like gentlemen.''

The judges' historic decision needed the proper setting. We got it. The Old Courthouse, in the shadow of the Gateway Arch. The National Park Service let us put our brains under their dome.

Judge Bommarito insisted on professional tasting standards. He wanted "cool water and French bread to clear the palate."

"If Vince is doing that, I better give up my cigars," said Alderman Villa.

Judge Michael Porter washed his taste buds with suds.

Under the stern stone pillars on the Courthouse's west portico, the cooks were frying their hearts out.

Grandma's, the sole Illinois finalist, fried quietly in the corner. The four South Side saloons brought their own cheering sections and plenty of beer.

Loyalist Kim Besserman admired the symmetry of Pirone's sandwiches. "See the slight sprazzling of pepper," he said, lifting the rye to reveal the crusty brain. "The single pickle is set in the center like a jewel."

It was a good brain. Judge Bommarito's notes said it was juicy. But it still wasn't the best.

Billie Ferguson of Ferguson's Pub served an awesome brain the size of an ostrich egg.

"What do you serve it on?" asked a spectator. "Wheels?"

"You mash it," said Billie, firmly.

The judges gave her big brain third place. Now it was tense. The two remaining finalists were a South Side tavern, and Grandma Dot's, the Belleville brainmaker. What if the best brains in St. Louis were in Illinois?

The judges declared Grandma's brains were crispy. And worthy of second place.

And the winner? It was O. "Bud" Dieckmeyer of Dieckmeyer's Restaurant & Tavern.

Dieckmeyer's bar is in Alderman Villa's ward, but Villa said there was nothing funny about his decision.

"Sure, I've eaten Bud Dieckmeyer's brains," he said. "But I've also seen them cleaned."

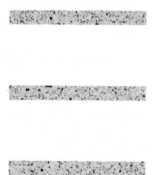

*The old Route 66 runs through the tiny Village of Marlborough, on the edge of St. Louis. Marlborough is famous for two things: a landmark speedtrap and the Coral Court Motel. It's the ultimate no-tell motel. Each glazed brick unit had its own private garage.*

*But when it looked like the Coral Court might be torn down for a shopping center, St. Louis finally discovered this Art Deco motel has other architectural features. So started one of America's strangest preservation efforts.*

## (1) Saving the Coral Court—A Modest Proposal

Zoe Mance thinks it'll be a sin if we don't save a St. Louis County landmark.

She's talking about the Coral Court Motel on Watson Road, the old Route 66. It's an amazing place. It's been around since 1941, but few St. Louisans admit they've been there. Now the motel may be razed for a shopping center.

"The buildings are of great architectural significance," Zoe said. "It's our duty to save them. Won't you help?"

How?

"We could picket," she said.

How?

"We could wear paper bags over our heads," she said.

"There's got to be some way to save the Coral Court Motel. I'm not ashamed to stand up for it."

Have you ever stayed there?

"No," she said. "Now I may never get a chance. That's why I want to save it.''

That's the problem with the Coral Court. People who've never been there would like to save it. Many people who have would like to forget it.

This is the only modern landmark I know of that has to be saved by people who haven't seen the inside.

''I've never seen a whale,'' Zoe said, ''but it's my duty to save them, too.''

The Coral Court is usually associated more with wolves than whales.

Just how much the Coral Court deserves its racy reputation is unknown. After all, the eminently respectable St. Louis Convention & Visitors Commission has it on its list of recommended motels.

The director of the Landmarks Association of St. Louis calls it ''one of the most significant pieces of roadside architecture in the country.''

Scholars rarely mention the architectural feature that made the motel such a success—the private garages.

The glazed-tile buildings are nifty—but only if they remain a motel with the same appearance of absolute respectability.

Otherwise, what could we do with them? Make them into a museum and give tours? Make them into a shopping mall like Union Station? What would you sell there?

You can take your kid to Union Station and say, ''This old building is important to our family history, dear. A long time ago in World War II, this was a real train station. This is where your grandpa said good-bye to your grandma. He was a soldier. He said if he came back from the war, he would marry grandma.''

''Gee,'' says the kid, ''was it an exciting wedding?''

''Yes. Grandma was beautiful. Grandpa wore his uniform. Ask Grandma to show you the photographs.''

Now, imagine driving by the Coral Court and saying, ''This building is important to our family history, dear. Your grandpa Mark took your grandma Sandy here after the prom. He promised to marry her.''

''Gee,'' says the kid, ''was it an exciting wedding?''

''Yes. Especially since great-grandpa had a shotgun.''

That may be the Coral Court's fascination for those who've never been there. Zoe, the woman who wants to save the Coral Court, graduated from a ritzy local girls' school. She says just knowing about the motel used to be the height of teen-age sophistication.

''I was always so jealous when the other girls at school pulled out their Coral Court matches,'' she said.

''I've never even seen the place up close. The closest I ever came was when I was bike riding with a friend. We rode by, and I said some day I'd like to go there.''

What happened?

"He moved out of town.

"We save everything these days," Zoe said, "whales, seals, wolves. We can save part of a city fantasy. I've thought of something that would get the message across better than picket lines."

What?

"Snappy T-shirts," she said. "I have the slogan: 'The Coral Court Motel—Love It and Leave It.' "

## (2) Keeping the Coral Court: Parking and Recreation

We've finally found a man to lead the fight for the Coral Court Motel.

He's Esley Hamilton, an architectural historian with the St. Louis County Department of Parks and Recreation.

Don't laugh. Parking and recreation is what the Coral Court is all about.

"Actually, I've never been to the Coral Court," he said.

That's what they all say. The motel has been around since 1941, but few St. Louisans admit they've been there.

"That's not true," said Esley. "When we had our petition, one guy asked if it was OK if he signed it—he'd only been there four times.

"Another man said his life would have been very different without the Coral Court."

How?

"He said he'd have to use those depressing downtown hotels."

So what's a nice guy like Esley doing saving a place like that?

"It's a fine example of Art Deco architecture. It was in the county's book on historic St. Louis area buildings. When I heard it was endangered, I felt it should be saved."

For awhile, it looked like the Coral Court would be razed for a shopping center. Now the motel manager says, "We're here. We're staying. We're going to be here for quite awhile."

But Esley says that's not enough of a guarantee.

"The owner is in her 70s. The motel could be sold—and lost—at any time."

Esley wrote a lyrical description of the Coral Court in an architectural journal.

"The green of the lawns, the black of the pavement, the yellow and red of the tiles, and the blue of the sky combine to lift the spirits of any lover of America's commercial archeology," he wrote.

And, speaking of lovers, Esley wrote about an important Coral Court feature.

"The absence of visible parked cars enhanced the surreal beauty of the Coral Court and set it in sharp contrast to the average motel.

"The garages also assured the guests anonymity. It is this feature of the motel that contributed to its local reputation, which seemed to induce whispered asides and loud laughter."

Nobody laughed when the president of the Society for Commercial Archeology, based at the Smithsonian in Washington, saw the Coral Court in September.

He was impressed. "He said the Coral Court was a most unusual example of the motor court. Most are single cottages of flimsy frame construction. The society will have a consultant come to St. Louis to make recommendations on how to help the motel's business."

Perhaps the consultant knows about the Coral Court's innovative packages.

Any place can have a weekend package. But the Coral Court makes every hour count. It has an hourly package: four hours for $20—a $10 saving on its daily rate.

Keeping the motel financially healthy is one way to help save it, Esley said.

"We'd like to see the village of Marlborough make the Coral Court a local landmark. Only that will protect it if the owners want to tear it down.

"Right now, the village seems reluctant to get involved. I believe their legal counsel has advised them if they made the Coral Court a landmark, the owner might sue them. Marlborough can't afford a lawsuit, even if it wins. It only has 2,000 people.

"An organization called the Volunteer Lawyers and Accountants for the Arts is looking for an attorney to advise us.

"And if we had some money, we might be able to help with legal fees— or help the motel owners."

The Coral Court has a nifty fund-raiser, thanks to OTR Enterprises, a Maplewood T-shirt firm. Susie Hochman won't give you the shirt off her back, but she'll sell you one.

Their $12.95 Coral Court Preservation Society T-shirt is a hot number. One dollar goes to the preservation fund.

"Tell everyone it comes in a plain brown wrapper," Susie said.

## *(3) Deer Season: There's Wild Life in Bars*

"Deer season is coming," said my friend. "I can hardly wait."

That's odd. My friend is not the outdoor type. He thinks he's roughing it when a hotel has no room service. Wild life is what happens in a riverfront tavern after midnight.

So why the sudden enthusiasm for deer season?

"Deer season is when thousands of husbands and boyfriends take off to the woods," he explained. "At the same time, some of their wives and girlfriends head for the singles bars and discos.

"I've never gone deer hunting with the boys, so I can't tell you what goes on in the woods. But the hunting here at home is great."

These women are mad. They feel deserted. They want revenge.

Not to mention a little fun.

A 27-year-old St. Louis bachelor claims "after the night before New Year's Eve, deer season is the best time for picking up women. They're looking desperately for someone, anyone. Even you.

"I found out about deer season two years ago," he said. "I noticed the neighborhood disco was wall-to-wall women, all new faces. Most were in their late 20s, early 30s. I recognized some of them as women who'd dropped out of the singles scene 5 or 6 years ago to get married. I saw a girl from the office who regularly brushed guys off with, 'Sorry, I'm married,' go home with a guy. I couldn't believe it.

"Then somebody told me it was deer season.

"The women only come out during the firearms season in mid-November—not the bowhunters season. You'll never see them any other time."

His motto is: Be prepared.

Our man has even written Ten Rules for Deer Season. He says these rules are useful year-round, but especially in November. He also says if I use his name, he can't go back to these places again.

RULE 1: Never arrive at the bar or disco before 11:30 p.m.

"Women like to play 'I know I can do better than you,' " he said. "You may hit it off with a woman early, but she'll drift off—usually after you've invested several drinks. She's looking for someone richer, thinner and better-looking.

"Later in the evening, when she realizes Mel Gibson isn't drinking in St. Louis, she plays another game: 'You may not be my type, but I guess you'll do.' Therefore, never arrive early. All you'll miss is a chance to blow a bundle. If you can't score from 11:30 to 1 a.m., get out of the game."

RULE 2: Get a seat by the bar.

"This old rule is known to anyone who's done hustling outside the VFW hall. Take a seat by the bar in a crowded spot. The women will have to lean over you to order a drink.

"If you spot someone particularly attractive, offer her your seat. This technique should be reserved for your best shot.

"If you can't get a seat by the bar (and you probably won't) stand in the path to the ladies' room. They all head there sooner or later."

NOTE: The ideal spot is a seat at the bar near the ladies' room.

RULE 3: Act like a regular.

"During deer season, you have a lot of women who are unsure of themselves. They've been out of the singles scene for awhile. If you act like a regular, she will feel more comfortable. This will allow you to lead the conversation in your direction."

RULE 4a: If you dance, you're in luck. All married women like to dance. All husbands hate to.

4b: If you can't dance, say, "I can't believe they're still doing that dance. I wouldn't want to embarrass you by doing something that's so out of style."

RULE 5: Always keep eggs and bacon in your refrigerator.

"The first thing every woman wants after the bars close is breakfast," our man says. "I don't know why, but they do. First take her to the most crowded place you know, like Denny's. Obviously, it will be tomorrow morning before you can get a table. Mention that you have eggs and bacon at home and you'll be glad to make her breakfast. No woman can resist the thought of a man cooking her breakfast.

"Once you get there, if she's really hungry, make her fix it herself."

RULE 6: Always keep your house or apartment clean. But not spotless. If it's immaculate, she'll think you're married.

RULE 7: Women seem to respond favorably to guys who read books.

"Almost every woman I bring to my apartment asks about my books. Books can be obtained by the box for two or three dollars at any garage sale. I prefer law books, medical books and thick, outdated government manuals. Atlases stack up real nice."

RULE 8: Keep your high school or college yearbook near the sofa.

"Every woman will be tempted to leaf through the pages, and ask

questions like, 'Is that really you?' You will need to take a seat beside
her to answer. Then lead the subject around to things like how long her
husband or boyfriend will be out of town. You are now poised for any
number of activities."

RULE 9: Remove your phone number from your telephone.
"This will keep her from writing it down. You won't see her after deer
season. The last thing you want is your phone number falling out of
her purse two weeks later when her husband, the steelworker, asks for
a quarter.
"Also, avoid business cards during deer season."

RULE 10: Never, never ever go to her home.
"Try to find all possible excuses, like allergies to dogs, kids or baby-
sitters. You never know when her husband will step on a rusty beer can
and come home for a tetanus shot.
"Remember, hunters carry guns."

## (4) The St. Louis Stop

"St. Louis stop signs look just like the ones at home," said a visitor
from Portland, Ore. "So I stopped just like at home. You know, foot
on the brake. Speedometer at zero.
"Everybody started honking. Some people got mad and drove around
me. One guy accused me of trying to cause an accident."
The visitor says St. Louis stops are not like any other city's. This is
not a criticism. He finds the local custom exhilarating.
"A well-executed St. Louis stop takes skill and nerve," he said. "There's
an element of danger. It's like the running of the bulls at Pamplona.
Sometimes I find a seat near an intersection, just to watch the St. Louis
stop in action. The cars approach the intersection, slow down to a cruis-
ing speed of 15, look around, and roll through the stop at about 10 miles
an hour. Meanwhile, the other cars are doing the same thing. Nobody
ever makes a full stop to check out the intersection. They get through

on a kind of radar.

"It's beautiful," he said, his voice full of admiration. "It's poetry in motion.

"The St. Louis stop is one of the city's trademarks. It's known coast to coast. Ask anyone."

I did. Local drivers agreed with everything the Portland visitor said. They bragged of being ticketed from New York to Texas for their St. Louis stops.

A St. Louis man was nabbed by the Illinois highway patrol with this line, "You're across the river now, friend. We stop over here."

A Texas Ranger told a St. Louis woman, "Down here, ma'am, when the sign says stop, it means stop. You're not in St. Louis." The cad gave her a ticket.

"They also got me in Cleveland," she said. "Evidently, stop means stop up there, too."

A taxi driver reports that when he lived in Syracuse, N.Y., and worked for a fried-chicken franchise, he was ticketed for rolling through a stop. "This ain't St. Louis, pal," the cop told him.

"I never heard of a St. Louis stop then. Four years later I ended up here driving a cab."

And rolling through stop signs.

"It's all those four-way stops here," he said. "In any other city there would be traffic lights at those intersections. St. Louisans are coping the best they can."

Another St. Louisan noticed some peculiar behavior in the nearby town of Fenton. "All those people were taking an abnormally long time at a stop sign," he said. "They were just sitting there, stopped dead. I thought maybe it was something people did in small towns. Then I realized they weren't making St. Louis stops."

A former policeman confessed, "I never gave a ticket unless the drivers failed to pause at a stop sign. They couldn't stop completely—they'd get hit in the rear. This worked OK until the drivers left the city. Then they got nailed with a ticket."

Presented with this body of evidence, our man from Portland conceded there might be even more to St. Louis driving than the stop.

"I've noticed St. Louisans run red lights, too. They always look first to see if anyone is around. Then they run it. St. Louisans also tailgate a lot. And they speed. So maybe it's just not the St. Louis stop. Maybe there's a whole St. Louis driving style."

A Washington University professor has the best story. When he first arrived in St. Louis, he made a full stop.

And a police car hit him in the rear.

# (5) Uncle Sam's Reefer Madness

Psssst! Wanna know how to grow marijuana? You can get the straight dope from the government.

Way back in 1915, the Department of Agriculture published a handy little booklet telling you how to grow marijuana for profit. It's Farmers' Bulletin 663, "Drug Plants Under Cultivation."

The booklet offer practical advice for growing digitalis, cannabis and other nifty plants.

The 73-year-old booklet was revised in 1920 and "slightly revised" in 1935. That's when somebody took out the cannabis section. That's also about the same time as the movie "Reefer Madness."

The Agriculture Department discontinued the booklet soon after. But you can still check it out through an inter-library loan from your local library. It's part of a bound collection of Farmers' Bulletins on hoof-and-mouth disease, cutworms and cultivating the native persimmon.

Reading "Drug Plants Under Cultivation" is like falling down the rabbit hole. Some of these circa 1915 statements can still raise howls.

The book begins innocently:

"Interest in the possibility of deriving profit from the growing of drug plants is increasing yearly."

Nobody's going to argue with that.

But then the booklet becomes bolder:

"Annually, large sums of money are expended for crude drugs imported from other countries," it said. "As a means of guaranteeing the future supply of crude drugs and of lessening the dependence on importations, attention is now being turned to the cultivation of drugs plants with a view to increasing domestic production."

The 50-page pamphlet is curiously unbiased. There are no statistics, studies or moral arguments for or against cannabis. In fact, it never says what the stuff is for.

"The plants mentioned were selected for discussion because information regarding their cultivation is in constant demand," the book said.

Also true.

There's more good advice: A cannabis grower "cannot give too much attention to the problem of securing a satisfactory market for his product. . . in many situations, the local marketing of crude drugs in quantities will not be possible."

This is Uncle Sam's advice for the marijuana farmer: Plant cannabis seeds in the spring. Two or three pounds of seed per acre should give a good crop. Manure is the recommended fertilizer. Use about 20 tons per acre.

Another handy hint: Harvest the cannabis flowers with a cranberry scoop. It's quicker.

Today, the Agriculture Department is very straightforward about Farmers' Bulletin 663. It's there in the department library. The department is happy to answer any questions. A department scientist said cannabis had about the same uses in 1915 as it does now. Some people liked to smoke it. Others thought it made a dandy tea. Sort of like sassafras.

"There's a lot of interesting folklore about cannabis," the scientist said. "It's believed to be an excellent insect repellent. In parts of Afghanistan farmers alternate a row of cannabis with a row of cotton, to keep away bugs. Some people use it in salads. In the Far East, you see cannabis floating in chicken soup."

No wonder it cures colds.

The biggest use, of course, was for rope. "Cannabis was grown commercially, especially in South Carolina and Virginia, for fiber," the scientist said. That's rope fiber, not cereal.

The booklet's agricultural advice is OK, but outdated, he said. Cannabis cultivation has improved in 73 years.

There are other changes, too. The booklet reports top price for cannabis in 1920 was 35 cents a pound.

## (6) UP-Manship: The Elevator Game

Do you know about the Elevator Game?

The object of the game is to embarrass a fellow traveler in a crowded elevator. The game takes timing and skill. Not to mention nerve.

The Elevator Game is played at noontime, when the elevators are crowded and the audience is alert. Early morning is a bust. The spectators are so soundly asleep they have to be awakened at their floor. In the evening they're all so anxious to leave they aren't listening.

The Elevator Game calls for subtlety. Here, listen to this:

A man and a woman are waiting for the office elevator. It's lunchtime and the elevator is packed. As the doors open she turns to her companion and says, "Edward, the rabbit test is not infallible."

Then there is silence. A very loud silence. At least until he gets off.

You have just witnessed the Elevator Game.

OK, so it isn't nice. Nobody said it was. But it sure is fun.

Alfred Hitchcock played the Elevator Game. There's a story that Hitchcock turned to an unsuspecting companion in a crowded elevator with, "I never thought there would be so much blood."

Then he got off.

The Elevator Game is celebrated in literature and film. In "Barefoot in the Park," the bride follows her husband to the crowded hotel elevator. He's dressed for the office, she's in a pajama top. She says, "Call me any time you're in New York, Mr. Wilson."

One victim was so acutely embarrassed by the Elevator Game he got off at the wrong floor. Once he took really drastic measures and WALKED down five flights of stairs. I wish I could report he looks fit from all this walking, but he doesn't. He's clearly showing signs of strain.

"I don't like elevators," he said. "I have this fear of people listening in on my conversations. Even innocent conversations sound dumb on an elevator.

"It seems to me that proper elevator etiquette demands you plaster yourself to the nearest wall, stare at the lighted numbers and shut up. Then those people started tormenting me."

The tormentors say they are driven to playing the Elevator Game. They are irresistibly drawn toward their victim, like a snowball toward a top hat.

"It's his attitude," said a woman gamester. "He asks for it. We'll be having a conversation and then he gets on an elevator. Suddenly he turns into a pillar of salt. He just freezes and stares straight ahead. We aren't discussing anything the whole world couldn't hear. But he clams up.

"So I'll turn to him and say, 'Just TRY Preparation H.' "

This gamester says it's not what you say, it's how you say it. "Deliver the line just as the elevator doors open. Look surprised, then give a quick downward thrust to the head, and study your feet for the rest of the ride."

She warns it's tacky to say anything gross, like, "Your fly is unzipped."

"The simplest lines are the best. If your victim is a man, you can nail him with one word. Just stand next to him, and as the doors open, deliver an emphatic, 'NO!' "

Then ride down in silence.


## (7) Meals on Wheels

"I eat breakfast as I drive to work," said the man at the next desk. "Eggs, bacon, mug of milk. Today I had honeydew melon with lime.

"Think of it," he said. "There I was with the only honeydew melon on Highway 40."

Probably the only lime, too.

Over on the Forest Park Parkway, another office worker was eating an onion, cheese and tomato omelet. And steering with his knees. He finished his omelet, plugged in his electric razor and shaved.

This is his regular morning routine. The omelet is a diner carry-out— truly fast food.

Most people think morning traffic just sits there, clogging the highway. Maybe the cars aren't moving. But inside there's plenty of activity.

Women are picking curlers out of their hair. Guys are tying ties, buttoning shirts, tying shoes. And everybody's eating breakfast.

In case you come to work on the parkway, the guy who eats his omelet while he steers with his knees drives a green VW. His name is Bob.

"First I eat my omelet, two slices of whole-wheat toast and coffee," Bob said. "Then I shave. You have to eat before you shave, or you get whiskers in your eggs."

I'm told some people do nothing but drive to work. But I couldn't track any down. Incidentally, folks like Bob don't consider themselves traffic hazards—they're just practical. "I spend 1 hour and 15 minutes each morning on the road," he said. "I hate to waste that time."

And Bob has to eat while he drives. He gets funny looks when he's stopped.

"My omelet and coffee are hot and people stare at the steam rising from my lap. Besides, every time some chick looks over at me, I've got eggs falling out of my mouth."

Jan puts on her makeup at stoplights. She has it timed. "There are only five stoplights between my house and work," she said. "Stop One, I find the tube in my purse. Stop Two, I take off the top. Stop Three, I put lipstick on my upper lip. Stop Four, I get the lower lip. Stop Five, I blot and check.

"On extreme mornings I also put on shoes and scarves or wriggle into jackets and vests. But I always wear a skirt and blouse to the car."

Pat puts on shoes, belts, jewelry and nail polish while she drives. But mostly she goes fishing.

Fishing?

"I've got five kids, ages 7 through 15," Pat said. "In the morning four people are after the hair dryer. Three want the curling iron. Everybody's after the one shower and 30 gallons of hot water. I'm getting dressed in the middle of this. The only time I can go fishing is in the car.

"After you dry a big load in the dryer, some of the smaller pieces stick to your clothes. In the car I detect the odd lumps in my dress, and fish out the stray socks and underwear."

I asked another worker if she dressed on the way to work. She only laughed.

Why? Too organized?
"No," she said. "I take the bus."


## (8) What Soda Goes With Red Meat?

Soda drinking is an art, but it's not that difficult to master. There are rules, of course. Colas go best with red meat, white soda with chicken and fish. But these are just guidelines. Even the worst soda snobs will not sneer at those who order 7-Up with their steak. Drink what you like is the cardinal rule.

Consider the story of the gentleman host. He planned to serve an unpretentious little cola that complemented the beef admirably. The gentleman was nervous. The cola, Shasta, was a discount brand he found at the grocery. Worse yet, it was served in cans. All the soft-drink guides recommended Pepsi and Coke with red meat, and they would never—never—think of serving canned soda at anything but a picnic. But our host was sure that his audacity would amuse his guests.

"Don't be discouraged from indulging your personal preferences by snobbish glances or sly asides," wrote soda connoisseur Earl Shorris.

Shorris is the last word in soda snobbery. Also the first. And possibly the only. About 1970, Shorris wrote THE soda-drinking article for a California newspaper.

Shorris is the soda connoisseur who originally advised people on red-meat, white-meat soda selection. Shorris has only one firm rule, and it's based on common sense.

"Don't serve colas or other dark sodas with fish," he wrote. "The flavor of the fish tends to sour them on the palate." He recommended 7-Up or any other lemon-lime soft drink.

With the dark colas comes the question of dryness. Pepsi is considered drier than Coke. A few soda snobs claim that diet soda is driest of all. This sparks a real controversy. True soda aficionados complain that diet soda tastes of chemicals and doesn't even attract flies. Diet soda's defenders say they know what flies like. They'll stick with diet soda, thank you.

Ginger ale and bitter lemon are two light dry sodas. They go with just about anything, though red meats tend to overpower them. These two sodas are also good with mild cheeses. The more robust Roqueforts and sharp Cheddars need the dark sodas.

Cream soda is the traditional choice for corned beef and pastrami. Experienced soda tasters also recommend celery tonic. The master, Shorris, claims "for the adventurous, an egg cream may be most pleasing."

Dr. Pepper is primarily a pasta and pizza soda. Particularly cold pizza the morning after.

Root beer is excellent with Coney Islands, but only if the Coney Island is heaped with chopped raw onion.

Orange soda goes well with duck.

Sweet sodas—grape, strawberry, chocolate—are dessert sodas or aperitifs, although some soda drinkers say they are an excellent accompaniment to potato chips and peanuts.

Soda should always be served cold, but connoisseurs argue endlessly on how it should be chilled. Some prefer ice cubes, others say that crushed or shaved ice cools the soda more thoroughly. A few, no doubt influenced by the English, think soda should be served chilled but with no ice at all. These soda drinkers also recommend decanting the soda for three minutes before serving.

## (9) A Rehabbed House Is Not a Home

Yesterday I heard a story that gladdened my heart: A home decorating editor for a fancy women's magazine, after years of advocating the joys of restoring an old house, began believing what she wrote. The editor and her husband bought an old barn—or was it a grist mill?—in upstate New York, and completely restored the thing. The project took three years, and when it was over, the couple was bankrupt and divorced, and she had a nervous breakdown . . .

Lately, there seem to be enough local and national articles advocating restoration to fill Lafayette Square. This is a most admirable cause. Old houses are lovely places, some of the last available homes with character. But the stories about them have the sameness of a row of suburban tract houses. They go something like this:

**(1) The Sting:** The couple, usually young, attractive and of a slightly liberal bent (she is a sociology major, he works for Legal Aid) find an enchanting Victorian (Georgian on the East Coast) home in what is delicately called a transitional neighborhood. This means the home buyers are one step ahead of the guys with the headache ball, who are about to transform the house into that St. Louis architectural specialty, the parking lot.

The couple sees that the house has problems. There are no walls in the second-floor rear bedroom, and a home will have to be found for the family of rats in the basement. But the house has great Potential.

The couple buys it for practically nothing.

**(2) The Horror Stories:** This is the part everyone loves to read.

"We hauled out 25 truckloads of trash before we could begin the restoration work . . ."

Or, "It took two months to strip the paint off the mahogany mantel. Imagine, they used white deck paint on that old beauty."

The stories of stripping, scraping, rewiring and refinishing are endless, for there are endless things to go wrong with an old house. Finally, after several exciting months, our couple triumphs.

**(3) The Happy Ending:** This is celebrated in Before and After pictures with the couple beaming like proud parents in the midst of their redecorated splendor. There is no doubt this story has a happy ending.

The story, alas, is a delightful bit of whimsy. No one ever lives happily ever after in an old house. That's a fairy tale. Living in an old house is more like a soap opera.

Don't get me wrong. I like my old house. I wouldn't live in any other kind. But people ought to be warned before they go into restoration wide-eyed and innocent. These are the best years of your life. You may not want to spend them with a hammer and crowbar, knocking out plaster.

There is nothing romantic about it. Restoration is filthy, expensive, difficult work. It is a strain on your marriage, your temper and your bank account.

Here is a set of restoration tips you'll never see anywhere else.

**(1) Restoration is never finished.**

When you've restored all the rooms, the roof will begin to leak. When you've repaired the roof, the basement will develop odd cracks. The porch will sag.

Old houses just don't have antique woodwork and old-fashioned stained glass. They also have antique plumbing and old-fashioned wiring. The problem with an old house is that it is old. Remember that old car you used to own? After you fixed the starter, the brakes went out. Then the muffler, and the clutch.

You get the point. An old house is an expensive hobby. You may want a cheaper pastime—a stable of race horses, maybe, or a yacht.

**(2) Know your handyman.**

If it will make you feel better, check the Better Business Bureau to see if he's reputable. But that's not the big question. Instead, ask yourself: Do you feel you could spend the rest of your life with this man? Because the handyman is going to move in with you for six months to two years. You'll see him more often than your spouse.

Make sure your relationship is based on mutual trust and understanding. If the first thing he says is, "We'll get rid of this old molding.

Too much dusting. And lower those 10-foot ceilings—that's wasted space,''
he is not the man for you.

The relationship will be a lot like the early stages of love. You will
spend long hours waiting for his call, hoping that today maybe he will
come see you. Handymen are an independent breed, who work when
they feel like it.

NOTE: There is a movement in restoration circles to do all the work
yourself. This way lies madness. It's much cheaper to have a professional
do it right the first time. Ask yourself, could an amateur do your job
at the office?

**(3) Nothing in an old house is ever standard size.**

Especially the windows. Those large gracious windows that you so
admired are at least a foot longer than any regular-sized windows. This
means storm windows and curtains will have to be custom-made. These
usually cost more than the house. Some home owners partially solve this
problem by not having any curtains. One of these houses is on our block.
The lights are always on at night, revealing four neat, orderly rooms
and no people. I think the inhabitants go from room to room by crawl-
ing on all fours.

**(4) Every project becomes complicated.**

The company stopped making parts for your plumbing in 1927. Your
wiring has been obsolete for at least 50 years. You can spend all Saturday in the hardware stores looking for one part.

Nasty surprises are everywhere. There is that one wall you judged
basically sound, except the wallpaper had to be removed. Strip off the
wallpaper and you will discover that's what was holding up the wall. There
will be a four-day delay while you buy and put up wallboard.

**(5) House restoration can cause severe personality changes:**

(a) You become boring.

While your friends are analyzing foreign affairs or the latest movie,
you discuss the merits of a new wood stripper, and where to buy wallboard
for 79 cents a sheet cheaper.

Because no one else understands your problems so well, old house
owners tend to seek the company of other old house owners, where they
can discuss the fine points of restoration to their hearts' content.

(b) You become strange.

When you enter a house, you no longer admire the stained glass, woodwork and antique light fixtures. What really awes you are flawless,
uncracked ceilings. Showers, garbage disposals and other modern con-
veniences are endlessly fascinating.

You'd do anything to have them. Except move to a new house.

# (10) It's Never Too Late for Romance

He was an old bachelor—white- haired, round-faced, with crinkly lines around his eyes. He wore a polka-dot bow tie, and looked the perfect sugar daddy, except he was a smidge too old. About 70.

He had a story about "a couple of South Side girls." From the way he said it, I knew the "girls" were about the same age as the old boy.

"The girls have a pipeline to a local funeral home," he said. "A funeral home employee tips them off when a likely gentleman becomes a widower. The girls tip off their single friends.

"One dresses in black, and goes to the funeral home to check him out. If he looks pretty good, she introduces herself, and says something like, 'You don't know me, but I was a dear friend of your wife. I know you're too confused to talk right now about Martha and how much she meant to you. But next week, when things are quiet and you're all alone, why don't you come to dinner at my home? I'll fix you a good home-cooked meal.'

"The widower usually accepts. At dinner, Martha is too painful a subject to bring up. But he does notice what a fine cook the woman is, and how clean and comfy everything looks."

He may also notice that he's low on shirts and socks, and has been eating scrambled eggs three nights in a row. If the widower's not a total drag, she'll invite him back for dinner again.

And again. And again. And again.

"The girls tell me if you can get a new widower in the first three months, he's nabbed," he said. "Then you either have a husband or a permanent roommate, depending on your Social Security."

But there was something about this story that bothered me. Why would a woman knock herself out for the privilege of cooking and cleaning for some old geezer?

These women are at least 65 or older. They've had a lifetime of heavy-duty housework. I couldn't see them signing up for more.

The answer came from an unexpected quarter. George was complaining about his 71-year-old father.

"The old goat," he said. "He's worse than my teen-age son. His wife died three years ago. She was hardly buried before his phone began ringing off the hook. He used to go out every night. He finally moved in with a nice widow of 67. That's stopped the phone calls."

Why are women so anxious to cook for an old goat?

George rolled his eyes. "Cook? Dummy! Those dinners are just a blind. The women are looking for lovers. If it doesn't interfere with their Social Security they may even marry the guy. The dinners are a chance to check the old boys out and see if everything is in working order before they sign up for anything permanent.''

I think this story will give young people new hope for their declining years. In about 40 years, if you recognize me hanging around the local funeral parlor, remember: My intentions are strictly dishonorable.

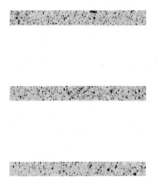

## (11) Wanted: The Man Who Paved His Lawn And Painted It Green

The man is a St. Louis legend. A symbol of the eternal struggle with the elements. He returns every summer, when spring's bright promise has shriveled. In other words, when the local lawns are shot.

He is the Man Who Paved His Lawn And Painted It Green.

The story is always the same: "Some guy in our neighborhood got tired of mowing his lawn. One day he had the whole thing concreted and painted green. I don't know the exact address, but here's the street. You can't miss him."

But I do. I can't find him anywhere.

I first heard about the man three years ago. He was supposed to be "just off Virginia, near I-55."

He wasn't. He's also been reported on the North Side, in South County and once, in wealthy Ladue, paving over a dazzling expanse of lawn. This summer, the first sighting came in late July. He was back on the South Side.

"Lives over on Delor," the caller said. "He was fed up with his lawn. They look so scraggly this year. One day he had the whole thing concreted . . ."

I drove 12 miles up and down Delor Street. Not a trace.

But I understood the admiration in the caller's voice. The Man Who Paved His Lawn And Painted It Green is a folk hero, an urban rebel. Many home owners dream of destroying their lawns, but few have the courage for such a bold stroke.

There's nothing more useless than a lawn. You can't eat it, you can't put it in a vase and it doesn't give shade. It just gets green, and by August, it won't even do that.

Lawn care takes the choicest times of summer—the soft, warm evenings and the sunny afternoons are spent mowing and watering it. And after you've given the grass the best years of your life, does it try to make something of itself, and comfort you in your old age? Nope. It rises up next spring and expects the same treatment.

Think of it. The Man Who Paved His Lawn now lives a life of ease. A fresh coat of green paint in the spring, a little tuckpointing or whatever you do to concrete, and his time is his own.

At first I thought the man would be a leftover hippie, who refused to sell out to the system. But he'd probably cover his lawn with something organic. Only the older generation would be brave enough to use something so solidly unnatural.

I imagine him as about 70, a crusty old guy with a heart and several teeth of gold. He lives an otherwise ordinary life. Occasionally you'll find him pottering about on his patch of concrete, thumping it with his cane, then setting out a comfortable lawn chair to watch his neighbors cut their grass.

As August grinds on, long and dull as a Sunday visit, he is an inspiration. But we need to know: Is he a real person or an urban legend?

I'd like to institute an all-out search for the Man Who Paved His Lawn And Painted It Green. If you know of his whereabouts, or better yet, if you are the man, write to me.

Include all the details, including the complete address. I need concrete evidence.

## (12) Found: The Man Who Paved His Lawn

The search is over. We've found the Man Who Paved His Lawn And Painted It Green.

In fact, we found two men and a woman.

And, just as I suspected, people who pave their lawns are remarkably cheerful. Those studies are right: Grass does have a harmful effect on the personality.

A lawn is expensive and useless. Since you probably already have a brother-in-law, you don't need a lawn, too. But most of us don't have the courage to quit. Here are a few who did. We honor them today:

Joseph Lightfoot has moved to New Madrid, Mo.—"good fishing and good hunting." But in the summer of 1960 he lived on the South Side, and he paved his front lawn. It's still there.

"I did it out of necessity," Lightfoot said. "The lawn is steep. Nothing would grow there. I seeded it. I sodded it. I dug up everything and made a rock garden. It all looked terrible.

"I got disgusted and decided to concrete it.

"My wife said, 'No you don't.'

"I said, 'Half this house is mine. I'm going to concrete my half of the yard. I'll leave your half grass. You can mow it.' "

Lightfoot researched the subject. He discovered that three inches was the proper concrete thickness. He put wire mesh underneath to prevent cracking. He mixed green dye in the top layer. "Otherwise, I'd have to paint it every two or three years.

"My neighbors would tease me, but on Saturday morning, as soon as I heard the mowers start up, I'd get me a cup of coffee and go tease them. Everyone thought I was crazy. But my lawn looked fine, and I wasn't wearing out any mowers."

Two months later, Mrs. Lightfoot asked Joseph to concrete her half of the lawn.

Richard Sippel owns the house now. "The lawn has cracks in it," Sippel said. "My wife would like me to tear it out and put in railroad ties and moss. Looks just fine to me."

Anthony LoRusso's lawn on The Hill, the Italian section of St. Louis, is meticulously neat. It's paved and painted deep green, and surrounded by a concrete fence painted battleship gray.

The small, terraced lawn with the three-foot drop-off gave Anthony trouble. "I used to be golf course superintendent at Forest Park," he said. "I had my fill of grass. My 'lawn' is thick—four inches. A drain pipe washed out the dirt underneath. I had to have clay pumped under the concrete, and holes drilled in it. Cost me $400. It still beats cutting the grass."

And what about Doris Radford? Her concrete lawn came with the place.

Mrs. Radford's South St. Louis ranch house has a steeply pitched front yard. Roughly two-thirds is paved and painted forest green.

Does she have any problems?

"Yes, they didn't go far enough," Mrs. Radford said. "I wish they had concreted the whole lawn. I don't know who did it, but I'm very satisfied. All I do is paint it every three years. Looks nice and neat. I'm tempted to call a concrete company and have them finish the job. "

Harry Mellman still regrets he settled for less.

"Over 20 years ago, to cover an unwieldy and unsightly back lawn, I planned a complete concrete back yard. However, Mrs. Mellman and the concrete man insisted on a large but 'reasonable' size for a patio. And the concrete is painted green, which shows up best when wet.

"PS: What remained of the back yard is still unwieldy and unsightly."


## (13) Vintage Guide to Wine Tasting

Here are the latest words in wine tasting, straight from New York. They are: Road tar.

That's from Terry Robards, the New York Times wine critic who said three California zinfandels tasted like road tar. He meant that as a compliment. See for yourself.

(1) Buehler Vineyards zinfandel 1979.

"Very dark, almost black color. Spicy bouquet, with suggestion of melting road tar. Peppery and spicy in flavor. "

(2) Calera zinfandel 1977.

"Dark color. Perfumey bouquet of truffles and hot road tar. Crisp and dry on the palate."

(3) Carneros Creek zinfandel 1978.

"Very dark color. Sweet bouquet of lilacs and road tar. Full-bodied and very rich in flavor."

Notice the delicate variations in road tar. There's "melting" tar and "hot" tar. When teamed with lilacs, the road tar is strong enough to stand on its own.

The hot tar and truffles combination is puzzling. I've never tasted road tar, but I have tried truffles. Personally, I think the delicate bouquet of the truffles would be overpowered by the road tar.

There's also the question of what kind of road tar. Country road tar is thicker and more full-bodied than city tar. Hot road tar is thin, but has a pungent bouquet.

Sometimes, Robards' criticism is so personal, you'd think he was at an encounter group instead of a wine tasting.

In the same road-tar column, he says seven zinfandels were "not seriously flawed, but simply lacked strong character and in some cases, seemed somewhat hollow or boring. "

Another zinfandel was: "Young, immature and slightly awkward, but should improve." Sounds like a teen-age boyfriend.

A local wine lover says this is "cocktail party criticism." But he was

dark, thin and sour, with a suggestion of bitterness.

Lilacs, road tar and truffles may be a little vague for wine pros, but they evoke such wonderful moods. The descriptions are awkward, but should improve with age.

Perhaps I can offer the notes from my own wine tasting. They may be used for any wine, domestic or imported. At cocktail parties, they are great for dancing chic to chic.


### A Vintage Guide to Wine Tasting

**The wine was . . .**

Redolent of a summer night at a drive in.

**The wine had . . .**

The bittersweet taste of a $5 raise.

The muddy color of a sale dress.

**The wine was . . .**

Young and awkward, but well-meaning.

Young, smooth and over-produced, like Brooke Shields.

**The wine had . . .**

A spicy bouquet suggesting A-1 Sauce and garlic.

**The wine was . . .**

Dark and subtle, with a hint of paint thinner.

Like a singles bar—dark and smokey, with a bad aftertaste.

**The wine had . . .**

A light, airy bouquet of lilacs and roses, set off with ivy. The bridesmaids carried orchids trimmed with ferns, and the mother of the bride wore a wrist corsage.

A grassy bouquet of Zoysia, bluegrass and AstroTurf.

Finally, here's an all-purpose phrase by another New Yorker. It will introduce any wine, especially one you're not sure of:

"A modest wine, but I'm sure you'll be amused by its pretensions."


# (14) James Bond Got His Job Through the Want Ads

Want to be a spy? Check the help wanted ads.

The CIA advertises in major newspapers, including the Post-Dispatch. If you think the new James Bond is a wimp, wait till you see the CIA in there along with companies looking for machinists and management trainees.

The ad features a bold eagle silhouette and this headline: "Central Intelligence Agency. We're looking for men and women with special talent."

The word "spy" is never mentioned. But you get the point: "The primary task of the Central Intelligence Agency is to gather information to help protect the international interests of the United States. We seek men and women with special talents and skills to begin careers with the select group that helps gather this information by living and travelling abroad."

Another recruiting ad says the CIA "offers adventure, travel, pay, benefits, security and positions of responsibility . . ."

Applicants must have "U. S. citizenship, a college degree, language skills or aptitude, and an interest in international affairs."

Also, no sense of irony.

The CIA is "an equal opportunity affirmative action employer."

Its motto is chilling: "It's time for us to know more about each other."

But when I did want to know more, the CIA was distressingly cheerful and straightforward.

"Oh, sure, we run those ads all the time," said the chipper man at the local CIA office. "We're just another big company. Like IBM. Let me give you someone in Washington who can answer your questions better."

That was Dale Peterson, spokesman for the CIA public affairs office. He said they were not quite like any other big company, "but we do run recruitment ads. We've always advertised for technical people. But in the last few years we've started running these ads for our operations abroad. Most people would say we're looking for spies. They will be primarily collecting information and recruiting people who have access to information.

"One reason we started advertising is that the draft is no longer in effect. The kind of person we wanted—who had a degree, language skills, some experience of the world, possibly military training—was often found on campus.

"Now, we literally have to advertise for them."

I thought the CIA would be more cloak and dagger.

"If we want to get the people we need, we have to say what we do."

Next I talked with the Midwest personnel representative in Chicago, James Jones. "That's my name," he said. "You can quote me."

Jones wouldn't answer some questions. But he sounded like a businessman worried about the competition. "I don't think I can tell you how many people answer the ads," he said. "My area is recruiting.

"It's a myth to think we're looking for people who are going over there with guns. This is a career-training program for people interested in becoming intelligence officers. We're looking for people with drive, who like to work with foreign people. We are seeking the type of person who would go into multi-national companies or foreign service."

The ads are also a good way to pick up "a variety of other people, including economists, engineers, computer scientists and linguists."

The languages are no surprise: Middle Eastern, Oriental, Eastern European and Russian.

If I had any more questions, Jones said, "call me at my office. I'm in the phone book under CIA."

One more thing. If anyone wants to send a resume, it's Personnel Representative, PO Box 2144, Chicago, Ill. 60690.

"Thanks," he said. "It's good advertising."


## (15) The Woman Who Crashed the Academy Awards

If I'm somewhere I don't belong, I get caught. Attendants ask for my ticket, guards escort me to the door, receptionists tell me I did NOT have an appointment. So Alice Joy Brown has a special fascination for me.

Alice crashed the 1980 Academy Awards ceremony. Except crashed isn't the right word. Alice strolled in the front door and picked a nice center seat. Then she went to the dinner afterward. Alice says the food was delicious, but not worth $200.

I'd feel better if Alice looked especially fierce or commanding. But Alice has a small, soft voice and big, round glasses. She looks much younger than 26. Alice is not even a starstruck fan. She's a university English major who wouldn't be caught dead with a movie magazine.

"I didn't do this on my own," Alice said in that silvery voice. "Becky Gross, my best friend in L. A., has been sneaking into movie star parties since she was 17. She's 31 now. It's her hobby.

"Becky always takes three or four friends with her. I was out in L. A. for a while, and I went to the Awards. While the guard was checking someone else's ticket, we walked in. Becky said if you act like you belong, everyone will believe it."

How do you act like you belong to that group?

"Act snobby," Alice said. "Don't talk to anyone. Everyone's so caught up in themselves, they won't notice you."

What if someone asks what you're doing there?

"Becky just says, 'I know someone.' If they ask who, she says, 'I promised not to tell.' "

Alice didn't even wear an evening gown. She had a short peach cocktail dress she bought on sale.

Alice and Becky waited about 15 minutes until everyone was seated, then found empty seats. Alice said Oscar host Johnny Carson is much funnier in person. After the ceremony, they picked up two more of Becky's friends, Bonnie and Pearl, and headed for the Awards dinner at the Beverly Hilton. This time, they didn't go in the front door.

"Bonnie showed me the kitchen entrance," Alice said. "She'd been there before. The people are so busy, they don't notice you. I went straight on through to the dining room. Bonnie got stopped. I didn't look back (another of Becky's rules). None of the others got in. I was on my own, and scared.

"I pretended I couldn't find my mother, who had our reserved tickets. I was really searching for an empty seat. Finally I sat down at Table 138 in the back.

"The only people who questioned me were two New York girls at the table. They said, 'What are YOU doing here?' I asked what THEY were doing there. That shut them up. Everyone else was very nice. A waiter winked at me.

"I noticed Sally Field, George Hamilton and Johnny Carson at the front tables, but there really weren't that many movie stars. Becky said movie stars are working people who get up early, and they don't attend many parties."

The menu, in best Hollywood French, included lobster with "Louie dressing," roast duck, snow peas, "panache of wild rice," strawberries and coffee.

Then Alice produced the final convincing detail—she had tea and dessert with a British TV producer who thought Hollywood was unbelievably crass.

"He was anxious to get back to London the next day. He said that L. A. was too much for him.

"The powder room had great gossip. No movie stars there, either, but plenty of rich girls. One said, 'His dad owned a dress factory. He promised to give me a blouse if I'd go out with him.'

"After dinner there was dancing in the ballroom and a small disco. The only star on the disco floor was Robert Hays from the TV show 'Angie.' I also danced with an Argentine romantic, a married producer and a handsome hunk." The hunk asked her home, but Alice said no thanks.

The party was over early, about 1 o'clock. Alice packed up her souvenir bottles of perfume and cognac. She had a wonderful time. That year she and Becky crashed even bigger and better parties.

This year Alice will watch the Academy Awards on TV, like the rest of us. She hasn't crashed a party since she returned to St. Louis. Not even the city's biggest society event.

"Nothing seems worthwhile," she said. "Even the Veiled Prophet Ball looks so boring."

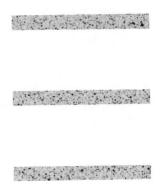

## (16) Scrooge Was Right

Scrooge has always gotten a bad rap, and until recently, I thought he deserved it. But after rereading "A Christmas Carol," I see the man was maligned. Scrooge is a victim of press persecution.

The writer, Charles Dickens, was biased. He introduced Scrooge as "a squeezing, wrenching, grasping, clutching, covetous old sinner." After that, you're naturally going to think the worst.

But examine Scrooge's statements on their own, and you'll see what a farsighted man he was. These are the famous "Bah, humbug!" lines that got him in such trouble:

"What's Christmas-time to you but a time for paying bills without money; a time for finding yourself a year older, and not an hour richer, a time for balancing your books and having every item in 'em through a round dozen of months presented dead against you?

"If I had my will, every idiot who goes about with 'Merry Christmas' on his lips should be boiled with his own pudding, and buried with a stake of holly through his heart!"

Scrooge sounds like a regular consumer advocate, warning against the dangers of buying on credit. That last sentence may be a little strong, but the man was tired.

You can guess what it's been like at his office for the last month. It's impossible to get any work done. Everyone Scrooge calls is either on vacation till January, or gone for the rest of the day. At 1 o'clock.

The aluminum Christmas tree on the office file cabinet falls over every time he shuts a drawer. Even worse, Scrooge's co-workers have been bringing in Christmas food.

Like most successful executives, Scrooge is weight-conscious. But to be polite he's had "just a taste" of fruitcake, eggnog, gingerbread cookies, homemade wine, peppermint sticks and a punch made from lime sherbet, Jell-O and cheap champagne.

Dickens starts his story on Christmas Eve, and doesn't take any of this into account. Scrooge is still trying to get some work done, when his smarmy nephew barges into the office. He wants Scrooge to come to Christmas dinner. Scrooge refuses. The kids will be tearing around the place, and a bachelor is simply not used to the noise.

The nephew cannot take a hint. He keeps asking. At last, Scrooge says flat out that he can't stand the nephew's wife.

OK, it was a little abrupt. But it marks Scrooge as a man of rare courage. Most of us can't stand our in-laws. But we go to one dreary dinner after another, and keep our mouths shut.

Scrooge has also been criticized for refusing to subscribe to a charity. Let's look at that scene again. Two "portly gentlemen" show up at the office. Scrooge probably figures this well-fed pair is from one of those charities that squanders the donations on executive limousines and banquets for the volunteers.

"What shall I put you down for?" the one says, boldly.

"Nothing!" says Scrooge, just as bold. The charity looks like an operation that deducts your donation from your paycheck, and your promotion is based on how much you give.

Finally, poor Scrooge goes home and tries to get some rest. Instead, the spirits of Christmas drag him around all night, telling him to shape up and enjoy himself.

Scrooge wakes up scared. He sends the usual turkey bonus to his employee, Cratchit, then goes to his nephew's place for dinner, after he's already told them no. Naturally, they had to find him a place.

According to Dickens, Scrooge is a reformed man.

If you ask me, he sold out.

## (17) Guide to Society Stories

Every fall, society launches a dazzling array of parties. And reporters launch a dazzling array of adjectives.

Elegant. Distinguished. Charming. Lavish.

In New York and Cleveland, St. Louis and Seattle, the story is always the same: The hostess is gracious. The decorations are lavish. The crowd is elegant.

And yet, a nagging doubt remains. Are all society parties created equal? Of course not. For "society" substitute "charity benefit" and give many of the folks there your sincerest sympathy. They have been blackmailed into attending this function by friends, relatives and colleagues.

Some would be happier at home in front of the TV. Others would rather be at a real society party, where there are no reporters. Remember the last good party you went to? Would you want someone lurking about taking notes?

There is a way to decode a society story. We present a glossary of terms, useful anywhere in the country. Notice how many apply to women. Men are usually ancillary to society, except as escorts.

### AMERICAN GUIDE TO SOCIETY PARTIES

A STUNNING GOWN: Low-cut. Also, too tight.

BUBBLY: Brainless, flighty. See also, Enthusiastic.

COLORFUL: A gentleman who appears in ads for his own business; one who wears gold brocade dinner jackets.

COZY: 400 of the 500 people invited did not show up.

DANCED TILL DAWN: The press went home early.

DANCED TO THE BIG BAND SOUND OF . . . Not a musician under 50.

DEBUTANTE'S DELIGHT: A young man who dances well, is nice to homely girls, writes thank-you notes and lives with his mother. Permanently.

DEBUTANTE'S PARENTS WITH A DOUBLE ADDRESS: Pay attention! This kid's loaded. Must be "Mr. and Mrs. Gotrocks of Ladue and Bar Harbor," not Crestwood and Lake of the Ozarks.

DISTINGUISHED: Hasn't much to say.

DOMESTIC CHAMPAGNE: Cheap. With a plastic cork.

ELEGANT: Ordinary. The usual crowd. Also, boring.

FAMILY AFFAIR: The guest list is positively incestuous.

FAMILY AFFAIR, CATHOLIC: The archbishop is present.

FESTIVE: Drunk.

FINGER FOOD: A skimpy buffet featuring stuffed celery.

FLAMBOYANT: Overdressed. Also, drunk.

FLIRTATIOUS: Falling out of her dress. After all the men.

GRACIOUS: Panting to have her name in the paper.

HEAVILY LADEN BUFFET TABLE: A buffet of mostaccioli, potato salad, cold cuts.

HONORARY CHAIRMAN: Does no work. The committee hopes his/her name will sell tickets.

IMPROMPTU: Disorganized.

INFORMAL: Disorganized. Also, homemade.

INTIMATE: Couldn't sell tickets.

LAVISH: The charity gets zilch.

LEISURELY: Tedious.

LIVELY: Drunk.

MAJESTIC: Fat.

MAJORING IN LIBRARY SCIENCE: A homely debutante.

MAJORING IN LIBRARY SCIENCE AND EXQUISITELY DRESSED: Homely, but very rich.

ORIGINAL: When used to describe food it means, ''I've never seen anything like this. Not on a table, anyway.''

OUTDOORSMAN: Any man who takes off his tie.

QUEENLY: Fat.

REGAL: Stuck up.

ROCK MUSIC: Used to indicate a younger (under 50) crowd. Could mean anything since the jitterbug.

SIMPLE: Cheap. See also, Unpretentious.

SPORTY: Nothing he's wearing matches.

STATUESQUE: Fat.

STILL YOUTHFUL: She looks terribly old. Not to be confused with a gentleman's ''youthful'' companion. That means he's cradle robbing.

STRIKING: Can't believe anyone would dress like that.

TASTEFUL: Stuffy. Probably monogrammed.

TROPICAL: Used for outdoor galas. Means the guests would be more comfortable sailing down the Amazon.

VIVACIOUS: Drunk.

WE'RE HAVING A WONDERFUL TIME: Used to indicate acute ennui.

## (18) The Other Woman

She called herself the Other Woman, just like in the movies. She said, "I want the rat punished."

It sounded like the old story. It wasn't. Maybe we haven't heard them all.

The rat was 45, and "going through midlife crisis. He took up racquetball, jogging and me—all at once.

"He was a salesman, and good-looking. Blue eyes, gray temples, you've seen the type. Our office was one of his accounts. This started eight months ago. I went in with my eyes open. I knew he was married. I didn't want him to leave his wife."

The Other Woman is a 30-year-old executive, pretty, a little plump, but "hardly homewrecker material."

She told her story over lunch, sipping delicately at a bourbon and water.

The wages of sin, she says, are lousy. No roses, candy or shopping sprees at Saks. "He couldn't write those off. I discovered he put our whole affair on his expense account: The little lunches for two, the drinks after work. We met in parking garages, and he even put that on his expense account—under parking.

"He treated his wife even worse. They never did anything deductible."

Besides, he liked some weird stuff. "He said he wanted dinner on the table every night. And he wanted his shirts IRONED.

"It was time to write him off," she said, stripping the bread off her sandwich.

The Other Woman felt guilty. She lost a few pounds and cried. The wife didn't look too happy, either. The only one who was chipper and guilt-free was the husband.

"The rat was getting away with it," she said. "I wouldn't mind if he'd treated me badly and was good to his wife, or vice versa. But both of us? He must think we're saps. It's an insult to women to let him off scot-free."

She crunched down on the last potato chip.

"I blame his wife. All she had to do was look long-suffering for a few days, until he got the point. Then she could have racked up the goodies: A new car. A trip to the Bahamas. A fur coat. At the very least, she should have demanded that he come home on time every night.

"Finally, I went to her house one afternoon to explain things to her."

You told her about the affair?

"No, she knew about that. I told her about the golden opportunity she was missing. I certainly knew how tough it was to get money out of him. I said a divorce was a little drastic, but if she wanted one, I'd even testify for her.''

What happened?

"Nothing. She's going to let him get away with it. There's such a thing as standards, you know. The rat ought to be punished."

She reached for a lemon slice from the pile of garnish, and squeezed it dry. I reached for the check.

"You have an expense account, too," she said. "I know all about those."


## (19) The Sap Rises and Goes to the Country

Every Spring the sap rises, gets into his pickup and heads for the woods.

At least, that's how Don H. sees it. "I don't understand," he said. "If God wanted us to go camping, he wouldn't have given us hotels."

The wilderness is a challenge, Don H. Camping makes people self-reliant.

"How self-reliant is it to sleep in a $159 down-filled bag protected by a $250 nylon tent?

"In the city, people still know how to rough it. There's a guy in my neighborhood who camps out on a park bench. He needs only a newspaper and a bottle of Rosie O'Grady to keep warm. He's tough.

"Campers have grown soft and lazy. They need expensive entertainment. Fiberglas canoes. Trail bikes. Cute little rainbow-colored RVs that cost $15,000.

"City folks are used to simpler pleasures. With a $1.39 deck of cards, I can have a poker game that keeps people entertained for hours. And with a couple of dice I can get . . ."

Raided?

"No, the rent. City folks also know how to live off the land. Last winter I was up a creek: Two days before payday, I was broke and desperate. My checking account was empty. My credit cards gave off steam.

"A camper would have been reduced to eating roots and berries. But I knew how to provide a hearty meal. I foraged for empty soda bottles in the park. Empties are a cash crop. I found enough returnables to buy dinner at White Castle. I even had money left over for Tums."

Must have been rough.

"You have to know where to look. The big parks are picked over by neighborhood kids."

Some people like to go camping to get closer to nature. They want to know the ways of the wilderness. Like: Still water runs deep. Moss

grows only on the north side of the trees.

"I know those," Don H. said. "When a tree has an orange Day-Glo X spraypainted on the trunk, that means the highway department is going to chop it down.

"But few people take time to learn city lore. I know how to find a bottle of good wine on Sunday. And which dry cleaner sews on buttons.

"I know you should avoid bars where off-duty cops drink—but doughnut shops that give free coffee to cops are safe places. They're never held up.

"I know there's no such thing as a happy hour, only a bartender maximizing his cash flow.

"I know how to elude the wily city inspector. How to make a burglar alarm out of sticks and cans.

"I know city folklore. In certain districts, you watch the couples walking together. The rule is: 'Outside, the lady is for sale; inside, the lady's for show.' "

At least you must admit the country has fresh air.

"I don't breathe anything I can't see."


## (20) Cousin Kurt Gets Revenge on His Boss

Like millions of Americans, Cousin Kurt hated his boss.

Unlike them, Kurt did something about it. That got him led out of the place in handcuffs. But he still thinks it was worth it.

Kurt worked at a grocery, and considered himself a model employee. Sure, he had his faults. He filched candy bars, but everybody did that. And one Halloween he showed up dressed as a flasher.

But Kurt says he was as conscientious as any American worker. He's probably right.

Then Kurt crossed a supervisor. The supervisor hinted Kurt should leave. To help him get the point, he transferred Kurt to another store. The employees called it Devil's Island.

"They sent me to the toughest guy they had," Kurt said. "His specialty is firing people. He offered the security people a bonus to catch me. They couldn't. I really cleaned up my act. I didn't even steal a grape."

The strain must have been terrible.

"It was. But I did it just to spite them. I also bought a pocket tape recorder, and kept it on me at all times.

"You couldn't believe how that guy treated his employees. The store was trying to eliminate its full-time help. Part-time people are cheaper.

They get less benefits and vacation time. They're also desperate. They toe the line to work a few hours a week. He'd yell at cashiers until they cried.''

Kurt knew it was time to leave. Besides, he'd landed the job of his dreams: Hot tub salesman.

"But first, I wanted some fun," Kurt said. "The boss was upstairs in his office. I hid my tape recorder in my pocket and said I wanted to talk. I told him he humiliated his employees.

"He said, 'There ain't nothing you can do about it, Kurt.'

"The next day, the boss asked if I'd had my tape recorder with me. I did. I didn't have it on, but he didn't know that. He said he hadn't slept all night. I knew I'd won. He'd lost sleep over me. He said he wanted to hear the tape. I said I'd have to talk to my lawyer. This went on for several days.

"Finally I said, 'Why don't you buy me out?' I had two sick days, a birthday, three weeks' vacation and a week of comp time. He let me have everything but the extra week. It came to $1,350."

On Kurt's last day he picked up his check early and gave it to a friend, along with his car keys and wallet, "in case I got arrested."

"My plan was to throw him in the trash, because that's how he treated people. I took all the sharp objects out of the store dumpster, and brought out my Special Mix. I'd been saving garbage for a week. It was nasty stuff: Old lettuce leaves. Cabbage. A melon. Some tomatoes for color.

"I had to get him down there. He's worried about theft, and comes running if anything unusual turns up in the dumpster. I baited the trap with two 12-packs of beer and unplugged the security camera. Then I called him on the house phone. But someone must have tipped him off. He wouldn't come downstairs.

"So I walked into his office, grabbed him by the collar and said . . . never mind. You couldn't print it, anyway. I tried dragging him down the stairs. He was too heavy to carry far. At the landing I sat on top of him and said, 'How does it feel to be on the bottom?'

"He said, 'Call the cops.'

"Somebody did. A cop showed up and handcuffed me. As he hauled me off, I yelled, 'My cousin writes for the Post-Dispatch!'

"While they decided what to do with me, I told the cop the whole story. He said, 'Hey, everybody has a jerk for a boss. If they all did what you did, I'd never get anything done.'

"The store decided not to press charges. I said goodbye to all my friends. The cop had to escort me, right out to my car."

Then Kurt drove to the other store and threw a blueberry pie at his supervisor.

## (21) How to Tell If Your Neighborhood Is on the Way Up

Don H. returned from a scouting mission, waving a beer bottle and smiling happily. "The neighborhood is on the way up," he said. "Look what I found in the gutter."

A beer bottle?

"That's a HEINEKEN beer bottle," Don H. said. I looked at him dumbly. At least, that's how he thought I looked.

"Heineken and Michelob bottles are signs that a city neighborhood is on its way up," he said. "Rosie O'Grady and half-pints in brown paper bags mean decline."

Don H. is in on the great city gamble: Will my neighborhood make it? Some people look for the obvious: No vacant buildings. Fewer boarded-up windows.

But Don H. reads the city's subtle signs. He has lived on the South Side for 16 years. He is streetwise and cagey. He knows the city like an Indian knows the forest. I tested him anyway. A man is nothing if he cannot be tested.

How do you know the Heineken bottle wasn't tossed out the window by a suburban social worker passing through?

Don H. laughed scornfully. "I checked the newspapers blowing down the street. There were *Wall Street Journals* and a book-and-arts page. When I moved here, it was nothing but *Modern Screen* and the *National Enquirer.* Bad news.

"For weeks, the only motorcycle parked in front of the apartment house has been a little Moped. It's a city law: The more expensive the cycle, the lower the income."

Don H. agreed to tell us some of his city lore. These are his **City Signs of Success.**

**You know your marginal neighborhood will make it when. . .**

The neighborhood restaurant puts up an awning.

The joggers come out. Especially joggers in bright-colored warmup suits.

There are fewer campers and more foreign cars.

The pawn shops move out. (On South Grand, a pawn shop sold out to a florist, a sure sign of success.)

The neighborhood saloon charges $1.50 for draft beer to keep out "undesirables." A few years ago, undesirables were the only customers.

There are more small, yappy dogs in the backyards than Dobermans and German shepherds.

There are Christmas lights and other homey decorations. (This is true only during the holiday season. Christmas lights in the summer are a bad sign. So are curtains hanging out an open window. Especially in winter.)

A survey of bumperstickers turns up more symphony than country music stickers.

The city repairs the pot holes on your street, and puts in streetlights, sidewalks and other capital improvements.

The neighborhood association organizes a house tour and charges for tickets. In bad times, you can't pay people to visit.

The neighbors put in new tennis courts or swimming pools. Points off for horseshoes and corkball games.

And nothing is sold on the street but newspapers.

## *(22) What High School Did You Go to?*

Steve is new to our city. He doesn't understand the local customs.

"When two St. Louisans meet for the first time," he said, "they always ask, 'Where'd you go to school?' Casual-like. They mean high school.

"Why would anyone care? Most of them graduated at least 20 years ago."

You have to understand St. Louis, Steve. You can't say, "Pleased to meet you, Mr. Smith. Does your family have any money? What's your religion? Any social connections?"

In some cities people are conveniently stereotyped by last name or neighborhood. But the best way to put St. Louisans in their place is by their high schools.

A St. Louis businesswoman explains: "If someone went to U. City High about the same time I did (she's 38) I automatically assume: They're Jewish. They went to college, either Yale or Wash U. They were in at least one anti-war demonstration. Maybe it's wrong to type people, but it's an easy shorthand."

Based on interviews with native St. Louisans, here's how we type one another. Our main guide is Mrs. Old Family. The Old Familys all but ran the 1904 World's Fair and started the Art Museum.

Mrs. O. F. warns that her observations are accurate "only if you've been to at least your 10-year reunion. And they're even more accurate if you're older. As for today, Lord knows what's going on."

**Where the Elite Meet:** Mary (or Mary I, only outsiders call it Mary Institute), Burroughs (nobody says John Burroughs), Country Day.

Mary and Country Day used to be thought of as social but dumb. Mary is losing that reputation, Mrs. O.F. says. Burroughs kids are supposed to be the smartest.

"Back in the Dark Ages (before the Pill) the real reason children were sent to private high schools was so they wouldn't have sex," Mrs. O.F. said. "Some, like Mary and Country Day, worked on the theory that this catastrophe could be prevented by sending boys and girls to separate schools.

"Burroughs and its kindergarten-to-sixth feeder school had the daring idea that if boys and girls went to the same school from the sandbox, they'd know each other so well the incest taboo would take hold at the critical stage. You not only knew each other's parents, you knew they'd be hysterical if anything happened. It just wasn't worth it.

"Priory, and before that Chaminade, was the place for well-bred Catholic boys. St. Louis University High varies. Sometimes it's a social zero. Now it's better, partly because moneyed families are moving back to the city and want their boys in a private school."

No, not because they're worried about the kids getting pregnant.

"For Catholic girls, the No. 1 school is Villa Duchesne," Mrs. O.F. said.

**Clayton:** If you must go to a public school, this is it—the Beautiful People of the public-school set, the kids who play tennis and read Kierkegaard.

**Parkway high schools:** Rich suburban. Very new money.

**Hazelwood district:** Like all North County schools, Hazelwood is supposed to be blue collar. It doesn't help that the newer high schools look like factories. But Mrs. O.F. warns that the North County is tricky. There are pockets of old rich and new money. Never assume anything.

**Ladue:** Rich. Highly stratified.

**Kirkwood:** If "Father Knows Best" was set in St. Louis, it would be here.


## (23) Militant Moms

I have a confession to make. Many years ago, when I was very young, I was a child. An extremely small, wet version of a child, known as a baby.

My parents realized I was simply going through a stage. They kept me locked in an attic until I outgrew certain disgusting personal habits. When I was large enough to hold a cocktail glass, I was ready to mingle with society.

Nowadays, many parents are not giving their children the same advantage. They are exhibiting babies at all sorts of unseemly times. The people who see these children have long memories. Fifteen years

later, they will remind Jennifer she used to run around with a pink bow taped to her bald head. Jennifer will never recover from the trauma.

There is a time and a place for parents to display babies. I'd nominate the Arena parking lot at 3 a.m.

I am not advocating that babies be banned. They are useful citizens. Babies give full-time employment to grandparents. Babies give you something to talk about at pointless gatherings.

You: "Nice baby you got there. Looks just like his dad."

Mom: "Yep, they're both bald."

Sensible parents and their offspring are fun. What you have to watch for are the Militant Mothers.

The Militant Mother is easy to spot. She's been through all the '60s and '70s fads. A few years ago, she wanted to Free the Chicago Seven. Now she's a LaLeche League sympathizer.

Militant Moms wear flat sandals, and they use "sharing&caring" as one word. They do not drink, do dope, smoke cigarettes or chew Wrigley's spearmint gum. That would affect their milk.

Next to a Militant Mom, June Lockhart would be arrested for neglect. Moms make their own baby food in the Cuisinart and paint the baby's room with intellectually stimulating graphics. They also bake bread. But Militant Moms scorn advice from their own mothers, who are too middle class.

Militant Pops are even worse. The mothering Militant Pops take "parenting" courses. While a Militant Mom will admire only her own child, a Militant Pop drools over any kid. That way you can congratulate him on his sensitivity.

You don't need to. He's already congratulated himself.

Here is a paradox: Militant Mothers are not glamorous. Babies are.

Princess Di rushed out and got several. Soap stars and other motherly types have babies. What these mothers will do when the fad is over and the babies are outdated is another question.

Somehow, a Militant Mom can take the cuddliest baby and reduce it to a pile of inefficient plumbing. Once, at dinner with a Militant Mom, I feasted on an exquisite vegetable pate and dandled the curly-headed offspring on my knee. Here was an opportunity to combine Mom's top two subjects, health food and the kid.

"If there are any leftovers, little Rachel will eat well tomorrow," I said.

"Certainly not," said the indignant Militant Mom. "Carrots give her gas."

Almost everyone enjoys baby pictures. That's because a photo never burps. A Militant Mom never shows pictures of the baby. She shows pictures of the birth.

If a Militant Mom tells you she keeps the placenta in the freezer, call the police.


## (24) Guide to the South Side

Now that the rest of the St. Louis area has discovered the South Side, it is time to discuss proper etiquette when you visit this quaint region. Well-meaning tourists are accidentally offending the charming native people.

Naturally, you are welcome to visit the South Side, especially if you spend money and get out by sundown. Understanding the local customs will avoid needless offense and unpleasant scenes.

Auntie Elaine, our local guide, lives near Tower Grove Park, where she regularly picks up small children and soda bottles.

### Auntie Elaine's Guide To The South Side

**Q:What do I call a South Sider?**
**A:** Many South Siders are of German descent. There is also a large Oriental community, Indians, Mexicans and many Americans of English stock who originally settled in Kentucky and Arkansas.

All these diverse peoples are deeply offended by the term "ethnic."

The proper name for a South Sider of German ancestry is "Kraut." A term of endearment among long-time married couples is, "You hard-headed old Kraut."

South Sidese is similar to Chinese: The voice inflection may change the meaning. Deliver the same hard-headed Kraut statement forcefully in a bar, and it's guaranteed to start a fight.

South Siders of English ancestry are called "rednecks." Sometimes you will hear the term "hoosier." That is a pejorative term, used only when the saloon owner is planning to redecorate.

Here's what you say about all other ethnic groups: "They work hard, mind their own business and keep the property up."

**Q: Do South Siders really scrub the front steps on Saturday morning?**
**A:** Please don't ask a South Sider this question. We must hear it once a day. At one time, it was true. But the modern scrubby Dutch scorn such compulsive behavior. They do, however, trim their lawns with scissors.

**Q: Do South Siders drive on the left or right-hand side of the road?**
**A:** Neither. They drive squarely down the center. After all, they paid

for the whole street.

Things move at a slower pace here. Especially the cars. South Siders stop their cars in the street to chat or unload groceries.

Don't honk. That marks you as an outsider. The driver won't move anyway.

**Q: Last Saturday, a gentleman told me to go to a tavern because it had great brains. Auntie Elaine, is this a place where intellectuals drink?**

**A:** No, foolish child. This is where the elite meet to eat. Deep-fried brains are the haute cuisine of the tavern: brown and crispy on the outside, white and cloud-soft inside. Brains are usually served with the traditional accompaniments—salt, pepper, ketchup and onion.

Unfortunately, as fern bars continue to infest the area, there's a brain drain. Even the standard South Side cheeseburger is endangered. To find a good cheeseburger, follow a mail carrier. Like truckers on the road, mail carriers always know where to eat.

One warning: Never drink the water in a South Side tavern. The wine is even worse. But the beer is the coldest in town.

**Q: South Side repair persons do good work, but I find them difficult to deal with. Help!**

**A:** Obviously, you don't know how a customer should act. When you take your car to the garage, the repairman will say he can't fix it. He's too busy, the car's hopeless, you're hopeless, etc.

Look stricken. Hunch your shoulders. After 10 minutes, shuffle your feet.

This is the handyman's signal to begin work. The car will be finished by 5.

**Q: I'm invited to a South Side wedding. What should I expect?**

**A:** A good fight. A South Side couple may not be legally married unless there's one fist fight. Remember, you can hit anyone but the groom. That is the bride's prerogative.

## (25) Why Soaps Are Better Than Football

Lonely? Depressed? Tired of spending your weekends alone?

Then you're probably married, and your husband watches football. Every fall these women ask advice columnists, counselors, clergy—even me—how to cope.

At last I have an answer. In all modesty, I can say that my plan is so good it may end family strife, boost the economy and get me the Nobel

Peace Prize.

Here it is: Quit fighting football. Get the same thing for yourself.

First, examine the arguments men use. Men tell you that watching football with their friends promotes camaraderie and manly ideals. What they're really doing is staring at the TV for six hours, drinking beer.

I'm not knocking this. It's wonderfully relaxing. But women who sit around all weekend and drink are handed magazine articles on "Depression and the New Woman."

Women don't dislike football. We just demand more excitement than the sport can give. But I've found the perfect substitute. It has a built-in following. It can be organized into teams and leagues. With some minor adjustments, it could have everything that football has now.

I'm talking about soap operas.

First, the soaps would need expanded network coverage. Under my plan, soaps would run all day Saturday and Sunday, plus Monday and Thursday nights. Women soap fans would camp out in front of the family-room TV all weekend, or escape to soap bars. There they would swill diet soda and talk soap.

Soap talk is as intricate and trivial as sports lingo. Soap fans can recite the bios, stats and records of top players. They regularly discuss their team's intercepted passes, which players scored and who fumbled.

Really dedicated soap fans also keep track of players' marriages, brain tumors, mental breakdowns and auto accidents clear back to the '50s.

They can explain the soaps to newcomers and answer these questions: Will Cecille be shattered to learn she's illegitimate? Is Kevin or Victor the father of Nikki's baby?

Soaps are like great sports in another way. You can bet on them. In fact, people already do. Bookies from London to Las Vegas gave odds on who shot J.R., and newspapers carried the results on the front page.

Once big-league soaping is established, it would inject excitement into regular sports betting. Which would you rather do: Put money on whether Amaryllis waits till her wedding night to confess she was a hooker or worry about the point spread between Dallas and Washington?

Soap fans share something else with big-time sports. They are loyal. Critics say soaps are stupid, but fans know those guys are effete snobs. Soaps are tough. They tackled subjects like homosexuality when prime time was still running scared. Soaps teach you about psychology, law and medicine. Hating soaps is un-American.

As in any sport, soap fans can participate on an amateur level, especially with affairs, illegitimate children and divorces. But these are one-on-one activities, usually conducted after work. Soap fans still look to the big leagues to see how the pros perform.

## (26) Why Is There Always One Shoe
## on the Side of the Road?

Did you ever know anyone who lost one shoe on the highway?

Think about it. The roadsides are dotted with abandoned shoes. One tennis shoe. One old boot. One high heel. You never see two shoes.

This is not a frivolous inquiry. It is one of the three great questions of our century. Answer them, and you will understand the universe.

The first question is by Roger Miller: "How come a chicken can eat all the time and never get fat in the face?"

The second is by Robert Benchley: "Why is the person you're waiting for at the depot never the first one off the bus?"

And the third question is, in all modesty, by me. It contains a lifetime of philosophical speculation. One gentleman spent an entire vacation in Nassau pondering the question. Instead of watching single women, Bud sat on the beach thinking about single shoes.

"Did you ever notice how many of those shoes aren't untied?" he asked his wife. She had him checked for sunstroke.

Bud has abandoned his original theory, that the shoes were lost in car accidents.

The Missouri Highway Department doesn't know where they come from, either. "Ma'am, you wouldn't believe what we find by the road," said Frank Kriz, district engineer at the Kirkwood office.

"If I had to guess, I'd say the shoes are lost by kids, probably fighting in the family station wagon. They toss the shoes out the window. I've never seen any percentages, but I'd guess most were kids' shoes.

"Some items fall from garbage trucks. We see a lot of odd things. Billfolds with money and no identification. Dead animals. Dogs, cats. Deer, cows, horses. We bury the small animals on the right-of-ways, but we can't handle a cow or a horse. We call a rendering plant. I've wandered off the subject, haven't I?"

Yes, Frank. But you did an admirable job. Less patient people would have called the guard. Even some of my friends look edgy.

Mrs. Old Family considered the question seriously. She has never personally lost any shoes. "That's because Mother was a big name-tag lady," Mrs. O.F. said. "She put my name in coats, sweaters, even the instep of my shoes."

This is a common Old Family practice. Old Families like to put their names on streets and trust funds and public buildings, and they never let go of anything.

Mrs. O.F. presented several theories. "I figure the shoes were piled on top of a redneck mover's truck, and one blew off.

"Or, someone stretched out in the back of the car, with their feet on the open window, and lost one shoe.

"Or, someone is really chucking two shoes, and one rolled into a culvert. Have you looked for the second shoe?"

What about the fighting children theory?

"That's very good. But it doesn't explain the red satin high heel you see by the road."

What satin heel?

"Well, can't you make one up? The high heel is the traditional feminine weapon. As I see it, a man and a woman are in a car. He threatens her. She whips off her shoe to defend herself. They wrestle. He grabs it and throws it out the window . . . "

We left Mrs. O.F. with her tongue hanging out—of her brogues.

John A. had one more theory: "Maybe the single shoe is a hoax, like Big Foot, if you'll pardon the comparison. "

Why would someone travel the country dropping shoes?

"Maybe," said John, "he's footloose."

In desperation, I'm turning to readers for help. Remember, you found The Man Who Paved His Lawn And Painted It Green. If you know someone who lost ONE shoe on the highway, write me in care of the Post-Dispatch.

I expect much sole-searching.

## (27) The Answer Is a Shoe-In

The question no one dared ask has been answered. I asked it—but you've answered it.

"At last, someone wrote about this subject," a Ferguson woman said. "I tried to discuss it with my husband, but he won't talk about it. He thinks I'm crazy. It's something I've wanted to know all my life."

Mrs. F. E. was too embarrassed to give her name. Take comfort, dear. You are not alone. Mail has been pouring in. Readers from as far away as Paducah, Ky., responded to this question: "Did you ever know anyone who lost one shoe on the highway?"

Some readers called it the Single Shoe Syndrome. Cindi Hill Longwisch of Bethalto, Ill., shows what SSS does to people:

"From the time when I was first able to look out a car window, I wondered about those shoes. They have bugged me for years. I can't account for most of them, but I do know about one.

"My husband drove through a flooded intersection and drowned out the car's engine. He had to push it out of the way in calf-deep water and mud. In the process he lost a slip-on loafer (brown, 10½ D, a Florsheim, no less).

"We went back after the water receded, but the shoe was never heard from again. If anybody has found it, they can have the mate. Single shoes sell poorly at garage sales."

Now Cindi is wondering "about the women's underwear along the side of the road." If anyone knows how it gets there, DO NOT write. This is a family newspaper.

The Single Shoe Syndrome has several categories. They are:

**Sex and the Single Shoe:** Now that I have your attention, it's awfully wedded sex. Six readers blamed newlyweds. Dave Gillette of Bridgeton gave this first-person account. "I photograph weddings. Honeymoon cars pull a bunch of cans and shoes. They fall off on the street."

St. Louisan Susan Meier added: "Perhaps no one ever gathers those shoes and trashes them because they're a symbol of freedom. After all, they're single, right?"

Donna Ayers knew about a Clarence, Mo., wedding where the shoes were on top of the car. A groomsman planned to dress at the church. "He carried his tux on a hanger in his left hand and his shoes in his right. He put his shoes on top of the car so he could open the door, put the tux in the car and drove away.

"When he got to the church only one shoe was on top the car. He had to borrow shoes for the wedding. In about two weeks his shoe showed up hanging from the stop sign at the main intersection."

But newlyweds can't be blamed for all the single shoes. This leads to our second most popular theory: **The Fighting Kids.**

Frank Kriz, district engineer for the Missouri Highway Department, believed shoes are lost by kids, "fighting in the family station wagon."

"North County Teacher" thinks her idea is even closer: "The shoes and other articles of clothing (have you ever noticed T-shirts, jeans or underwear?) are thrown by kids from school buses. I am a teacher and have second-hand knowledge of how the highway gets its clothes. Goodwill should send crews out each day to gather donations."

But children do not toss these shoes lightly. Carol Donner of Paducah sent this classified ad from the local Sunday paper. It is really a tribute to a brave lad.

The ad said: "LOST. Little boy's new black & white saddle oxford shoe size 5½, on roadside between Reidland & Draffenville on Highway 68, where he threw it out of the car."

The ad was placed by Camilla Rippetoe (honest, that's her name).

Her 2-year-old nephew, Drew, tossed the shoe after church on Easter Sunday. "He has blond, curly hair, blue eyes and a cleft chin," she said. "He looks like a little angel."

Camilla doesn't know why he threw the shoe, but I do. Drew's mom dressed the kid in a sailor suit and matching $25 shoes. Kids who look like Drew are often subjected to these outfits. Only a young man of firm character takes matters into his own hands.

**Sole Survivors:** Other readers have been literally knocked out of their shoes. During the big snowstorm of 1982, a semi slid off the road and hit Shawn Scott's stranded car. Fortunately, the Scott family was not hurt. But Shawn is personally responsible for one stray shoe on I-44.

**Sole Mates:** Melvin Sylvester, who used to be a liquor salesman "down east of Jefferson City," actually stopped and picked up a pair of women's shoes on the road.

You may wonder where to turn in these lost shoes. Melvin took them to a bartender. The bartender knew the owner. It seems that a couple had come to town that morning to sell a load of grain. Then they celebrated at the saloon. They "stayed too long and got into an argument on the way home," Melvin said. "She took off her shoe to tap him on the head. He took it away, threw it on the road and would not go back after it. She said she could not walk with only one shoe, so she threw the other one away.

"By the time I came along, the couple had come back to town and everything was peaches and cream."

**Lost & Found:** M.L. Jernigan says a friend found something even rarer than a single shoe—a hitchhiker wearing one shoe.

During the mid-60s, Jernigan's friend spotted a hippie with his thumb out on a Florida highway. "He wore only one shoe, a dirty white canvas loafer adorned his right foot."

The kindly friend stopped, opened the car door and said, "Poor fellow, you've lost a shoe."

The hitchhiker said, "Aw naw, man. I found one."


## (28) How to Meet Men

Now there's another book with advice for single women. It's "101 Creative & Effective Ways to Meet Worthwhile Men."

As usual, it treats the single state as a handicap. But it's your own fault. If you'd fix yourself up and smile, you wouldn't look half-bad. The book's Creative Way No. 97 includes this motto: "Every pot finds its lid. "

I didn't see my friend Selma's favorite saying, but Selma enjoys being single. "Men are like fish," she said. "Once you catch them and keep them around the house, they stink."

The book does have some creative ways to meet men. Who'd ever think to attend shareholders' meetings? Check the obituary pages for fresh widowers? Use your children and dogs to lure subjects? Wander around "lost" in courthouses to snag lawyers? Not to mention the ever-popular Join Clubs and Activities.

But do you really want to take up square dancing, just to meet a man? You could spend the rest of your life with someone who wears a bolo tie.

These advice books are too coy. Women need a more modern, realistic guide. So here it is:

### Nine No-Holds-Barred Ways to Meet Men

**Hospitals:** Where else can you find someone who needs you? And what better place for a romance. Just like "Love Story."

Look for a good prospect, a man who's rich but not too healthy. Remember, love doesn't last forever. Stand by him in his final days, and he'll leave you enough to keep his memory green.

Make sure he's of sound mind, if not body, or the will won't be valid.

**Men's Rooms:** Why join all those boring clubs? They let in too many single women. Think! What place is always filled with men? The men's room. Walk right in. Every eye will be on you. It's a great way to make a lasting impression.

**Singles Bars:** Women don't do well in singles bars, because they don't know how to talk to men. Men are interested in good conversation, but you don't have to sound overly sophisticated.

Try this sample opener. Order a Coke and tell the man next to you, "I have to drink this. Even one glass of white wine makes me forget all my inhibitions."

You'll be surprised how quickly he begins talking to you. Most men are so nice, they'll even buy you a glass of wine.

**Locker Rooms:** Walk in after a game and pretend to be a reporter. It's a great chance to ask nosy questions. Don't forget your notebook and pen. Be sure to get the cute guys' names and phone numbers.

**Military Induction Centers:** Talk about men! This place is loaded with young, vulnerable men. One friend always wears a motherly dress, like Jane Wyatt in "Father Knows Best," and fills her purse with fresh-baked brownies. Works wonders.

**Gas Stations:** Ever see any women hanging around gas stations? You'll have the field to yourself. Don't pick a self-service station. Those horrors attract the wrong kind of men: Wimps, liberals and cheapskates.

**Meetings:** Forget meeting men at the supermarket. Everyone knows about that. Laundromats are old news, too. A smart single avoids competition. Hang around auto-parts shops and hardware stores. If you're attracted to athletes, bowling alleys and pool halls are unexplored territory.

**Taverns:** Tired of pretty boys who weigh less than you do? That's what you get for going to singles bars and cocktail lounges. Real men go to taverns and drink beer. Don't worry about his marital status. If he's sitting at the bar most nights, and he's not single, he ought to be.

**Adult Book Stores:** Obviously, these men are looking for women. There's a real good chance they can read, too.

## (29) Just Like Romeo and Juliet

I saw "Romeo and Juliet" at the theater last weekend. I'd always thought this play was about passionate young love. Shows how much I know.

Sitting right next to me was a woman who gave the play a whole new perspective. She said, "Romeo and Juliet aren't star-crossed lovers. They're a couple of dumb kids."

Maybe she has a point. Juliet got a lot of bad advice, and she was too young to know it. Juliet was not quite 14 when she met Romeo, and her parents were pushing her into marriage already. Friar Laurence tried to save her with a sleeping potion. It was a nice idea, but it didn't work. The family feud didn't help, either.

But this is a more enlightened age. What if Romeo and Juliet were alive today? Could this tragedy have been prevented? Suppose Juliet had our advantages. Suppose she wrote to one of our many fine syndicated columnists for advice.

DEAR FRAN: I am 13 going on 14. I met a guy at a dance last night. We danced once, and then he kissed me.

I'm in love, Fran, and we want to get married right away.

There's just one problem. His family doesn't get along with mine. They fight all the time. They've been arrested for disturbing the peace three times.

What do I do? Our parents will never give their consent to our marriage. In the meantime, I have to meet him on the sly. I don't like sneaking around like this.

## IN LOVE AND DESPERATE IN VERONA

THIRTEEN IS MUCH too young to get married. You have your whole life ahead of you. You should be dating other boys, and getting to know them. One dance is no way to choose your life's partner.

It's difficult to tell true love from infatuation. But ask yourself this question: Does your heart say, "I must marry him right away. What if he falls in love with someone else?" Or does it tell you, "Our love will last forever. I can wait."

Remember, when love's hot desire is gone, you may have to face him cold turkey. Don't do anything I wouldn't do. If you can't be good, be careful. Write me back, dear.

DEAR FRAN: Thank you for your wonderful column. I cut it out and put it in my wallet. Everything you said was right, Fran, but we ran off and got married this afternoon.

I think we're in real trouble. My cousin picked a fight with my husband (I'll call him Romeo) and Romeo killed him. It was self-defense, and a good lawyer could get him off easy. But we haven't even had our honeymoon yet.

Fran, what do I do? Romeo may have to start over somewhere else. I'm not sure Romeo can get a job in another city—he doesn't have any connections there.

Also, I don't think I'm close enough to my parents to talk to them. They want me to marry someone else. I'll call him Paris. He's a wimp.

Please help.

REALLY DESPERATE IN VERONA

YOU NEED counseling right away. If you don't trust your parents, perhaps you know a mature, older woman you can talk to. Otherwise, look in the Yellow Pages for a good counselor. Or see your clergyman.

DEAR FRAN: Thank you for answering so quickly. I do have a clergyman, and I'm very close to him. I'll call him Friar Laurence. He's promised to help me and Romeo. He says not to worry, we'll be together forever. Thank you, Fran.

DELIGHTED IN VERONA

**Is it true love? Or pure lust? How do you know you're really in love? To find out, send 50 cents for Fran's new booklet, "Much Ado About Nothing."**

## (30) Why Women Don't Like Football

This anguished letter arrived just before Super Bowl Sunday. It's from Thelma B., a woman obviously married to a football fan.

She said: "Please print a treatise explaining the game of football so that women can understand to the point that maybe we'll sit by the TV and the men will be in the kitchen."

Of course women don't understand football, Thelma. It's another sign we're smarter than men.

A football team contains many perfect specimens of humanity. A quarterback, for example, is about 6-foot-2 and weighs 210 pounds. A hunk, as we used to say.

When you see something like that, Thelma, do you want to let him outside, where he can get hurt? Do you want to have him tackled by some brute, so he can spend the rest of his life in knee surgery?

Of course not. You want to take the young man home and protect him. Lock the door. Throw away the key.

That's a reasonable reaction—and a humane one. After a few years of playing football, the poor lad will be almost crippled, and reduced to endorsing pantyhose.

Every season, the football question torments women. The standard advice is appeasement. "Watching football is a traditional male activity," the columnists say. "Learn to enjoy football. At least you'll spend the day with your husband."

Wrong. Needlepoint and macrame are traditional female activities. Ever see this as advice to husbands: "Learn to needlepoint, Sam. At least you'll get to spend the day with your wife."

Watching football is an incurable disease. It's in the genes. Passed down from father to son.

I believe women could wipe out football-watching. Here's my plan: Refuse to marry a football-watcher. If you must marry one, don't have children. If this genetic abnormality is not passed on, football-watching will eventually die out.

You made your mistake years ago, Thelma, when you married Mr. B.

You knew the signs: He was young then. Sometimes on Sunday he'd have a couple of beers with the boys and watch a game. But he said he really wanted to spend the day with you.

You kidded yourself. Football-watching gets progressively worse. By the time a man is 40, it's every Sunday and all Monday night in front of the TV. In advanced cases, he even tapes old football games and watches reruns.

It's too late for you, Thelma. But there's hope for the next generation.

The answer is public education. Young women should be taught to detect the early signs of football-watching in their dates. When a young man shows even a casual interest in football—drop him. Remember, football-watching has no cure. You can only prevent it.

Through education, football-watching could be eliminated in two or three generations.

Picture this scene, Thelma: It is the year 2022. Education has begun to take effect. Your daughters have married non-football-watchers. One Sunday, your great-grandson brings home his new bride. She is a lovely young woman. But you know the dark cloud that hangs over her. You take her aside and tell her gently, "I know you love him, dear. But there's something you must know. His maternal great-grandfather is a football-watcher. We've been clean for a generation. But there's a 1 in 4 chance your sons will be football-watchers. It's a risk you'll have to live with."

Her beautiful eyes dim with tears. Then, from the depths of the living room, you hear great-grandpa's dreaded cry: "Thelma! Commercial break! Get another six-pack!"

You owe it to the future, Thelma.


## (31) A Dictionary of Euphemisms

A foolhardy gentleman once described me as "30ish." He did not understand why I was outraged.

"It's the truth, isn't it?" he said. "You're around 30."

You are technically correct, sir, but dead wrong. Ask any woman: 30ish means "frump." Meryl Streep and Diane Keaton have all passed 30. Ever hear them described as 30ish? But you have seen those wrinkle creams for "women over 30." You've just called me a frump. A quick survey of female colleagues proved me correct. So I broke a chair over his head. Sometimes the truth hurts.

To promote understanding I present here a brief list of euphemisms. You know what these words are supposed to mean. Now, here's what they really say:

A MODEST HOME: A dump. Poor.

A WELL-KEPT MODEST HOME: Deserving poor. No home in Ladue is ever called well-kept.

AN A-STUDENT AND AN EAGLE SCOUT: A teen-age nerd.

AGGRESSIVE: Obnoxious.

ARTICULATE: Won't shut up.

AVERAGE: Dumb.

BLONDE: Fast.

BUXOM: A fat female. A fat male is husky.

CAUTIOUS BUT UPBEAT: A business term meaning "expecting a disaster."

CREW CUT: A right-winger.

COLORFUL LANGUAGE: Foulest mouth west of the Mississippi.

CONSERVATIVELY DRESSED: Good for men, bad for women. A conservatively dressed man wears $600 suits. A conservatively dressed woman wears sensible shoes and looks like a field hockey coach.

CONTROVERSIAL: A crook, or a crazy.

CRUSTY: A rude hick.

DELIBERATE: Slow, dull.

ENERGETIC CHILD: A brat.

ENTHUSIASTIC: Fanatic. As in, Mrs. Ronald Social is an enthusiastic theater-goer. Or backpacker. Or tennis player.

FIESTY: Short. No tall person is ever described as fiesty. Tall people are enraged. Average-height persons are angry.

FIFTYISH: Old. No one is ever 60ish.

FLAMBOYANT POLITICIAN: A loudmouth who smokes cigars. Chicago aldermen are controversial and flamboyant.

FUNLOVING: Drunk.

GREAT SENSE OF HUMOR: Enormous stock of dirty jokes.

IMMACULATE HOUSEKEEPER: Complusive.

IMPOSING: Fat important person. Fat likeable person is portly.

INDIVIDUALISTIC: Doesn't get along with anyone.

INNER CITY: Slum.

INTELLECTUAL: Any academic job, including gym teacher.

MAJESTIC: Fat rich person.

MAVERICKS: Politicians who get their names in the paper, but never accomplish anything.

METHODICAL: Dull but crazy.

MIDDLE-AGED: Dull. Period. The deadliest combination in the language is "middle-aged housewife."

MISCHIEVOUS CHILD: Sets fire to the babysitter.

PLAINSPOKEN: Rude.

POETIC: Weird.

PROMINENT LAWYERS: Wear gold chains on their vests.

QUAINT SMALL TOWN: Any place that has a festival every year. Also, no new buildings.

QUAINT SUMMER COTTAGE: No plumbing.

REGAL: Fat and rich.

REPUTED: Certainly is. As in, "reputed mob figure."

RESERVED: A rude rich person. Often used to describe politicians' wives.

RESPECTED POLITICIAN: One who agrees with you.

SLEEPY SMALL TOWN: Dull.

SOLIDLY. BUILT: Fat.

SPRIGHTLY: Any old person who can move.

SUBURBAN HOUSEWIFE: Even worse than 30ish. Ever hear of an urban housewife?

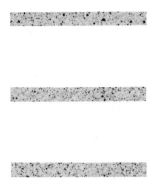

## (32) The South Side Wedding

Dave, a foreigner from Illinois, married a South Sider six years ago. "Please explain what happened at my wedding," Dave said.

You're a lucky man, Dave. A South Side wedding is a memorable event. We have a rich and meaningful tradition. Our young couples are saved from the chilly ceremonies designed by department-store etiquette experts.

"But why do you serve mostaccioli?" he said.

A South Side marriage could be annulled unless mostaccioli is served at the reception. You pronounce it MUSK-a-choli, by the way.

The rest of the menu is ham, roast beef, two kinds of potato salad and slaw. Some health nuts include a relish tray with carrots, sweet pickles and stuffed olives.

The food is served buffet-style. Sit-down dinners at hotels are not proper. You could get germs off the silverware.

The VFW hall is the socially correct choice. The hall must be large enough to accommodate at least 400 "wedding and funeral relatives"—second and third cousins seen only at these events. One aunt can explain how they are related. If she dies, the key is lost.

Traditional decorations are white bells and crepe-paper streamers. The guests stake out seats at long cafeteria tables covered with white paper cloths. At the wedding will be:

**The drunken uncle.** One family member is detailed to watch him. This precaution fails. About 12:30 a.m. the uncle will walk up to your divorced cousin and his date. (That's Mack, the one with the mid-life

crisis.) Drunken Uncle will ask, "Hey, Mack. Is that your wife or your daughter?"

**The red-hot mama.** She's pushing 50, but kept her figure. Mama wears hot pants or a miniskirt and a long mane of hair. You'll find her in all the "misty-art" wedding photos.

**The hotshot cousin.** He's made it big and everyone knows it. But at what a price! He abandoned the family religion. He turned Republican.

**The feud.** Most of the family does not speak to the rest. Engage a big hall, so all the warring parties can square off. A parking-lot fight is part of the nuptials. Tearful reconciliations are the entertainment at funerals.

**The bridesmaids.** These are six of the bride's dearest friends. Or anyone with $90 for a dress and dyed-to-match pumps.

Everyone will tell you: "It doesn't look like a bridesmaid's dress. You can wear it New Year's Eve."

When is the last time you went to a New Year's party in pink chiffon with streamers?

Oh, I forgot. The groom. Well, everybody forgets him.

They will remember the band. When the engagement is announced, three people know "a great rock band you can get for $200." The band goes the way of the great little apartment for $350.

The bride's mother finds a last-minute compromise: Five guys in iridescent green tuxes who do rock and polkas. The band has an accordion and a guitar player.

The bride will see those tuxes in the wedding album. No expense is spared for the wedding photographs. It's the only way the dazed couple will remember what happened.

The bride and groom will disappear before midnight. The bride wants to stay and dance, but Mother is afraid someone will think they've been living together. Besides, once the couple is gone, the guests can have a good time.

Everybody takes home a piece of wedding cake in a monogrammed napkin.

Someone stands by the table to tell the unmarried guests: "Put your cake under your pillow. You'll dream of your true love."

The next morning it's the same old thing. More crumbs.

## *(33) Equality Marches On: Women Master the Wolf Whistle*

"WOW! WOOOOOOEEEE! Look at those legs!"

I could hear the yells and whistles when I walked down the street. Young ruffians. There they were, sitting on the library steps. I could just make out three forms in the deepening dusk.

Ignore them, that's all. I kept walking.

The noise started again. "Wow! WOOOOOOEEEE! Look at those muscles!"

Muscles?

Wait a minute. Those are girls. They're whistling at the boy in the cutoffs.

Well, that's different. At last, I am proud of the younger generation. Thanks to them, we have achieved equality. I didn't know young women had such well-developed whistles. These three whistled with strength and volume. They whistled with authority. You could hear them a block away.

These whistles had something more—that insinuating quality that amounts to a verbal ogle.

I am pleased to announce that women can now execute the classic wolf whistle.

For a long time, I've known we have had the physical capability. We also had the mental capacity. I've heard my friends describe actors and rock singers in terms that would make the porkiest Playboy reader blush.

Women have even told newspaper columnists that they admire the taper of a baseball player's thighs and the curve of his tush. But they still spoke anonymously. Women weren't bold enough.

They'd never stand on a street corner and whistle at men. Well, I knew one woman who did once. She whistled during a demonstration at a construction site. But that was a protest. This was whistling for pure entertainment.

The three whistlers were named Jennifer, Tina and Laura. They're 12 years old, and in junior high school. They wore perfect tans, shorts and white tennis shoes with red shoe strings. Each carried a can of soda.

The following philosophical discussion took place on the library steps with Jennifer, Tina and Laura. Except sometimes it was Tina, Laura and Jennifer. They answered all together. They answered one after another. Until I got so lost I couldn't figure out who was talking. But the message came through, loud and clear. It even has a certain clean, spare look, like Beat poetry.

**How do guys react when you whistle at them?**

Sometimes they turn around.

Sometimes they whistle back.

Sometimes they tell us to shut up.

Sometimes they ignore us.

**Do you whistle a lot?**

Sometimes. Not all the time.
It's something to do . . .
. . . while we finish our Cokes.
We just go outside, and if we see somebody we like we whistle at them.
Sometimes we do it to be ignorant.
If somebody's ugly.
**Do the ugly guys know you're making fun of them?**
They think we're serious.
Most of the time, we are.
**Do you get whistled at?**
Sometimes.
**How do you feel?**
Embarrassed.
If they're ugly, it's gross.
If they're cute, it's embarrassing.
Usually we whistle at them, and they whistle back.
Sometimes they think we're gross.
**Do you think women whistling is a sign of equality?**
Equal?
You mean are the men equal to us?
Or are we equal to them?

# (34) Mixed Marriage: The Story of Muffie Van Der Venter Gravois

This sad story was in my morning mail. Let it be a warning to any woman who stomps on her roots. The unfortunate bride will be called Muffie Van Der Venter Gravois.

"I am the victim of a mixed marriage," Muffie wrote. "I am a full-blooded West County suburbanite. My husband is a third-generation South Sider.

"The marriage has not been without conflict. Choosing a home site was more difficult than deciding which faith to raise the children." The couple settled on neutral territory—southwest county.

"I probably wouldn't have been entrapped in a South Side marriage if I'd been a St. Louis native. My family came here when I was 18. I spent most of my time away at school. I met my fate on a summer job."

A smooth-talking South Sider seduced the naive girl with exotic stories.

"My future husband would spend hours describing the colorful South Side, portraying it as a sister city to St. Louis."

Now she saw her family home through his eyes. "He explained my subdivision had huge, overpriced, prefab boxes with hollow-core doors. The window sills were too small for knickknacks and mugs. We didn't even collect and display souvenirs."

South Side collections leave others speechless. Muffie must have been dazzled by the Frankoma pottery acquired on Ozark vacations. She'd probably never seen salt-and-pepper shakers from all 50 states.

"My enlightenment increased with each date," Muffie wrote. "I visited his parents' second-story flat and had many questions.

"Who gets the backyard? Is it divided down the middle or do you rotate days? Are alleys one-way? Does the string in the bathroom turn on the light or flush the toilet? Can the old woman watching me from the adjacent house hear me? Where are the privacy fences?"

Muffie studied the parking customs. "It may be a public street, but you don't take Fred's parking spot.

"I soon learned my beau's tales left out quite a bit. There are no automatic dishwashers, double garages, weeping willows, Coors beer or people under 16. There are ceramic swans, front porch First Communion parties, vigorous street sweepers and militant caned pedestrians.

"If you want to keep it private, don't say it in the backyard. If you have an announcement, take it to the tavern."

Muffie learned the language. On the South Side, a cooler was a beer box, a pub was a tavern and a basement a rathskeller.

Muffie even picked up the fine points of tavern etiquette. A gentleman "talks sports, brewery or not at all. Laughs loud at all jokes but doesn't make any of his own. Carries cash and doesn't charge. Ogles any female who comes in. Says 'doll' instead of 'chick' or 'fox.' "

Well-bred women "drink beer only, and try to drink more than their husbands. Buy cigarettes even if they don't smoke. It's OK to touch strangers on the shoulders and say, 'hon.'

"The marriage is holding up," Muffie said. "We've tried to expose the children to both cultures. They attend South Side parish carnivals. They have sampled Ted Drewes Frozen Custard, the Pretzel Man and Hodak's chicken. They've seen electric lawn mowers.

"In the county, they've been to shopping malls and Queeny Park and gone horseback riding.

"My husband is allowed to use South Side lingo in front of the children: 'Youse guys,' 'sunda' and 'warsh.' But the kids are forbidden."

You've tried, Muffie. But you cannot help your children make their most difficult decision:

Will they proudly display the South Side emblem of adulthood, the beer gut? Or will they return to their mother's people, and work out at Nautilus?

## (35) Executive Sweet: Office Etiquette

She was an executive with a St. Louis company. She was also furious.

"How could he be so rude?" she said. "He asked me: 'Does my husband mind if I have a job?' Can you believe it?"

Sure. Female executives are still rare enough that some people may not understand the new office etiquette. They do not deserve our scorn. The poor slobs need help.

Delicate situations are so easy to avoid. Just ask yourself this question: Would I ask Donald Trump that?

See how easy it is? Only a twit would ask Mr. Trump if his wife minds if he works.

You don't need to know who cooks or cleans the house—unless you want the name of a good domestic.

I asked St. Louis women about other difficulties they've encountered. These are real executives, not vice presidents for environmental concern at major polluters. Here are some occasions you may wish to note:

THE BUSINESS LUNCH: When you see a female executive at lunch with a man, it is impolite to assume she is cheating on anything but her expense account. It is also impolite to use the wrong knife on the executive's husband.

"I was at a business lunch," the woman said, "and I ran into my husband's boss. He could hardly wait to get back to tell my husband. 'Maybe I shouldn't say this, but I saw your wife at lunch with a man.' "

"That's OK," the husband said. "I know she eats."

PERSONNEL QUESTIONS: It is never polite to ask a woman executive if her husband minds if she works late.

Long office hours are a sore subject with any spouse. Remember the basic rule. Would you ask your CEO if his wife minds his hours? She probably does—unless she's working late at her office.

One woman gives this answer: "Whenever someone asks something rude I say, 'How lovely you feel you know me well enough to ask such an intimate question.' "

Here's another handy hint: Do not assume the woman behind the desk is a secretary. Even if she is, don't call her honey.

And if she's the only woman in the firm, don't ask how it feels to work with men. At least one woman answers with a disconcerting, "I wouldn't know."

An attorney says she is sometimes mistaken for a secretary. But when her own secretary treated her like one, it was too much.

"I fired her. She knocked on my door and said, 'I can't understand Mr. Jones' handwriting, and he's so busy I don't want to bother him.' "

Another lawyer, sensitive about his height and her position, told her, "You remind me of my first secretary."

"That's funny," she said. "You remind me of my first secretary, too. But he was so much taller."

EQUAL PARTNERS: When married couples are partners in a firm, do not make jokes about sleeping with the president. They've already heard them.

Do not assume the wife spends her time typing and filing. It could be he's the cute bit of fluff with great legs. It's even possible two intelligent people could marry each other.

Some questions are better left unasked. "A lawyer was trying so hard to sound liberated," said one partner-wife. "He asked my husband, 'Does your wife work with you, or for you?' "

YOU CAN BE TOO POLITE: "I was on a trip with other executives," said a businesswoman. "We came to an escalator. This whole big string of men stood aside to let me on. They fell all over themselves. They meant well, but it was ridiculous."

Don't overlook the advantages of equality. "I took a man out to dinner," another woman said. "He was my client. It was my invitation. But the poor man felt compelled to reach for the check. It must be inbred in men."

When you see the check on the horizon, just act as you would normally. Head for the restroom.


## (36) Beware of Life's Side Effects

Almost every day, Jim H. spends a few moments with a small book he keeps in his desk drawer. Jim only reads a few pages at a time, but the passages seem to have a profound effect on his life. Sometimes, the little book gives him great comfort.

"People never realize it," Jim H. said, "but this book is a bestseller."

He's right. "Prescription Drugs and Their Side Effects" is a national bestseller.

"Even the commonest drugs have weird side effects," Jim H. said.

"Look at this section on Darvon. A mild painkiller, right? Well, the book says you can't take it with alcohol, tranquilizers and sleeping pills. Look at these side effects."

Jim H. began reciting 13 unpleasant possibilities: "Dizziness, sedation, nausea, vomiting, headache, weakness, euphoria . . ."

Why pick on Darvon? Almost any common prescription drug has a long list of side effects. "If people only knew. . ." Jim H. said.

It would have no effect at all. You know the side effects of cigarettes and alcohol. You use both. In fact, we know the side effects of most things we do. It doesn't stop us. What if the side effects of marriage, jobs, children and pets were listed scientifically? Would that help?

Just in case, I present the new and revised:

Common Events and Their Side Effects: A Complete Guide

MARRIAGE: An effective cure for loneliness and boredom, marriage can have serious, long-term side effects.

Side effects: Brief period of euphoria, followed by nightmares, headaches, drowsiness, confusion, nausea, changes in sex drive.

MID-LIFE FLINGS: Frequently used to alleviate symptoms of male menopause. A fling can make a fortyish male feel younger, but it has serious, even life-threatening effects.

Warning signs are sudden weight loss, followed by acute urge to buy small, shiny sports car.

Side effects: Nervousness, constant headaches, shifty eyes, pain in the neck. May result in paranoia, permanently enraged wife and in some cases, divorce.

CHILDREN: Children are prescribed to fill empty hours, empty rooms, provide companionship. They are said to be a comfort in old age. Children are used less successfully to save ailing marriages.

Prolonged exposure to small children can impair adult speech and reasoning capacity.

Side effects: Fatigue, nagging headaches, restlessness, sleepless nights, cabin fever, permanent crippling from stepping on Fisher-Price toys in the dark.

PETS: Pets are sometimes used as child substitutes.

Side effects: Dizziness and irrational behavior.

In some cases, pet owner may begin to look like pet. Dog lovers could have red eyes and drool. Less serious effects are unsightly deposits of hair on furniture and in butter.

Warning: Prolonged exposure to pet owners may cause nausea and vomiting in other people.

JOB: Drastic but effective method to stop hunger. Jobs have many serious side effects. A job is usually taken under strict supervision. Jobs

should not be combined with the use of drugs and alcohol.

Side effects: Ulcers, hair loss, allergic reactions, headaches, muscle aches, rapid changes in blood pressure.

NEW CAR: Frequently prescribed after the death of an old car, a new car can be an effective anti-depressant.

In some cases, serious psychological dependence can develop. Watch for these signs: Refusal to remove sticker. Frequent snorting of new car smell. Severe cases may show photographs of car. Often cured by a slight scratch on the fender.

Side effects: Aggressiveness, excitement, fever, light-headedness, flat wallet and debilitated bank account.

## *(37) Lil Harvey and Ron Reagan Pray for Their Lunch*

Lillian Harvey has raised an important question, and I don't think we have to wait for the courts to settle it. In fact, I can answer it right now.

Lillian Harvey is the 71-year-old Ferguson woman who filed suit against the U.S. Department of Health and Human Services. For three years, she took the bus and ate at a federally financed lunch program for the elderly in nearby Dellwood.

"The lunch is good," she said. "I like sitting with my friends."

But before lunch, everyone stands up and prays. "The people who object, object quietly. Because if you don't, you're not welcome back.

"My friends say, 'Why don't you just sit down if you don't want to pray?' But you don't want 150 people looking at you when you sit down. You feel stupid. If you stand up and don't pray, that's not so stupid. But it's wrong. I object.

"I want to stop the salute to the flag and the prayer. It's unconstitutional."

The courts can worry about that part. I'm more interested in Lillian's other question. She says praying is a common practice at these centers.

"I want to stop it in senior citizen centers all across America. Not just Dellwood. I want this for old people everywhere."

Do all elderly persons have to pray before they eat their federally financed lunches?

What about that spry gentleman of 77, President Ronald Reagan? Does he stand up and pray before his lunch? He's eating a federally financed meal, too.

Lillian asked and answered that question in her complaint. "Does President Reagan stand up before lunch and pledge allegiance and have prayer time?'' she wrote. ''No.''

Surely, this is an unjust assumption. Our president has such a great interest in prayer for our young people, he must want it for the old, too.

I called the White House press secretary's office with this question: ''A 71-year-old woman wants to know if President Reagan stands up and says his prayers before lunch.''

There was a long silence. Undoubtedly, the press aide was waiting for inspiration. ''I wouldn't have that information,'' the aide said. ''I have seen the president eat his lunch. He may bow his head, but I don't believe he stands up and prays and makes a production out of it.''

Let me get this straight. The president may pray before lunch, but he doesn't stand up and make a big production out of it.

''Don't put that last part in. We don't want to make light of the subject.''

Certainly not. Not when our president wants to make a really big production out of prayer in the schools. He'd like a constitutional amendment to require voluntary prayer. At least, I think that's how it goes.

President Reagan called for his prayer amendment this way: ''The time has come for this Congress to give a majority of American families what they want for their children—the firm assurance that children can hold voluntary prayers in their schools just as the Congress itself begins each of its daily sessions with an opening prayer.''

This is an interesting insight into the power of prayer. If Congress is pulling all those shenanigans after a daily prayer—what would it do without one?

Now that we know the answer to Lillian's question, I feel it's time for Reagan to stand up for his beliefs.

If the president is eating out of the federal trough, so to speak, we should ask for a constitutional amendment requiring him to stand up and pray before his lunch.

He may be praying silently already, but how do we know? And we should. We pick up the tab for his lunch. We finance the limos, the helicopters and bands playing ''Hail to the Chief.''

How can the president object? I know his prayer would be voluntary. The amendment would protect him. What if a godless Communist or a Democrat got in office and didn't permit presidents to pray any more at lunch?

The president could say he was bowing his head and praying. But he could be studying the waterspots on his silverware for all we know.

We need a constitutional amendment. We must guarantee the president the right to stand up and pray.

We can't have him sitting down on the job.

EDITOR'S NOTE: The Mid-East Area Agency on Aging, which operates Lillian Harvey's lunch spot, now says it "neither encourages nor discourages" prayer and patriotic activity. It also says no person is required to participate in any way and no one is denied service if they do not pray.

Lillian's case was dismissed in April, 1984.


## (38) Why Did the Cars Cross the Bridge?

What sits on Eads Bridge, wears a handlebar mustache and likes corn? Charlie the toll collector.

Every morning, Charlie Immethun greets commuters with the corniest joke he can find. He posts the joke right on his toll booth.

Charlie only puts up the first half of the joke—the commuters try to supply the rest. In Charlie's case, half a joke is NOT better than none. Here's proof:

Q: What's the hardest job in the world?
A: Wheeling, West Virginia.

Q: Which fly in the kitchen is the cowboy?
A: The one on the range.

"See what I mean? Those are dumb jokes," Charlie said. "But people look for them every day."

Sure enough, a regular stuck out a dollar for change, examined the day's joke line and said, "OK, why does the Indian wear feathers?"

"To keep his wigwam," Charlie said.

The man groaned. The bridge shuddered. Charlie swears it was just a bus going through in the other lane.

Many of these wounds are self-inflicted. "I get most of the jokes from people going through here. When I use their joke, you should see them beam—even when they've stolen it. A bus driver steals jokes off a bank sign and gives them to me.

"Some people say, 'You need better jokes,' and bring me the awfullest joke books you've ever seen."

The other jokes? "I'm very light-fingered."

Crime never pays. Charlie even had the nerve to ask this question:

Q: What do you get when you cross a bridge with a car?
A: To the other side.

"OK, Charlie, what's the answer today?" said yet another regular. Charlie delivered his punch line and waited.

"That's what I figured," the man said.

"He always knows the answer," Charlie said, "but I have to tell him."

"Some people don't get the joke. They ask me to explain. If I have to explain they'll never understand."

Charlie's right. You try telling someone why Santa wears tennies. (Because ninees are too small.)

"You should be here during rush hour. You'd hear me tell the same joke 15 times in a row." The prospect of hearing Charlie's Indian joke 15 times drew only a luke-*WAM* response.

Charlie tried again. "Did you hear about the man who had his left side amputated? He's all right now."

I looked out the tollbooth window, and cursed what had created this monster—the Poplar Street Bridge.

"Years ago, before they built the Poplar Street Bridge, I couldn't do this," Charlie said. "There were too many cars taking the Eads Bridge between Missouri and Illinois."

Charlie's daily joke started in the summer of '81. "My daughter made one of those signs wishing you a nice day. I liked it so much I hung it on the booth. Gradually, the sign evolved into jokes and puns, mostly puns."

Charlie believes "at least one or two people take the toll bridge to see my joke. But no more than that. A few think they could get through faster without the joke."

They're wrong. Charlie hands out your change and his line together.

He has jokes stockpiled days ahead. "I can't put up off-color jokes. I have to clean them up and cut them down." Charlie's jokes are 8 or 9 words.

"I work and work to cut them down to size. There's one I love, but I can't get it to fit." You're not going to miss this one. Not if I had to hear it:

Q: Willie McGee hit a ball into the outfield, a pig ran up and ate it and Willie got a home run. What do you call it?
A: An inside-the-pork home run.

Charlie stopped when an old man, wearing a blue flannel shirt and gray stubble of beard, pulled up. "I want to go to Indianapolis," he said. Charlie gave him directions.

"People ask for directions all the time. One woman about 60 drove up in an old car. In that car was everything she owned. She said, 'I want to go to California.'

"I told her how to get there. Six months later, she comes driving across the bridge, hands me a $2 tip and says, 'You give good directions.' "

Charlie's spent 37 years on the bridge. "I enjoy the people I meet here. And I try not to take life seriously."

Even serious things turn out un-serious for Charlie. "Last year, I saved a woman who tried to jump off the bridge. I was honored for it. The mayor even named a Saturday in June for me. Two jewelry stores rewarded me with a diamond ring.

"I got the proclamation a week after my day took place, and it was a woman's ring. They gave me a day I missed and a ring I can't wear, but I'm still honored.

"I've got a joke just for you," said Charlie. "Why do reporters sleep on corduroy pillows?"

I give up.

"They make headlines."

Charlie's stockpile has a joke just for him:

Q: What's worse than one of these jokes?

A: Two of them.

## (39) Real vs Fake Cafes

You've probably noticed the new style in restaurant decor—the fake cafe.

The fake cafe has many authentic fittings: leatherette booths, tile floors, neon signs. Some have chrome-trimmed counters with genuinely uncomfortable stools.

The fake cafe is usually found in fashionable neighborhoods and rehabbed buildings. The food can be good and the clientele quite stylish.

The fake cafe is a refreshing change from those blasted rain forest restaurants. But you must never think it's a real cafe, any more than the Fonz is a real 1950s hood.

The same ingredient is missing in both—grease, the staff of life. The human body must have its insides oiled regularly. This reduces friction.

Grease is a versatile substance. The true cafe finds many uses for it. You fry food in grease. You put it on the cook's hair. A little grease sprinkled on the walls gives the restaurant a distinct ambiance.

Anointing the salt shakers with grease helps the customers maintain a low-salt diet.

Over a breakfast soaked with this nourishing substance, I conducted a panel discussion on what makes a real cafe. Our panel dines regularly at real cafes. They also eat at the fake ones, but only when someone else pays.

Here are eight signs of a real cafe:

**(1) Waitresses.** Fake cafe waitresses wear tuxes, tell you their name is Nedra and they are happy to serve you. Later you may learn they are studying voice or drama. They are nice, but can you respect them? These women have abdicated the function of a true cafe waitress.

Cafe waitresses are the last social arbiters. Step out of line, and you'll know it.

One afternoon I erred at an Illinois diner. The place had "homestyle atmosphere." I thought that meant the red-checked curtains. Then the waitress said, "Want any dessert, honey? And quit playing with the butter."

By George, that was just like home. I sat up straight and took my knife out of the butter tub.

Besides, it was for my own good. Only regulars are worth chastising. You truly belong to cafe society when you order fried potatoes and sausage and the waitress says, "You can't have that, you're on a diet."

Cafe waitresses are admired for their strength. "You know it's a cafe when you don't watch the waitresses wiggle," said a panelist. "They can't. They must move swiftly, and carry heavy loads."

He was obviously male. I never watch the waitresses wiggle.

**(2) Vegetables.** Fake cafes marinate and stir-fry vegetables. Some even have raw vegetable dips. True cafes know that vegetables grow in dirt, and are not safe to eat until they have been boiled many hours.

Crisp, green vegetables are a modern aberration. When America was great, those adjectives were for dollar bills. Muscles were hard. Vegetables were soft.

A real cafe maintains the old standards. Green beans are a proper Army green. Tomatoes are stewed with chunks of bread.

**(3) Decor.** A fake cafe has a tasteful color scheme: Pale gray. Aubergine. "A real cafe re-defines the color white," said a panelist. "There are stains in odd places. Ever wonder how that coffee got on the ceiling?"

Real cafes have orange or aqua Formica, fake wood paneling, dropped ceilings, and signs: "If you believe in credit, lend me five dollars."

Chrome and neon are a decorator's dream. That old stuff was ripped out of real cafes 15 years ago.

**(4) Coffee.** The glory of the real cafe, this coffee may save your life. It is hot and strong and served in cups that keep it that way. Some real cafes still use the old crockery, crisscrossed with cracks and suspicious stains.

**(5) Children.** Real cafes feed children. Loud children, cute children, runny nosed and whiny children.

"Look, there's a homey touch," said a panelist. "The kid is eating the plastic flowers.'' Plastic flowers are another sign.

**(6) Cafe society.** At a restaurant, customers who know each other nod. At a real cafe the customers table hop.

**(7) The waitress remembers your ''usual.''** You never have to order. Therefore, choose wisely. You may have to eat poached eggs, hash and juice for the rest of your life.

Real cafes coddle the customers. Does your diet require something that isn't on the menu? The real cafe will fix it. Want your toast burned a special way? The cafe will do that, too.

**(8) Roaches.** All restaurants have roaches. The finer places turn down the lights so you can't see them.

At a cafe, the roaches are friendly. They greet you. Once I noticed a small roach walking across the wall, and discreetly informed the waitress.

''That's nothing, honey,'' she said. ''You should see the ones in the kitchen.''

**You know you're at a real cafe when:**
The beer is American—and so is the mustard.
Ketchup is served without shame.
White wine is for the weak and degenerate.
The family runs the cash register.

The real cafe is summed up by the old roadside sign: EAT. That is a statement of purpose and a command.

## (40) The Man You Can't Live Without

I am older now. And wiser. I understand that men make promises they don't intend to keep.

But the first time a contractor said he'd fix the dining room, I believed him. Then he tore out one wall and disappeared, and I couldn't live without him.

It's always the same story. You've heard it. You have this old house with great potential—for bankruptcy. You hear about a terrific carpenter (plasterer, painter, tuckpointer). He doesn't charge much, either.

He promises to look at your house. He walks around the room, rubs his chin, and says, ''It's impossible. I don't have time now.''

You burst into tears.

The contractor looks uncomfortable and says, ''Well, maybe I can do it. I'll start Wednesday.''

You kiss the hem of his garment, and wait for Wednesday. He shows up on time, and works feverishly all day.

Then, when the wall is ripped out and plaster dust drifts across the floor, he disappears for two weeks. You beg him to return.

He shows up at noon and grudgingly works a few hours. But the fervor is gone. For months, you nag and beg until the job is finished. The work is beautiful, but you suspect he did it only to be rid of you.

Why does it always end like this? Are these relationships doomed from the beginning?

I asked my expert, Harold. You could call Harold a small contractor, but he's 6 feet tall. Harold has often starred in the drama I described. This is how he interprets Scene 1:

"The contractor is busy. He has too many jobs. He can't take on another. He wanted to say no, but he feels sorry for you. Besides, he needs the money. So he says he'll do it.

"Now he's committed himself. He starts your job.

"But the other job he's working on takes longer than he expected. They always do. The first one is pressuring him. He abandons your work to finish the first job. Then you start pressuring him, but by now he's taken a third job, and he still hasn't finished the first."

None of this would have happened if he'd shown some restraint.

"It's not our fault," he said. "Jobs always take longer than we expected because of the pointers."

A pointer is also known as a Kinda Sorta. They are identified by their plaintive cry: "While you're up there fixing the ceiling, could you kinda sorta do that crack in the wall? While you have the paint out, could you touch up that spot there?"

Maybe the paint fumes make pointers giddy. A careless holiday air prevails—until the bill arrives. The rat charged for those little touch-ups.

"I had a woman who wanted a simple drywall job," Harold said. "Then she asked if I could fix a few windows. By the time it was over, she kinda sorta wanted a new ceiling. The price had increased 100 percent.

"The classic pointer case is the Showcase Bathroom. It started as a simple $2,000 bathroom. But the woman had such good taste, she bought the best of everything: antique brass fixtures, fawn beige bathtub, ceramic tile.

"Naturally, the woman doesn't want her husband messing up this beautiful bathroom. So she builds him a shower in the basement. But she wants her husband to have the best, too. He winds up with a first-class built-in. She winds up with a $4,000 bill."

In my heart, I still blame Harold. Especially when I learned he was abandoning a woman with dreary plumbing problems for a cushy job in the county. "The woman will be mad at me, and I'll be another day behind."

But there is some justice. Harold is not a happy man. "My wife reads fancy home decorator magazines. Now she's seen this $30,000 kitchen. First, I'll tell her I don't have time."

Then she'll look sad. Harold will rip out one wall . . .

## (41) A Good Old Ladies Bar

Lil called at 4:04 in the afternoon. I wrote down the time, because I knew this would be a historic occasion.

Someday, Lil will be recognized as a great humanitarian. Future generations will rise up and call Lil blessed.

Right now, though, Lil would just like a few old ladies to call her "Bartender." If her plan goes through, Lil will preside over quite a joint.

Lil is 72 and wears a pink pantsuit. She lives in a suburban retirement community.

With a description like that, you may be tempted to call Lil spry. Not me. She's tough. One of the craftiest. And she makes a mean lemon bar. While Lil explained her plan, she plied me with brownies and lemon bars until my head reeled and I wrote down every word she said.

"I am an old lady," Lil began. "Most of my friends are about my age. Our husbands are retired. They're around the house all the time. Sometimes we feel pretty tied down. We just have to get out and get away.

"The whole thing started when I called my friend and said, 'Who wants a cup of coffee?'

"My friend says, 'Coffee! I want a drink.' Well, she's a retired banker's wife and very conservative. If she felt that way, I knew my idea would catch on."

This is Lil's idea: "I want to open a tavern for old ladies only.

"I've tried the idea out on everybody here at the apartment. Even women with no sense of humor laughed. I talked it over with my friends, and we thought about everything a good old ladies tavern ought to have."

Lil means a good tavern, not a tavern for good old ladies. "There will be a corner where you can show pictures of grandchildren —and a corner where you can't.

"We'll have a corner where you can wear tennis shoes. And a corner for Guccis.

"We are also debating a marriage broker for widowed and divorced women. Some women are against it."

The broker?

"No, marriage."

Naturally, you'd call your saloon Lil's Place.

"That's nice," said Lil. "I like the sound. But we already have a name. We'll call it either the Grocery Store or the Bakery. So when anyone asks, we can say that's where we've been all afternoon.

"I could also call my tavern Out, as in 'Where are you going? Out.'

"I found just the location, if I can steal the lease. There's a bank on one side, and a drugstore on the other. That's everything a successful tavern needs. You can cash your Social Security check before you come in and buy the bicarb when you leave.

"My tavern also has to be on a bus line. A lot of my customers are past the age when they should be driving."

Lil decided against the natural tavern habitat, the city's South Side. "I understand South Siders drink only beer. We want customers who'll buy expensive drinks. The bar should be in the better suburbs, either Ladue or Creve Coeur. We'll have a happy hour and hors d'oeuvres, but we want to make money on this.

"You haven't any idea how many people are taking this seriously. Two friends want to finance the project. Another woman in San Francisco wants the franchise there. I could also sell shares at $10 each. The beauty of this is the investors will come in and drink. It'll help their investment."

For the drinks, Lil consulted an expert. "My girl friend knows all about liquor. She can tell you what they drink anywhere in the world. Don't use her name. I don't want her husband reading that."

For music, Lil followed her own instincts. "No music that rattles the nerves. We'll keep to Bing Crosby and Perry Como."

Lil still has some problems to work out. "At first I thought I'd admit only ladies my age—70 or so. But now I think they should be 60 and over. That's the age when a woman starts needing to get away from at-home husbands and drop-off grandchildren.

"Now you can help me settle another problem. We can't decide what to do about this. Maybe your readers can help me. There are men who have worn out many pairs of shoes walking around the block—getting away from their wives. Should we admit them?

"If we do, what if they start getting together with the ladies? They're both in a similar fix. Then would we need a lawyer along with the marriage broker? These men really complicate things. My women will come there to be alone . . ."

But after a few drinks, men will start looking good again.

"That's it exactly," Lil said. "What do we do? I want to be fair. But we old ladies need a place to ourselves."

How about a men's night? You could let the old guys in one night a week, for atmosphere.

"That's good. Except we aren't much for nights any more. An hour to shower and in bed at 10. But we could have a men's afternoon."

## (42) The Night They Raided the Tupperware Party

In the gray month of January, I like to give readers something to hope for. Uplifting, you know. Inspirational.

And so, we honor Donna Margo Kochs. Her achievement should not go unrecognized. Donna did the impossible.

Her Tupperware party was raided.

Tupperware parties are like the product: They're wholesome and they last forever.

Once, at a Tupperware party, I heard a burp and thought maybe things were about to liven up. But it was just the Tupperware seal in action.

These parties are not formal affairs, but there is a correct way to issue an invitation. "It won't be as bad as it sounds," the hostess says, apologetically. "We'll have fun, honest . . . "

In Donna's case, it was true.

Donna refuses to take credit for her accomplishment. "I really owe it all to my friends, who are just great," she said, sounding like an Academy Award winner. "They're about my age, 27. I invited men and women. Men love Tupperware."

Donna's right. Men are fascinated with the stuff. Indeed, a man gave me my most valuable household hint. He discovered Tupperware is the only product that will keep the head on an open beer overnight.

Donna's party observed the Tupperware traditions: She held it at her South Side home, and she kept a Tupperware theme throughout.

"First, I made daiquiris in all the colors of Tupperware," she said. "That got us started."

Next, they played games. No Tupperware party is complete without them. The prizes are always Tupperware favors. "But we weren't going to play the dumb bridal shower games they usually have," she said.

The only way to get through most bridal showers is to grit your teeth and stare at the ceiling. I believe young couples live in sin only to avoid bridal shower games.

Donna's group played a variation of Rob Thy Neighbor. In this exciting game, players roll dice for prizes. After all the prizes are taken from the main pile, you start stealing prizes from one another.

When the dust settles at a shower, you may end up with an embroidered tea towel or a set of measuring spoons.

"We changed the rules a bit," Donna said. "You hid the prizes on your body—in your pocket, maybe, or your bra. There were certain Tupperware prizes everyone wanted: The shamrock-shaped cookie cutter. The strawberry plucker. The tea-bag squeezer."

A strawberry plucker removes stems from strawberries. I was afraid to ask what a tea-bag squeezer does.

"We really fought over those presents. My mother was the worst."

The party started at 7:30. By midnight, the relaxed dealer had sold $150 worth of Tupperware. "We were laughing and playing the stereo. The party was in full swing."

Suddenly, there was a knock at the door. Two policemen were on the porch.

"We've had complaints from the neighbors about the noise," said one cop, sternly.

"But officer," Donna said. "This is a Tupperware party."

"I don't care what it is," the policeman said. "Keep it quiet."

"Everyone was stunned," Donna said. "I'd never had a party raided by the police before."

Anyone can get raided over a little pot. Donna did it with a burpable bowl.

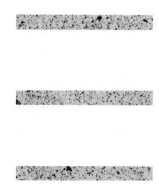

## (43) The Feds Clean Your House

Anita Riddle of Kirkwood sent me this letter, just in time for the spring housecleaning season.

"I know you have a deep interest in housekeeping, which I share," she said.

Anita must remember some of the household hints that appeared in this column. I was the first to reveal that Tupperware will keep the head on a beer overnight.

I also color-coordinate my cats with the couch, so the cat hair won't show.

It wasn't easy finding a plaid cat.

"I think you need the enclosed booklet from the Department of Housing and Urban Development," Anita said. "This handy guide sounds and looks as though it was written in 1930, but I swear I got it within the last 10 or 15 years."

The 24-page booklet is called "Simplified Housekeeping Directions for Homemakers."

"It's full of amusing chores," Anita said. Here are a few:

EVERY WEEK: "Defrost and wash the refrigerator, inside and outside.

"Give the stove a thorough washing, inside and outside.

"Scrub the floor with hot sudsy water and hot rinse water. Wax the floor, if it is the kind that needs a wax finish."

EVERY COUPLE OF DAYS: "Wipe each wastebasket inside and outside with a cloth wrung out of hot suds. Then wipe it with a damp cloth and end up by wiping it with a dry cloth. Give each wastebasket a real washing once a week.''

EVERY MONTH OR SO: "Empty the closets. Wash the closet walls, shelves and the floors. While they are drying, dust off the hangers."

Wash the light fixtures and shades. Wash the light bulbs. When you've dusted the hangers and washed the light bulbs, ''wax the outside of the refrigerator every couple of weeks if you want it to be shiny."

I never wax my refrigerator. I starch my freezer, to make it stand up straight. It's an upright.

The booklet recommends every month or so, you "wash, rinse and dry the furniture. When the wood is thoroughly dry, put on new wax or polish.''

After you wash everything that doesn't get up and run, wash what you've been washing with. The booklet explains how to wash the brooms, brushes, sponges and rubber gloves.

A woman's work is never done—and I do mean woman. No men clean house in this 1965 book. The women wear dresses, even when scrubbing floors on hands and knees.

"I suspect the motives of anybody who would write such a book," Anita said. "I consider it obscene."

I consider it the "Reefer Madness" of the homemaking set.

"So much sudsy water is used by the smiling little cartoon lady that I'm sure she, as well as everything else in her house, is covered with mildew, because nothing ever gets a chance to dry out.

"The front page said it was prepared for HUD by the 'Cleanliness Bureau of the Soap and Detergent Association,' " Anita said. "That should tell you something."

The SDA is an association of soap and detergent manufacturers. That may explain why so many tips begin: "Dip a big cloth or mop into a pail of sudsy water." The book has you dipping into "sudsy water" at least 61 times.

A helpful woman at the Soap and Detergent Association explained that the government no longer prints the booklet, but the SDA keeps a revised version afloat.

"The pamphlet was orginally developed for low-income people," she said. "It was designed to help people who were moving into public housing. We discovered it had many other uses. In some places, it was even used to help adults learn to read."

Aren't the housekeeping standards a little high?

"We prefer to set our standards a little higher.

"The new revised booklet will be more relevant," she said. "But I certainly hope you're not writing about it at this time. People would want copies. The new revised ones aren't available yet. The booklet is still being worked on.''

Then there may be time to include my favorite household hint. I will dedicate it to the entire Soap and Detergent Association.

Prepare a large bucket of warm, sudsy water.

Then soak your head.


## (44) The No-Tell Motel

This story could be about money and morals. But it's really about survival. Or maybe the man just has a good rationale.

He has a motel on Watson Road, the old Route 66.

''We've been in the motel business since the '40s,'' he said. ''There used to be motels on this strip for miles, all the way to Lindbergh.

''Now they're all but gone. The new highway killed us. People don't drive into the city this way anymore.

''We've been having to survive on traveling salesmen. And fellows who work in town and go home on weekends. Sometimes we get people waiting for their new house to be built, or looking for an apartment.

''People who spend their own money stay here. Not people on expense accounts. Those people stay at the big, new hotels.''

But he did get a boost from the local government. ''The crackdown on drunken drivers has pulled in a few. On a couple of occasions, the police have brought them in. The customers stay the night and sleep it off. It's cheaper than taking a cab, and they don't have to go back and get their car in the morning.

''Our units aren't as nice anymore. I don't see where it would do any good to modernize. We're out on the edge of the city. The business goes downtown.

''We're all just existing. When someone offers you a piece of change, you take it, and let them bulldoze the motel and put up a big store. When someone makes me an offer, I'll probably be gone, too.''

He paused. You could count the beats.

''Put down your pen a minute,'' he said, ''and I'll tell you how we really survive. We all do it along here. About 40 percent of my business is what I call tourist. The rest is local trade. Short rates. People who rent a room for a couple of hours.''

Is he right? Do all the strip motels really survive that way? Or is this the grownup version of ''It's OK, Mom. All the kids are doing it''?

He seemed a little uncomfortable. ''People who know me say, 'How can you do that?' I said, 'How do I know they're NOT married?' Do you carry your marriage license with you when you go to a hotel? Who am I to challenge you?

"Is everybody who rents a room at the big downtown hotels married? It's just how many bucks you got and where you want to go. And we'll give you a reasonable price."

The man said the local trade is different from the ordinary tourist. "There's very little theft. We have our names printed on the ashtrays. They never take them. They don't want to get caught with that in their purse.

"They don't even take the free matches.

"Another thing. We provide soap, but often it's not unwrapped. My clerk couldn't get over it.

"I said, 'Use your head. You come home smelling like Lifebuoy, and you use Dial, that's it. You're in trouble.' My customers bring their own soap."

But they aren't perfect. "Some don't care, you know. Some want the notoriety. They're rather proud of it. They keep one of my towels in their car. And some are just thieves. They'll strip the room—sheets, towels, drapes. Clean you out."

Your information could save some lives. "Maybe," he said. "I could cook a lot of gooses, too, if I ever started recollecting things. But that's all I'm going to say."

## (45) South Side Chic

For some time, I've suspected my South Side neighborhood was going downhill.

I saw the signs. The Fords and Chevys were giving way to BMWs and Audis. The plastic lawn ducks and concrete squirrels were becoming endangered species.

I kept kidding myself. I said there were still lots of aluminum awnings. People still grew sunflowers by the ashpit.

Now I know the worst. The South Side is fashionable. A West Ender told me he bought a South Side home.

Ten years ago, West Enders wouldn't have been caught dead on the South Side. Now they want to live in two-family flats.

There goes the neighborhood.

I wouldn't mind the newcomers so much, but they ask such dumb questions. For the sake of neighborhood harmony, I will answer Six Common South Side Questions.

(1) WHY DO SOUTH SIDE HOUSES ALWAYS HAVE THE BLINDS PULLED?

For two good reasons: You can snoop without being caught. And the sun won't fade the slipcovers and the carpet.

South Side floors favor the layered look. Carpets are covered with throw rugs. The throw rugs are protected with plastic runners. South Side sofas (couches are for shrinks) have two sets of slipcovers, good and everyday. Good slipcovers are saved for weddings and funerals.

You will see the actual sofa only once—at the estate sale. It will be in top condition.

(2) WHERE DO YOU GET THOSE PINK ALUMINUM AWNINGS?

The same place you get the white-and-green awnings. And the aluminum storm doors.

Note the initial on the storm door is not the same as the current owner's. When Mr. Zimmerman moved, he left a perfectly good door. Changing the initial is a waste of good money.

(3) WHAT COLOR SHOULD I PAINT MY PORCH? I'M THINKING OF PEACH WITH PERIWINKLE TRIM, TO SET OFF THE BRICK.

You're thinking wrong. South Side decorator colors are red, battleship gray, forest green and white.

Concrete steps and basement floors are painted red. Porch steps are battleship gray. Gutters are forest green. Lawn ornaments and bird baths are white.

If you are not sure of the correct color, paint it white.

(4) WHY DO THE LAWNS LOOK ARTIFICIAL?

Zoysia is the official grass of the South Side. If the grass doesn't look artificial, it isn't a real South Side lawn.

When the steps look artificial, they are. Some ritzy South Siders carpet their steps with AstroTurf.

(5) WHERE DO I HANG MY WIND CHIMES?

In your ear. South Side homes are allowed only the following ornaments: concrete swans and squirrels, plastic ducks and religious statues.

(6) HOW DOES ONE ADDRESS SOUTH SIDE ETHNICS?

Be polite but friendly. "How ya doing, Dutch?" is the proper way to address either sex.

Calling a South Sider an ethnic marks you as a social worker, federal employee or other undesirable.

## *(46) The Cutting Edge: Getting a New Haircut*

Mary Ann Faron, like millions of other Americans, suffers from a dreadful handicap. She lives in the suburbs.

"We're treated almost as if we're culturally retarded," Mary Ann said. "I'm your typical suburban housewife. I can understand why people make fun of the suburbs. But where else are you going to raise your kids?"

Recently, the whole issue came to a head. As Mary Ann sees it, a hair stylist condescended to give her the latest cut—without telling her. She was his own, personal suburban renewal project.

But did Mary Ann appreciate his efforts? Hah. Just read what she says.

"I had a nice, normal haircut," she said. "I hate when hair is named after a celebrity, but it looked like a Princess Diana cut."

Mary Ann used to go to a fashionable city shop. Then her stylist raised the price to $35, and Mary Ann rebelled.

"I went to another salon. A very reputable place. I told the stylist I wanted my hair layered."

Mary Ann came out a new woman. She had the haircut of a 14-year-old, and she couldn't give it back.

"He gave me a punk haircut. It's shaved in the back and on the sides. It's long in front and combed forward. It has a duck's tail. My husband has more hair, and he's going bald.

"But that's not the worst. It's two-toned. My hair is frosted, and it's cut so close on the sides, it's two colors now. The sides are black and the top is blond."

This is very important, Mary Ann. Did you tell the stylist:

(1) "I'm tired of this boring style. Do something interesting."

(2) "Could you take off a couple of inches?"

Those two sentences unleash terrible drives in hairdressers. It's like handing Lizzie Borden an ax.

"No, nothing like that. I said my hair needed to be shaped. He said, 'How about if I take a little off the back?' He never mentioned the sides.

"I said I wanted to be left with some hair. He left me with hair all right—a piece in the middle, like a Mohawk."

At first, Mary Ann did not realize her head had been rehabbed. "It was too wet to tell. Then I went home and took a good look in the mirror. I couldn't believe it. I called my husband at work and warned him. Then I waited."

Mary Ann's brother was the first person to see her new cut. "His mouth dropped open. He said, 'You look like you belong in a Van Halen video.' "

That was mean. But kindness was even worse. "People asked what happened. I pleaded brain surgery.

"I couldn't do anything with it. My hair was so short, I couldn't get a curling iron in it. I went out and bought a wig. The woman at the wig place called people over to look at my hair. Then I knew it looked really bad. She said it would be four months before my hair grew out. I burst out crying, right in front strangers.

"I called the beauty shop and said, 'I look like a rock star.' The hair-dresser asked, 'You don't want to look like a rock star?'

"I said, 'Not when I'm picking out bananas at the supermarket.' "

The next day, Mary Ann went to the shop and complained in person. "The stylist looked at me with such contempt. I could have crawled out of there. He said, 'It's the latest style from London.' "

That should have singed off Mary Ann's remaining hair.

"I don't have the cheekbones, the complexion or the clothes for this style. I said, 'You didn't tell me you were going to do this.' Besides, it looked choppy. He said my hair wasn't choppy. It was texturized.

"It was his word against mine. And I should have spoken up while he was cutting. Maybe I was a little intimidated. It was a lack of communication.

"He returned my money. But he couldn't give me back my hair."

And what about the man on the cutting edge—Mary Ann's hair stylist?

He told me, "We agreed on going shorter. I pulled her hair back and showed her how it would look. When she left, she seemed to like it."

How did it turn out two colors?

"She had her hair frosted, but it wasn't done by us. The cut uncovered an improper coloring."

But that wasn't the worst.

"It wasn't a punk rock cut," he said. "It was a modified layered wedge. It's nothing really unusual. There are hundreds like it."

That was the unkindest cut of all.

## (47) Slaughter on the South Side

When I got back to the office last Tuesday night, there was this message: "Joan called at 3:30 p.m. Return her call before 5."

It was after 6. Everything moved slower after the snowstorm—especially me. I called the woman anyway. "You missed a scoop," Joan said. "I was going to murder my neighbor at 5 o'clock."

Just my luck. I missed the call that could have made my career. Other columnists are always in the office when a murdering fiend calls.

I could have talked Joan out of the murder, written her story, and made the 6 o'clock news. If I failed, well, sorry about the neighbor. It's a good story, anyway.

Are you still planning to murder your neighbor, Joan? Where there's life, there's hope.

"No," Joan said. "A police officer talked me out of it."

He is one of St. Louis' unsung heroes. Read Joan's thrilling story of slaughter on the snowbound South Side.

"My husband drove to work Tuesday morning," Joan said. "In the afternoon, I shoveled him out a parking spot."

Forget Romeo and Juliet. When a woman shovels a spot for her man, that's true love.

"I finished about 3, and this neighbor pulled into the spot like I'd shoveled it for her. I was standing right there."

"You are going to move," Joan said.

"I'll try," the woman said, in a soft, infuriating voice.

"My husband gets home at quarter to five, and you will be out of there."

"I'll try," she said again.

Joan was outraged. The interloper had violated a sacred South Side custom —the inalienable right to the parking space in front of our homes.

Tradition says a South Sider owns that spot. When the natural boundaries are unclear after a snowstorm, we shovel out our spot and stake our claim with sawhorses, trashcans or old kitchen chairs.

Only a lowdown so-and-so would steal a freshly shoveled parking spot. That's just what Joan told the claim jumper. Then she called the police.

The officer explained the police couldn't do anything. "There's no law protecting your spot," he said. "But there's also no law that you can't sprinkle the snow in your yard with a garden hose. If their car happens to be in the way of your snow . . ."

He paused, meaningfully. "The water freezes doors and locks," he said. "It freezes tires to the ground. It took my neighbor four hours to chip his car out."

Joan asked, "But won't the police arrest me?"

"The officer said, 'Nah.' I asked for his name. He gave it."

We will protect this humanitarian's identity. The police would never advocate anything like that. Right, boys and girls?

## *(48) Ready or Not: A Dialogue*

The gentleman stood in his kitchen in deep despair. (Deep despair is an old family recipe. His mother makes it.)

"I'm stuck waiting again," he said. "Why isn't my wife ever ready to leave on time? She said she was ready to go. That was 15 minutes ago."

Surely, you've figured that out by now.

"Don't call me Shirley," he said. "That's my wife's name."

Lexicographers will tell you the phrase "I'm ready to go" has two accepted meanings. To find out which one your spouse or roommate uses, take this simple test.

You are going to dinner at the Hendersons at 7:30. They live 30 minutes away. At 6:50, you ask The Question. You get a cheery, "Yes, I'm ready to go."

This can mean:

(1) "I'm ready to go THIS MINUTE."

(2) "I'm ready to go . . .

(2a) "But I have to find . . .

"My shoes

"My glasses

"My car keys

"My coat in the hall closet

"And the scarf that goes with the coat in the hall closet. I think I left it in the bedroom.

"My gloves, which fell out of my coat pocket. I think they're on the closet floor. Would you mind turning on the hall light?

"Well, you don't have to be so crabby. I said I was ready."

It's now 7 o'clock. You are ready for the second part of this response. (2b) "I'm ready to go, but did you turn off the coffee?"

You'll probably answer, "Yes. I think so."

This answer is fiendishly designed to make the other person worry. On the way to check the coffee pot, which turns out to be unplugged after all, your spouse decides to look at the iron and check the stove. Both could still be on, and wouldn't you be sorry if the house burned down.

The next question is, "Did you close the bedroom window?"

Followed by, "Is the back door locked?"

"Did you let the dog out?"

"Do you have the directions to the Hendersons' house?"

By now, it is one-half hour since the initial question, "Are you ready to go?" was first asked. It is time for the absolutely final question, "Did you call the Hendersons and tell them we're running late?"

Women are blamed as the worst procrastinators. This is unfair. Women take the rap because their mothers told them to keep their dates waiting. "He won't appreciate you if you run right down," Mom warned.

The man never forgets those agonizing 15 minutes spent with his date's father. It blights the union forever. Once the couple marries, he never lets her forget what he suffered.

The other misconception is that this is the sign of a mismatch. Not at all. The sort of person who is ready on time invariably marries a procrastinator.

They make each other very happy, because this habit always leaves them an opening for a meaningful dialogue.

SPOUSE A: What can I do so you'll get ready on time?

SPOUSE B: What can I do to keep you from leaving your piles of magazines and papers all over the house?

SPOUSE A: That's not half as bad as your habit of leaving your shoes in the kitchen, where I trip over them in the middle of the night.

SPOUSE B: You wouldn't have tripped on my shoes, if you hadn't come in drunk Saturday night.

SPOUSE A: No wonder I was drunk. All I had to look forward to was Sunday dinner at your mother's.

And so on and on, until the couple has discussed many issues in an open and adult matter.

## (49) The Cultural Exchange Plan

A West County preppie with blond hair, red ears and a navy blazer asked me, "Do you like the South Side?"

Of course I like the South Side. I live there.

"But you say such terrible things about it," he said. "You make it sound like there's a bar on every corner."

There is. That's why I like it.

But the young man did not understand urban planning. I could have been talking another language. The South Side was a foreign country to him. That's when I came up with my plan.

West Countians go to London and Paris more often than Grand and Gravois. When they do visit south St. Louis, they see only the tourist spots, like Ted Drewes frozen custard stand. Consequently, they see us as a quaint people and do not appreciate our customs.

I would like to propose a foreign exchange program, where a young person from suburban Clayton or Ladue would live with a South Side family, and a South Sider would move in with the West Countian.

I believe both West County and the South Side would benefit from this experience, and they would learn to appreciate each other's culture.

AMBIANCE: Most people moved to the county because everything in the city is so old. Now they spend thousands of dollars re-creating an 1890s look. The city spends its money getting rid of the 1890s look.

DRESS: West Countians are colorful dressers. They prefer bright colors that South Siders frequently associate with lower income groups.

South Siders should remember that a Ladue man in a pink shirt is not a gigolo—unless the shirt is satin. If a West County man wears a blazer, he is not a security guard.

If a West County woman wears sequins, she's chic. In the city, she's a hooker.

Both the city and the county want prestige names on their sports togs. West County prefers Adidas. The South Side likes St. Gabriel's and St. Raphael's.

FOOD: It is impolite to comment on unusual food. South Siders like brain sandwiches and toasted ravioli, both high in that natural substance, grease. West Countians prefer horrors such as nachos with processed cheese.

On Sunday, county people go to brunch. City people go to church.

PARKING: West Countians cannot parallel park. They are proud of this deficiency.

The city has a highly developed parking culture. You can live there for years, and not understand all the rules. Here are some you'll need for survival:

(1) City residents own the parking spot in front of their houses. If you need a parking space, use the bus stop.

(2) Watch out for street-cleaning signs. St. Louis has such arcane rules as "No Parking Odd-Dated Tuesday 7 a.m. to 11 a.m." Forgetting this could get you a $10 ticket.

PLASTIC: City people use MasterCard. County people like American Express.

POLICE: Both the city and county are police snobs. In the county, the prestige police are Clayton and Ladue.

In the city, it's the Second District—Hampton Avenue. Rumor has it they won't check out a burglary without two references.

SALOONS: The South Side has neighborhood bars, with a walk-in trade. You can run a tab in a city bar, but not in the county.

The county has fern bars. They pay some ad agency to dream up cute names. South Side bar names are naturally quaint—Barge Inn and Big Daddy's.

In the county, darts is the bar sport. City people do not like objects whizzing past their heads. They play shuffleboard, cork ball and bottle caps. Bottle caps is played with a broomstick in the lot behind the tavern.

Both South Side and West County bars have tin ceilings. The West County has imitation tin, re-created by a nostalgia firm. The South Side has genuine tin. The paint is peeling off, and the owner will hide it with a drop ceiling as soon as business picks up.

City beer is American and cold. City bars prefer iced steins and fishbowls. Be careful. Once the ice melts, you can suffer serious injury when the stein slides down the Formica.

TRANSPORTATION: West County children take riding lessons. In the city, only the police ride horses.

WILD LIFE: The county has moles. The city does not. The city has rats. The county says it doesn't.

## (50) *Mama Said to Shop Around*

This story is about two star-crossed lovers. I call it "Kimberly and the Cute Guy."

You wanted Romeo and Juliet? Those names are too ethnic. They call this Yuppie love.

One night about 7 o'clock, Kimberly, a handsome single female, dashed into the Schnucks supermarket at Clayton and Hanley roads.

Kimberly is a busy executive. She wanted to pick up some avocados and Lean Cuisine. Other singles go to the Clayton Schnucks to pick up people.

When Mama said to shop around, she didn't mean go to the supermarket. But certain St. Louis supermarkets are chic—or maybe that's cheap—places to meet.

Kimberly was getting her amount-of-purchase check approved, when she saw a cute male.

"He eyed me, and I eyed him," Kimberly said.

Their eyes crossed.

"I thought, 'This is really nice. I would like to know him.' He seemed to be alone. But in produce, I noticed there was a woman beside him."

What a shame. He seemed ripe for romance.

"We skipped a couple of aisles. When I saw him again, the woman was gone. I never saw her again.

"We passed in the milk and yogurt aisle. I noticed how really attractive he was. We kept running into each other, accidentally.

"I wondered if I should start some kind of conversation with him," she said. "But I am really shy. It's hard to imagine that someone as successful as I am would be shy, but I am."

Kimberly looked deep into his cart. She liked what she saw. "He had to be a bachelor. I could tell by what he bought: Unmatched frozen dinners. One avocado. One frozen yogurt. All the things I had in mine. He might even be newly divorced. He was buying a broom."

Only divorced men buy brooms?

"It's a good sign," she said. "Usually, the ex-wife keeps their broom."

That was a sweeping statement.

"Finally, we were in line for the cash register. I thought, 'Either something's going to happen or it isn't.' He was standing in the shorter line. I was in the longer line. He moved over into my line. I was very nervous. Should I say something now?"

She hesitated.

"Then the cashier opened the next checkout line, and said, 'Miss, will you come to this register?' "

Kimberly said her first words to the Cute Guy: "Will you pardon me, please?" The Cute Guy followed her into the new line. Maybe he wanted to meet her. Maybe it was the fastest line. Kimberly wasn't sure.

"The cashier picked up my cabbage and asked, 'What is this?' 'I said, 'Savoy cabbage.' The Cute Guy chuckled."

Wait just a minute. What is Savoy cabbage?

"It's purply on the ends, and green toward the roots," Kimberly said. "It's a nice-tasting green that's purple."

The cabbage did not flower into further conversation. "I thought of letting him see the name on my check. Then maybe he would call me. I decided, 'No that's not safe. And it's not right. It's tacky.' "

She left with her yogurt and her pride.

"I walked out of there angry at myself," she said. "In the parking lot, I watched him get into a cute little red Volkswagen. He had trouble getting his broom inside. I have a bigger car. If I'd tried to talk to him, I could have offered him a ride home. I thought of going back to the store at the same time later in the week. But I know I'll never meet him again.

"There's a moral to this story," Kimberly said. "Dating must be difficult for men, too."

It is, Kimberly. But women can learn, just as men do. To help you, I've consulted the Schnucks Market in Clayton. Remember, their slogan is "the friendliest store in town."

"We're the matchmakers of Clayton," a store employee told me. "We see the singles hanging around here pretty much every day. But it probably increases toward the weekend—Thursday, Friday and Saturday. The busiest times are 3 to 7 on weekdays and 11 to 7 on Saturday.

"People used to meet in the tuna section and talk about their diets. Nowadays, they're into produce. They pick up a grapefruit or something and ask the person's opinion. They'll say, 'Do you think this is good?' "

Be careful, Kimberly. The wrong choice could be intimidating.

"Lately, I've seen them in the seafood section," the employee said. "They swap recipes, and talk about how to fix the fish. One thing leads to another, and before you know it . . ."

Hurry, Kimberly. It's not too late to run out to the supermarket and pick up something.

## (51) Suburban Superwoman Does Her Noontime Dance

Don looked out the window of his suburban Creve Coeur office and saw a young woman dancing down Olive Boulevard.

"She was wearing this Superwoman outfit," Don said. "Tights, sequins and a cape."

That's nothing unusual, if you work in the city. Every morning, I see people in weird costumes dancing, shuffling, mumbling, waving their arms and talking to themselves.

And these are just the ones going into my building.

But Don was amazed. "You don't see a lot of people in capes and sequins dancing around in a suburb like Creve Coeur," he said.

Don just won the Understatement of the Year Award, and it's only April.

"The first time, I couldn't believe it," he said. "She dances around lunch time, wearing headphones. She looks between 20 and 27 years old. What she does is somewhere between a dance and a strut."

Don sounded proud. "I'm glad she does it. I'm not complaining. Instead of eating a greasy hamburger for lunch, maybe we should all dance down Olive."

You could have a Creve Coeur conga line.

The Olive dancer has become a local legend. Everyone on the strip knew another story about her. There's a legend that she once caused a fender bender because a driver watched her dance.

Odie Smith, manager of the Standard station on the strip, says she's kind to animals and people.

"She says she's on a mission to catch and save stray dogs," Odie said. "Some people think she's three quarts low. I think she lifts everyone up. She's the kinkiest thing east of the Pecos.''

That's a compliment.

Most people are complimentary. She's become one of the sights of Creve Coeur. If there is any criticism, it's that sometimes she hangs around a place a little too much and talks to the help. A cape and sequins can be very conspicuous.

''She's a nice lady,'' said a supervisor, ''but those outfits make my men nervous.''

The dancer's outfits are part of the legend. A young woman who works in one of the Olive offices could describe them all.

''The Superwoman outfit is the most famous,'' she said. ''She also wears tiger-striped leotards. I've seen her dressed like a bumblebee, complete with antennae. Sometimes she wears feathers in her hair and sparkly belts. Her hair is very blond, and the guys like to honk at her.

''I don't know why she runs up and down this strip,'' the woman said. ''It's smoky and noisy. At lunch, I walk over to Denny's, and the exhaust fumes almost kill me. But you can see her kicking, dancing and spinning.

''Today, she's dressed quietly—blue striped leotard, blue tights, yellow socks and blue running shoes with bells on them. She has bands of blue sequins around her neck, waist and ankles. Wait! There she goes now.''

Sure enough, she was dancing down Olive, to the rhythm of a rock station and a chorus of honks.

The dancer says she is 31 years old, and a nurse's assistant at a hospital. She did not want to use her name. ''My nickname's Tiger,'' she said. ''Call me that.''

She says she dances down Olive from about 10 till 2. ''I work out every other day. You're supposed to give your muscles a rest. I'm very strong. Feel my muscle.''

I did. She is.

And she's not exactly dancing. It's some combination of jogging and aerobics, called the Jogger's Workout.

''I started this about 2½ years ago. I got sick then,'' Tiger said. ''I thought I was going to die. When that happens, it changes your life.

''Some people think I'm a hooker. Some try to run me down. But most get a kick out of me. They all know me. I'm harmless. I like wearing my costumes. My favorite is Superwoman. I do heroic people. Kids should see heroes in life and on TV.

''I try to help. I try to rescue stray dogs. Once, I saw a truck with its doors flapping open. I ran after it, and stopped it.''

Why don't you run in a park?

''I wouldn't do that,'' Tiger said. ''You have to run where people can see you. It's too dangerous in a park. People smoke pot and drink.''

Some people think you're crazy.

Tiger shrugged. The bells jingled, and the sequins glittered in the sun. "To each his own. I don't want to be critical. But I think this is better than coming home from work, eating dinner and watching TV."

## (52) In the Ring: The Wrestler's Wedding

Don H. opened the wedding invitation, and said: "Oh, boy! This is one wedding I want to see."

That's strange. Don H. hates weddings. He never goes, except at gunpoint. Even to his own.

Then I got a look at the engraved invitation. It said: "United Wrestling Federation presents the challenge of marriage uniting Jeanne and Insane Abdul . . ."

Yep, Insane Abdul Hussein, the wrestler who wears Arab getup and throws packs of Camels to the crowd, married sweet, red-haired Jeanne in a wrestling ring. Between matches.

Their wedding was the main event Thursday, after a UWF championship match in St. Charles.

Insane Abdul, like many wrestlers, conceals his real name. Jeanne doesn't. But she's going to have enough problems as Mrs. Insane.

Their wedding has been reported as a social and sporting event. But there's more to it. This was a trendsetting match, that managed to keep many elements of a traditional wedding.

The setting was a standard hotel ballroom, done in yellow and brown. In the center was a wrestling ring, about the size of a dance floor. The room smelled of popcorn, thanks to a refreshment stand. Parents hit with huge catering bills should know that guests and fans bought their own beer and sausages.

Wedding guests got in free. Wrestling fans paid $7 at the door.

Lenard, who sat next to me, asked, "Does the fight start before the wedding or after?"

After. Usually on the parking lot.

"Is this like any other match?" Lenard said. "Do we get to hiss the groom and cheer the bride?"

Please. Remember this is a wedding. Only the bride's family is allowed to hiss the groom.

This wedding had an emcee from a country station. Even that was traditional. He warmed up the audience with a couple of off-color jokes. Just like your uncle, who gets louder after midnight. Except this guy had a microphone.

The guests settled in to watch the preliminary wrestling matches. There were a lot of bottle blondes with beer guts bouncing around on the mat.

"Reminds me of the fight my mother had with the caterer," a woman said.

"Caterers are tough," Lenard said.

Guests recalled other championship fights before family weddings, mostly knock-down dragouts with florists and photographers.

No one talked about the groom's strange get-up. We'd all been in weddings before. We'd seen grown men in peach ruffled tuxes.

Finally, they cleared the ring, and hung it with white streamers and paper bells. The effect was festive, if you didn't see the blood smears on the mat.

"Ladies and gentlemen," the announcer said. "The wedding is in three minutes."

But first, he gave the Cards' score. They were winning. The crowd cheered.

Then the wedding began. To the tune of "Midnight at the Oasis," Insane Abdul arrived with his entourage. Abdul wore off-white satin sheik's robes, which opened to reveal his black bowtie and mauve wrestling togs.

He carried one perfect artificial leg.

The bride was escorted by her father, who helped her crawl through the ropes into the ring. She wore a white full-skirted wedding gown, and carried a bouquet. Her attendant wore a harem costume.

The couple was married by a distinguished-looking woman minister in white robes, known as the Jailhouse Angel. The crowd settled into a reverent silence. Until the minister asked, "Do you, Insane Abdul . . ."

Then everyone burst out laughing.

"Maybe they should say, 'In this ring, I thee wed,' " said a guest.

The guests spontaneously hummed "Here Comes the Bride."

After the wedding, Insane Abdul fought Bobby Valentine. The bride cheered and comforted the groom.

Valentine stomped Abdul's arm. The bride kissed it.

Valentine whomped Abdul on his head. The bride kissed it.

Valentine knocked Abdul on his rump. The bride shook her head no.

But she did lead the chant for her true love. The crowd roared: "Insane! Insane!"

At last, Insane won. The loser threw the wedding cake at the referee.

"Aren't they going to throw any rice?" said the romantic Lenard.

Why? They've already thrown the groom.

Most guests did not stay for the tag-team match. Instead, we talked with Abdul outside. "What did you think?" he asked.

It's the only honest wedding I've ever been to.

"Thanks," said Abdul. "Her father was against it. But I think he came around. Especially after I won the match."

## (53) There's One on Every Block

It's a neighborhood rule: "There's one on every block."

You know who they are. The ones who don't keep up the property. The family who doesn't quite fit in.

Their house doesn't look that different. The lawn is a little shaggy. The porch is one coat of paint behind the rest of the block. But look at the porch again.

That's how they always gave themselves away. They left up the Christmas lights. In July.

It didn't matter if the house was in low-rent Lemay or la-di-dah Ladue. The standards were the same.

Once, driving through Ladue, a gentleman pointed to a fancy home. "All that money, and look how they keep up the house," he said. He sounded disgusted.

At first, the place looked fine. Then I saw the tell-tale sign—it was Christmas in July.

When I was growing up, we lived in the suburb of St. Ann for a while. It was 1958, and our street was full of up-and-comers. One family had just bought a pink Edsel, which everyone admired. The house across the street had a color television. The whole block would go over there to watch Dinah Shore. She had green hair.

Then there was Bud's house. Bud's yard didn't look that bad. After all, he paid me 25 cents a bucket to dig out the weeds. And he didn't squash the weeds down in the bucket like other people did.

Bud was about 50. He had bluish tattoos on his sagging biceps, a tremendous beer gut and a long-suffering wife named Bernice. For years, I thought her first name was Poor, because everyone called her Poor Bernice.

Bud liked to get drunk every Saturday night. He'd pour himself a beer. Then he'd pour a bowl of beer for his dog. The two of them would agree that life was sad and the Cardinals were sadder. About midnight, they'd both start howling. Then they'd fall asleep.

Bud had a girlie calendar on the kitchen door and a fascinating set of salt and pepper shakers.

The shakers were the kind sold in Ozark souvenir stands—a reclining Daisy Mae. Her bosom was marked with a giant S and P.

Unfortunately, I didn't see much of these artworks. Whenever I walked in the house, Bernice would slam the kitchen door shut, and throw the toaster cover over the shakers.

The neighbors thought Bud was degenerate. When everyone gathered to watch the green Dinah Shore, they talked about him. The calendar was bad enough. And how could Bernice allow those disgusting salt and pepper shakers in the house?

But that wasn't the worst. Bud left his Christmas lights up all year-round. Even in July.

He turned the lights on at Christmastime, just like everyone else. For eight weeks, the block was content. Bud fit in.

But Bud never took down the lights in the post-Christmas sleet storm. He had a fine explanation. "Why should I put them up in November, if I'm just going to take them down in January?" he said.

I'd never heard a grownup use an excuse like that before. It was the same argument I'd used for not making my bed: "Why do I have to make the bed in the morning, if I'm just going to get back in it at night?"

People don't put up Christmas lights quite so much any more. Bud and his beer-drinking dog are long gone. But he remains a shining light.

This column is for you, Bud. Happy July.

## (54) A Hunter Down in the Dumps

He likes to hunt. But only if the animals deserve to die. "I don't hunt deer," he said. "Blowing away Bambi with a cannon is no sport for me."

No, sir. He goes to the dump and shoots rats.

"Rats are filthy and disgusting, and serve no useful purpose."

He is a police officer by day, a rat hunter by night. Some might say there's a connection between these two activities. But not our man.

"Naw," he said. "Rat hunting is relaxing."

And expensive. He uses a fancy $400 German air gun. Right now, he says there's no hunting ground worthy of his weapon. He likes to talk about the glory days of rat-hunting, when the old Hall Street dump was open.

"That was an endless dump—acres of garbage, lined up in long rows. Rats were everywhere."

Picture this scene: Our man is down in the dumps, setting up his rat blind. It is dusk. As the purple shadows gather, the dump begins to stir.

You hear the *clink!* of an overturned can, then a squeal.

"Rats don't come out before sundown," he said. "Their greatest activity is two hours later. They quiet down about midnight.

"I'd go to my favorite place, a cleared space between the piles of trash. It was a rat condo. I'd set out my blanket."

What's that for?

"You don't want to sit in garbage," he said. "That's disgusting. I'd take my gun and whatever I was drinking . . ."

You drink while you hunt?

"Rat shooting is thirsty work. On a good, clear night, you can see the rats moving. Heads would start popping out of the trash. I'd shoot them BING! BING! BING! I could get 50 to 100 rats an evening. The nice thing about shooting rats in a dump is you don't have to worry about disposing of the carcasses."

The hunter's friends benefit, too. We don't have to figure out how to cook rat meat.

And this hunter has no resentful wife waiting at home. "I take my wife along. At first, Joyce would just go with me and read a book, or be revolted.

"Then I explained that rats were nasty and spread disease. She decided it was OK to kill them. Now, she has a ball. We make a night out of it."

Joyce confirmed this. "I even got to where I could shake them," she said.

I don't understand hunter's slang.

"You stand on top a pile of trash," she said, "and jump up and down. The rats run down. Then he shoots them."

The officer said, "Rats are smart, and good at sensing you. I hit them with a light first. That makes them stand still. But only for a moment. You've got to be quick. You've got to hit them right behind the forelegs, or the head, to kill them. The head shot is more sporting, unless you're mounting the rat later.

"There used to be a guy who would bow-hunt rats. I had the highest respect for him."

Using a rifle is not sporting. And firing ANY gun in the city is not legal.

"Ever since the dump closed, I've been looking for a safe place to shoot rats. We've found a few spots. But you just don't see the vast numbers any more. Last time, I only shot a rat an hour. My wife and I are reduced to murdering beer cans."

Joyce yearns for the old, romantic invitation: "Wanna go to the dump and shoot rats?"

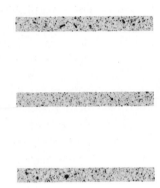

## (55) Controlling Comfort

Just when I thought there was no solution to this problem, I read a New York newspaper.

There was the answer, right in a Bloomingdale's ad for down comforters. The ad showed a couple of consenting adults under a comforter, regular $375. (That's the price of the comforter. But the adults didn't look cheap, either.)

The ad is devoted to an important bedroom issue: Who controls the thermostat?

It isn't clear who's talking in the ad, the man or the woman. But you can't fool me. I know it's the man who wants to keep the room ice cold.

Anyway, the conversation in the ad copy goes like this:

"What's this, the world's warmest down comforter?"
"Pretty close, I like it toasty warm when I sleep."
"Toasty? It'll be like the Sahara in there. I like it cold and crisp."
"Cold and crisp?"
"Yeah. Like New Hampshire in October."
"Well, I guess you'll have to learn to adapt."
"Adapt? Can't we compromise?"
"It's my apartment, remember? I make the rules."

Stick to your guns, sweetie. You know he really doesn't like the room cold and crisp, like New Hampshire in October. He likes it freezing, like the Yukon in December. If he kept the room the way he likes it, you'd think you were sleeping in a drawer, with a tag on your toe.

And you're right to make the rules. You can't compromise on an issue like this. There's a physiological reason why some people like rooms cold. They have a high fat content between their ears.

When this couple marries—and they will, these types always do—they will discover that marriage has its ups and downs.

She will get up about 2 a.m., and turn up the heat. He will wake up at 3:30, and turn it down.

In the spring and fall they will alternately open and close the windows. In the summer, they'll adjust the air conditioner.

Bloomingdale's has the first sensible alternative to the old, boring arguments. Those are usually variations on this theme:

"I'm cold."

"Big sissy."

Now, the couple has real ammunition. The new dialogue has crackle and snap.

He can say, "I like it cold and crisp, like autumn in Antarctica. So don't touch the electric blanket, honey. It was a present from my aunt. Your family gave us the ice maker."

She can respond, "Tough, sweetie. I'm turning up the heat. It's my house, remember? Daddy bought it for us as a wedding present."

Soon, she will be warmed by his heated protests. And he will be thoroughly chilled by her cold shoulder.

I admit Bloomingdale's solution is simply a test of economic clout. But what can you expect from a department store?

It's so good, Bloomingdale's may be entitled to their ad slogan: "What goes on in the bedroom is our business."

Do you think they know about Saks?


## (56) The South Side Jogger

Judy is new to the South Side. She is just beginning to appreciate the city scenery.

"He's beautiful," she said. Judy was drooling so heavily into the phone, I was afraid she'd electrocute herself.

"He's the Kingshighway jogger. He looks like a Nike ad. I see him every morning about 7:15, running down Kingshighway. All the other women see him, too. They slow down to get a look at him. Then all the men have to slow up. The men get very angry."

It's not easy watching this jogger. "I'm driving my daughters to school. They want me to scrunch down in the seat, so they won't have be seen with their mother. It's hard to drive, sitting on the car floor."

Judy tried to share this experience with her daughters. She pointed out the handsome young man. "The girls are mortified that I would be ogling the guy. They said it's disgusting—I'm an old married woman and I shouldn't look.

"He's perfect. Throbbing muscles. No rings around his neck. No rings in his ears. No tattoos. Perfect teeth."

Is he a racehorse or a runner?

"A runner. He wears these tiny little shorts and running shoes. Usually, the shorts are navy. One day he wore Hawaiian print shorts. It made my day. He's the best thing that's happened to me since I moved here."

That doesn't say much for the South Side. The high point of your life is watching a man run away from you.

"All the women at work know about him. They thought you could help us."

Do what?

"Tell us what we should we do next."

The same thing men do when they see a beautiful jogger. Wave. Honk. Leer. Yell crude things.

"I couldn't do that," Judy said. "He'd say, 'Look at that old broad.' "

That never bothers male honkers.

"If I honked, he might break his beautiful stride. We've thought of meeting him at the corner with fresh orange juice, but that might look too motherly."

Judy's problem needed a closer look. One morning at 7:15, I was at the corner of Kingshighway and Oleatha, alone and palely loitering. Fortunately, the Kingshighway jogger came by, before the cops picked me up.

Some men run so you can admire their $200 suits. Some run to show off their muscles. Some run to lose weight.

But the Kingshighway jogger ran effortlessly, for the sheer joy of running. He didn't seem to care if you saw him or not. For that reason, he was a pleasure to watch. Maybe he was part of the city beautification program.

There's no point in meeting the runner, Judy. Reality would spoil everything. He'd have a mother, a girlfriend and bills, like everyone else.

Just enjoy the view. The young man is poetry in motion.

He's like that line from Keats' poem, "Ode on a Grecian Urn"— "Forever panting, and forever young."

Except I don't think the lovers in the Ode were panting because they'd just run down Kingshighway.

## (57) A Classic Car

I saw another magazine article about "America's love affair with the automobile."

It's true. We love our cars. And we often fall for the wrong kind. Recently, I was seduced by something fast, flashy and expensive. It's beautiful, but I know it won't last.

But that's only half the story. Americans not only love the sleek new cars. We also love old cars. I'm not talking about snappy classics. These are family cars—dowdy, dependable, hardworking automobiles.

Some people call these old cars clunkers. What do they know?

It's true their bodies aren't what they used to be. Old cars sag. Their rear ends drag a bit. They come in colors you'll never see in a showroom—mud brown, hospital green, jaundice yellow.

Their looks have faded, but we love them anyway. We even name them. Old cars are called Sherman Tank. The White Whale. The Blue Bomber.

I had a Blue Bomber in college, an old Plymouth Fury, with a broken taillight and a butt-sprung seat. The man who sold it to me said it would get great gas mileage.

It did. Unfortunately, the Blue Bomber was an oilaholic. It slurped up the stuff, and belched out huge clouds of bluish smoke. Never mind. Oil was $1.98 a gallon then. The Bomber was cheap and dependable. I was too young to understand what a jewel I had. As soon as I got a full-time job, I sold the Blue Bomber.

Old cars live on in the family lore. How many times have you heard a tale that began, "Remember that old car we had? The floor was rusted out. Your cousin removed the board covering the hole when we were going 40 miles an hour and . . . . "

And that wasn't all. The back door lock had to be lifted with pliers. The radio was permanently stuck on a country station. The carpet rotted years ago. But you replaced it with a nice piece of yellow shag rug.

Old cars take care of themselves. You don't have to worry about them. The first scratch on a new car is always traumatic. The smallest ding means tears and a trip to the body shop. But on a good old car, another scratch is an honorable wound, a battle scar.

Fender benders don't faze them. Ordinary automobiles will be devastated by close encounters with your clunker.

Old cars are faithful. A good old car always warns you before it gets sick. It clanks and rattles for days. If you still don't catch on, it dies conveniently near a gas station.

There's only one thing you really fear: Death. If your car is destroyed in an accident, you know you can't replace it. The Blue Book says it's

worth $500, tops. There's no way you can make the insurance company understand the true value of a lumpy-looking car with 115,000 miles on it.

But it's paid for. And it always starts. Even on the coldest mornings, when nothing else will.

Of course, only you can start it. You have to pump the gas pedal a certain way. But that's OK, too. It's your car, and no one else can drive it.

You don't buy a good old car. You luck into it. And you pass it on, to friends and family, the same way you pass on baby cribs and wedding gowns. You hear that your widowed aunt wants to get rid of her olive green '67 Chrysler Newport. You inherit the white Ford Galaxy from your older brother, when he goes off to college. Your cousin sells you her purple Gremlin for $100. It's a great car. The only problem is the heater runs all year 'round.

These faults are part of your car's charm. You grow used to them, the way an old married couple grows used to each other's crochets.

You become very protective of your faithful old car. You began dividing your friends into groups: Those who say kind things about your car, and those who make snide remarks.

You never feel quite the same about someone who says, "Where did you get that thing?" You think twice about a person who snickers at the water jug you carry in the summer, in case the radiator boils over.

But anyone who says your car is "a classic," is a friend for life. Then you show them the map light and the Art Moderne ashtrays.

Sometimes, it's difficult to appreciate the true beauty of the family clunker at first glance. If you don't know what to say, try this: "They don't make them like that any more."

It's the truth.

## (58) Home Cooking: The True Story

I love reading about the current food fad—American home cooking, also known as "granny" food. You know it as the blue plate special: meat loaf, salmon croquettes, macaroni and cheese, bread pudding.

One reporter described a trendy New York restaurant where "customers excavate mountains of delightfully lumpy mashed potatoes."

Those were the words: "delightfully lumpy."

While the customers were taking their lumps, the restaurant owner said, "Everybody remembers when they were kids going over to Grandma's house for dinner. Some people get absolutely homesick over this kind of food."

Right. But I don't know if this information belongs in the food pages or Ripley's Believe It or Not.

I always enjoyed this mush. But now the food fad has gone too far. I've just seen the newest granny cookbook. It's called "Grandma's Kitchen: Recipes for Food the Way You Remember It."

"Grandma's Kitchen" is a collection of recipes from grandmas and aunts. The recipes have names such as Grandma Sadie's Banana-Lemon Cookie Cake.

Along with the recipes are reminiscences. Rosie Fugitt's Chicken Casserole with Homemade Egg Noodles is served up with this:

"Rosie was my maternal grandmother's best friend. . . . When we were first introduced to her, she told us to call her Grandma Rosie. She signed her letters, 'Love, Grandma Rosie,' and that's what we called her."

Good thinking, kid. But Rosie didn't give you much choice.

Too much sugar is bad for me. I barely made it to the last recipe, Mama's Chocolate-Mocha Almond Cake and Headache-Cure Cookies.

I also had some questions: Didn't anyone have any rotten relatives who were great cooks? Or even nice relatives who made lousy meals? Didn't anyone ever fight at these family dinners? Didn't you?

I thought so. These New Yorkers wouldn't be quite so homesick for Grandma's Sunday dinners if they really remembered them.

Grandma food, like most food fads, is for yuppies. The yuppies are over 35 now. So let's take them back home for a real Sunday dinner. The time is 1967.

The dining table is groaning with pot roast marinated in onion soup mix, mashed potatoes, lumpy gravy and Aunt Marie's heavenly hash cake. (It's a box mix, but she hopes you won't notice.)

The right wine is important: Mogen David concord grape, served twice a year, at Thanksgiving and Christmas. The rest of the time, store the bottle in the back of the refrigerator.

Remember these cooking tips: Fresh mushrooms are probably poisonous. Canned mushrooms are OK, but you don't use them except on special occasions.

Jell-O with celery is an appetizer. Jell-O with pineapple is a dessert.

There are three basic sauces: canned mushroom soup, canned tomato soup and dried onion soup mix.

Granny restaurants are chic. This is not the proper homey atmosphere. You're supposed to eat this food with your family. Let me introduce you:

Cousin Marlene and her husband, What's-His-Name, the good provider.

Uncle Merv, who chews with his mouth open.

Aunt Marie, who wears black dresses and Enna Jetticks, and talks about her operations. Marie has a real gift for description. She can make anything the surgeons find sound like a prize exhibit at the county fair.

"It was the size of a turnip," she'd announce. "And solid."

Speaking of turnips, there is Marie's son, Martin. He collects matchbook covers. Martin is 38 years old and lives at home.

Now, your family dinner needs some authentic conversation:

Sometimes, you discussed politics: "What do you mean, you don't think we belong in Vietnam?"

Or social issues: "Well, some people still call it living in sin. I say she's a tramp, and not welcome in my house."

Family dinners are a good place for fashion tips. Many spirited discussions start with, "Why don't you get a haircut?"

Most dinners could be livened up with these amusing one liners:

"Quit playing with your food."

"Sit up straight."

"Shut up and eat your red beets."

After dinner, the family still maintains the charming custom of the sexes withdrawing to separate rooms.

The women go into the kitchen and clean up the dishes. The men go into the living room, turn on the game, and snore.

Now, that's a real family dinner. Don't you have a warm feeling? It's called heartburn.


## (59) The Pro Jell-O Wrestler

By 10:30 Monday night, the wrestling pit was ready. The pit was plywood, lined in plastic. It was on the dance floor, under a dusty mirror ball. The pit was ankle deep in blue Jell-O. The pale blue Jell-O felt cold and flabby.

Monday night is Jell-O wrestling at the Bustin' Loose Nite Club on South Broadway. Bustin' Loose has this "Dress Code" on the door:

"No knives. No chains. No holey jeans. No leather jackets. No jean jackets. No bandannas. No motorcycle apparel."

The two Jell-O wrestlers were shooting pool before the match. They were small, slender women in their 20s. Peggy Sue was blonde. Teresa, the reigning champ, had dark hair.

Charmel was shooting pool, too. Charmel, a university student in search of the perfect pool room, even looked in Bustin' Loose. That's when she discovered Jell-O wrestling.

"Chauvinism is alive and well at this place," Charmel said. "But on

the other hand, no one hassled me while I played. I couldn't believe the whole thing. The men drink and make jokes, like you'd expect. But the women are dead serious. They really want to be professional wrestlers. This is the only wrestling work they can get."

Before the match, a rock station blasted over the speakers. No one listened. Anyone who wasn't playing pool was glued in front of the big-screen TV, watching football.

The patrons were an odd mix of big-bellied men with tattoos, businessmen with ties, and young working men and women in jeans and sweaters.

The emcee turned off the speakers to auction off four cans of whipped cream. The highest bidder was a bearded man with a scorpion tattoo. He bought one can for $5. The emcee said the whipped cream could be sprayed on the wrestlers.

The four buyers simultaneously sprayed the emcee.

Peggy Sue and defending champ, Teresa, both in one-piece swim suits, climbed in the ring. The match began. The winner took two falls out of three.

Charmel said, "The wrestlers try actual holds. But it's difficult. Between the Jell-O and the whipped cream, they mostly slide around."

The women wrestled earnestly, attempting headlocks and hip tosses. They sprayed great lumps of Jell-O on the crowd. The spectators squealed and backed away.

Melted Jell-O pooled in the wrestlers' ears and matted their hair. Sticky blue stuff ran down their arms and legs. Teresa was shivering. Peggy Sue stopped to wipe the Jell-O out of Teresa's eyes. Then they went back to wrestling.

"Teresa is going to lose," Charmel said. "Peggy Sue is more muscular."

Charmel was right again. The new champ, Peggy, stood up for the cheers. Teresa lay exhausted and motionless in the Jell-O. Some character sprayed her with whipped cream.

Both women went back to the shower, a portable stall rigged up to the restroom faucets. When anyone flushed the toilet, the cold water disappeared.

Never mind. They were athletes. They talked about match injuries. Teresa thought she'd hurt her ribs and should have them taped. "I injured them in a match in August," she said. Peggy said she had stitches three times in her wrestling career.

"Why do you do it?" Charmel asked.

"I need the money," Teresa said. "I have two kids to support. I get $25 just for going in the ring."

"Why not go out for the Sexy Legs contest?" asked Charmel. "That's

$100.''

"You can't win those," Teresa said, scornfully. Besides, she was an athlete.

Peggy started "on a dare. I stay because I love it. I've wrestled in mud and Jell-O. I like Jell-O better. My dream is to be a real professional wrestler—no mud or Jell-O. Once I had an interview with a promoter. He came to the door in his underwear and asked just how bad I wanted to wrestle."

Not that bad. She went back to Jell-O.

Teresa said, "People think it's degrading, because it's Jell-O. It's still wrestling."

Peggy said, "A woman can be feminine and athletic, whether she's in Jell-O or on a baseball field.

"What do you think of us?" she said.

I'm sorry you don't get the audience you deserve.

"Yeah, the audience here backs away from us. This group acts like they're going to melt."

Peggy was dressing for her return match. Out on the floor, a well-dressed woman borrowed a suit and jumped in the ring.

Why? She doesn't need the money.

"Female athletes are starved for something to do," Charmel said.


## (60) The Kit-Cat Klock

Once, many years ago, I had an easygoing aunt. She was a fine woman, but a failure as a housewife. Her domestic sins were much discussed:

The boys never had to clean their rooms. They filed their old socks under their beds.

They stayed up past midnight on school nights. They could read all the comic books they wanted—even horror comics.

Her house was clean, but cluttered. The cut-glass bowl on the dining table did not hold wax fruit. It was a repository for car keys, coupons and buttons.

Her husband watched TV in his undershirt, and put his feet on the coffee table. She never nagged him, the way any self-respecting wife would.

House-proud relatives would survey the wreckage and whisper, "How would you like to live like that?''

I'd like it just fine. Because my aunt had a black Kit-Cat Klock in the kitchen.

The kitchen was painted yellow, until you got to the refrigerator. Then my uncle found something more interesting to do, so the rest of the room stayed white.

The Kit-Cat Klock was on the paint border, over the refrigerator. I could watch it for hours, when I wasn't reading comics. It was a cartoon cat, with a bow-tie. The clock didn't just tick—it moved. The eyes went one way, the tail went the other.

I asked why we didn't have a clock like that. The house-proud relatives snorted. Then they rolled their eyes. Just like the clock.

Evidently the Kit-Cat Klock didn't go with French provincial.

Time passed, and I lost track of the clock. Then, 25 years later, I saw the Kit-Cat in the window of a West End shop. The clock had come up in the world. Now it was trendy. There was even a version with sparkly fake jewels. People who ate pasta instead of spaghetti started showing me their new Kit-Cat Klocks.

The real Kit-Cats are still made by the California Clock Co. of San Juan Capistrano, Calif.

Jo Horstman at California Clock said the Kit-Cat was ''developed in the 1930s, by a person unknown to me. The clock was originally made by the Allied Manufacturers of Washington.''

The Kit-Cats, or maybe the whole company, Jo wasn't sure, were sold to California Clock, ''a long, long time ago.''

''It's a classic,'' Jo said. ''But sometimes it's more popular than others.'' She thinks the current surge is because the ''Kit-Cat was featured in the movie 'Back to the Future.' ''

Unfortunately, the clock can be timeless. The clock has been known to die young. Some people think the motor gets confused, because the eyes go one way, and the tail goes the other.

''We've never quite understood that,'' Jo said. ''Some of our motors last 10, even 20 years. Some last five or even three years. But we have our own repair department. Our rates are reasonable.''

The clock costs about $38 plain, $40 with jewels. The basic black Cat is the current best-seller.

''Everyone loves that clock,'' Jo said. ''It's most popular with older women. But young men and women are right behind them. Some buy the clock for sentimental reasons. Some like it because it's trendy. It's a popular baby gift, believe it or not. Babies are fascinated by it.''

Time is on Jo's side. She knows those babies are the Kit-Cat buyers of the future.

## (61) Pitching

"I'm in a pitchin' mood," Jeanette announced. There was blood in her eye and a broom in her hand. "Pitchin' " has special meaning for St. Louisans. Anyone can throw something away. Pitchin' is serious. It is part of the city's favorite fetish—cleaning.

A pitchin' spell is brief but violent, like a summer hailstorm. And just as freakish.

If your mother, in a pitchin' mood, landed in your room, you could lose your best baggy sweat shirt. Or your jeans, worn to a beautiful soft blue. She might even give away your dog.

"They looked old, so I pitched them," Mom would say. You knew the death sentence had been passed.

Your father, who wasn't looking any younger, began to feel nervous. Before the pitchin' was over, his favorite sweater was packed off to the Salvation Army.

A pitchin' mood is intense, but short-lived. It lasts no more than four or five hours. And it has a beneficial side effect.

A pitchin' mood stiffens your spine. It gives you the courage to throw out useless things.

We looked at Jeanette with envy. You cannot bring on a pitchin' mood. It just hits you out of the blue—like a bright idea. Or a brick.

If I were in a pitchin' mood, I would have the courage to face anything. Even that mustard-colored blouse.

The mustard-colored blouse sat in the back of my closet for years. The blouse was a mistake from the beginning. That is an understatement on the scale of "except for World War II, 1944 was a good year."

The blouse had an impressive label. And a stunning price tag. I'd never worn that color before, but the saleswoman said it would do amazing things for my complexion.

She was right. The mustard color made me look like a deviled egg—an oval of dead white and a mound of mustard yellow.

The saleswoman also said it would last forever. She wasn't kidding. The blouse was jinxed. When I wore it, the boss chewed me out, and bill collectors found me.

Each year, the blouse got pushed farther back in my closet. First, I stuck it behind all the clothes that fit but were out of style and might come back some day.

Then, it was behind the three skirts the cleaner shrank, but I expected to wear again. (Have you noticed the way cleaners shrink clothes these days? Just around the hips?)

Finally, the mustard blouse even went behind the skirt that I bought while temporarily insane. That skirt had tiny green pleats. It looked like Kermit the Frog in a lamp shade.

And there the mustard blouse stayed. I couldn't give the blouse away. It cost too much. I couldn't wear it. It was too ugly. I couldn't even do the usual cop-out, and take it to the cleaner.

We have the perfect dry cleaner. Not only does he sew on buttons and make small repairs, he cut a deal with me and my husband.

Occasionally, we will take a violent dislike to each other's favorite clothes. For instance, Don H. had a baggy suede jacket. He said it looked lived in. It did—by a family of pack rats. I kept hoping he'd leave the jacket behind in a restaurant. It never happened. Proprietors would run after him, calling, "Sir, you forgot your coat." I guess they didn't want it, either.

Finally, I took the coat to the dry cleaner and said, "Look, if anything happens to this coat, I won't complain."

"You hate it, too?" the cleaner said.

Shortly after that, the coat died in a chemical spill. A flabby sweat shirt went the same way.

And I suspect my black imitation Persian lamb coat was slaughtered that way, too. All I know for sure is Don H. and the cleaner hated that coat, and one day the presser snuffed it.

I never asked any questions. I didn't want Don H. to inquire too closely into the death of his purple T-shirt.

Besides, it's a fair system. The dry cleaner never kills any clothes unless he hates them, too.

But I couldn't take the mustard blouse to the cleaner because I never wore it, so it never got dirty.

Finally, I got rid of it. Someone created an event just for it. A charity fashion sale wanted me to donate my old, wearable clothes. I wanted to help. But, unfortunately, I wear all my old clothes.

Then I remembered. I had this mustard blouse. It had a stunning label and an amazing color.

I said I'd be happy to pitch in.


## (62) Delicate Domestic Ecology

We gave away the dining-room table because the button came off the living-room couch.

That's the only way I can explain what happened. I laughed when I heard about the woman who cooked on a broken-down stove. The woman said she couldn't get a new stove, because if she moved the old stove, she'd have to retile the kitchen floor. If the floor was tiled, then the paint would look shabby. If the kitchen was painted, the curtains would look old, and she didn't want new curtains. It was easier to cook on an old stove.

I don't laugh any more. Now I understand the delicate domestic ecology. A house is like a sweater. Pull the wrong thread, and the whole thing unravels.

And my life was hanging by a thread when Don H. came into the room with a button.

"The button came off the couch cushion again," he said. We looked at the couch. It had more lumps than a bowl of rice pudding.

"The couch looks old," he said. "Maybe we should recover the whole thing."

I would, except the living-room curtains look shabby.

"Before you think about curtains," Don H. said, "it would be nice to have a place for the VCR."

I agreed. If I'd stopped there, everything would have been OK. Unfortunately I had a brainstorm.

When was the last time we used the dining-room table?

"Thanksgiving, 1984," Don H. said.

Let's get rid of the dining-room table. The only thing we use it for is mail. Do we need a 6-foot mahogany mail tray?

This was a bold move. I used to think you couldn't be married unless you had a dining-room table. Now I was proposing to ditch it. We would make the dining room into a practical room. There would be shelves for the VCR and monitor, the amplifier and speakers. We would have storage space for books and records, and two comfortable chairs.

When I came to, I was wandering around a furniture store, with a tape measure in my hand.

First I bought the two chairs. They were on sale.

Then I bought the shelves. I mean, the wall system with three lacquer finishes and precision German craftsmanship.

I wanted white shelves. But the decorator said white was a harsh color. She said the shelves would look better in eggshell.

The decorator was right. They would. Except our walls are painted white. If you put eggshell next to white, it looks like dirty teeth.

That was easy to solve. We bought the eggshell shelves. And repainted the dining room.

And the living room. You can't have an eggshell dining room next to a white living room. You can't have an eggshell living room next to a white hall. The eggshell hall looked lousy next to a white kitchen. And the eggshell kitchen didn't look so hot next to the white bathroom.

When we got back to the ex-dining room, we noticed the chandelier didn't fit in the hi-tech room.

So we put in track lighting.

The dining-room curtains sure looked strange with track lighting. What the heck. Might as well get new ones. After all, we were getting new curtains in the living room.

And having the couch recovered.

The whole project cost more than we planned. But we really use that room. We have to. We can't afford to go out anymore.


## (63) Check Out Your Library

It looks like a poster of five naked people in a clawfoot bathtub. That's no ordinary poster. It's United States Government Document E1.70:SA9, issued by the Department of Energy.

It shows that government documents come in all shapes and sizes.

You can find E1.70:SA9 at the St. Louis Public Library. The poster comes with a cardboard display rack, for pamphlets. The rack has some pieces missing, and the pamphlets never showed up.

But if you try to throw out the useless display rack, you'll be breaking federal law.

The law says the library cannot throw out these documents. Ever.

The government can even send out an inspector to check on the tub poster and the broken display rack.

The St. Louis Library has these documents because it is a federal depository library. Every year, the library gets more than 50,000 federal documents, if you count the microfilm. And you might as well—the librarian has to.

The documents range from the ridiculous to the downright scary. The downtown library has CIA maps of Nicaragua, Russia and China.

What do CIA maps look like? They're straight out of a spy novel.

Just check out the CIA street guide of Beijing. You can. It's Document PREX3.10/4:B39/5.

In the CIA street guide, you can find the Xuanwu Steel Mill, the Peasants' Recreation Center and assorted power plants. Plus the traditional meeting place for spies—the zoo.

Document D201.19/2:AV5/2 is a real card. Actually, it's a whole deck of flash cards called "Aviation Sea Survival Techniques." Just the thing for your next cruise.

One card asks solemnly (there's no other way to ask it): "What is the one *MOST IMPORTANT* factor in survival?"

The answer? "Will to live."

Don't confuse this with "the greatest menace facing the survivor at sea." You have four choices: "(1) danger from sharks, (2) exposure from the elements, (3) thirst, (4) hunger."

The correct answer is thirst, but none of them sound like any fun.

The sea survival flash cards are plastic, for easy handling on your life raft.

Document C55.102:F65/4/981 is really a flash card. A flash flood card, to be exact. It tells you what to do if there's a flood.

Our government is thorough. The first tip begins, "Keep alert for signs of heavy rain. . . ."

There probably won't be time to get to your concrete boat.

You think I'm kidding? The library has a copy of TD5.35:11-81—"Inspection Guide for Reinforced Concrete Vessels."

## (64) The Soldier Who Saved a Tank

It isn't everyone who can save a 35-ton Sherman tank. But Norman Braun fought singlehandedly for almost an hour. He says he saved it— from serious embarrassment.

Norman, almost 70 and semi-retired said, "I won a battle with City Hall."

That's the City Hall in suburban Florissant. If you ask me, Florissant really won. Here's the story:

"James Eagan is a good mayor," Norman said, "but he's so Irish, he wants to paint everything green. And I mean everything. The tank was the last straw."

Norman said the tank in Florissant's Bangert Park is "the city's pride and joy. Usually, they painted it a grayish color."

Norman, a tank driver in the 5th Armored Division in World War II, knew that color wasn't authentic, but he tolerated it.

"Then, one day last April, I drove by the park, and saw the tank was painted kelly green. The same color as the park trash cans.

"I said, 'That's it.' I drove over to City Hall. I got through to the mayor's office, and talked with his secretary. She's a super woman.

"I said, 'Now, look. This is the only Sherman tank I know of within 250 miles that's on display. It's a sacrilege to paint it that color.' "

Norman tried to buy the tank. "I said, 'I wish you would sell it. I'd take care of it.' ''

The secretary said the tank was not for sale. It was one of Florissant's prized possessions.

''I said, 'Then you shouldn't paint it kelly green.'

''The secretary said, 'Everything is green. The mayor loves green. Every hue and tint, every shade of green is beautiful to him. You ought to see his car.'

''I said, 'I'll paint the tank at no charge to Florissant. I'll even buy the paint.'

''The secretary said the mayor wasn't in, but she'd check with him. She called me back that afternoon. She said, 'Pardon my language, but you have the green light.'

''That was Step One,'' Norman said. ''Step Two was getting the paint. I needed Army OD. That's olive drab. If you want to buy olive drab paint in this town, forget it. I went to four different stores. None of them had it, none of them could mix it. I finally went to the Missouri National Guard at Lambert Field. I found out they bought their paint from the Porter Paint company.

''I told Porter I wanted three gallons of OD, and I needed it quickly. I had to paint that tank before the 40th anniversary of the German surrender on May 7.

''Porter wanted to give me the paint free. They were determined. I said I'd pay for the paint. Finally, I met them halfway—I paid half price. But they threw in all kinds of brushes, pails and paint stirrers.

''It took me three and a half days to paint the tank. I crawled around it, painting and swearing.''

I forgot to say that Norman swears. He also apologizes. He manages to make about one apology for every two cuss words. This fits his image somehow, like his pipe and his red Camaro.

''I must have met 500 people while I was painting,'' Norman said. ''Some were curious, some were hilarious. One old woman kept staring at me. Finally, she said, 'Excuse me, sir. Are you serving a jail sentence?' She seemed disappointed she hadn't met a real criminal.''

Norman tried to make the tank authentic, right down to the insignia. He also painted on his division's nickname—Victory. ''I can do that, since I'm doing the work.''

Some of the kids at the park helped paint the tank. Now they play on it. That's fine with Norman.

''The little monsters climb up and slide down the front here,'' he said. ''They use this tire to boost themselves. You can see where they rubbed off the olive drab. You can also see that kelly green underneath.''

Norman doesn't even get upset at the graffiti. ''I love Tessie'' is sprayed on one side. "That's OK," Norman said. "Kids do that. I have some OD left. I'll paint it out.

"This tank was the work horse of World War II," he said. "Right here is. . . " Norman stopped. "Aww, you don't want to hear that stuff from an old turkey.

"I got my wish. I've got the job of painting the tank for life. As soon as the weather warms up, I'll do some touch-up work.

"Eagan's OK, except for that one hangup. In my opinion, if he had his way, he'd paint the tombstones in the cemetery kelly green."


## (65) The Bank of Mom and Dad

The man on the phone sounded scared. "I'll tell you about the bank," he said. "But don't use my name. The bank would kill me if they found out I talked. Just call me John."

Right, John. Where do you live?

"Say I live in Fenton. The bank never goes to Fenton. That way they can't trace me."

What did you do, John?

"I borrowed money from the BM&D."

Never heard of it.

"It's the Bank of Mom and Dad," John said. "No Baby Boomer can survive without it. Check around your office. Almost everyone borrows money from parents."

Then why are you afraid?

"Do you want to face my mother? If she finds out you told, you're in trouble. The BM&D has one cardinal rule: Never talk about family finances with an outsider."

John gives the bank plenty of credit. He says the Bank of Mom and Dad is personal banking at its best. He ticked off the advantages.

"(a) The BM&D has the best rate of interest.

"(b) This bank never forecloses. I'm currently four months in arrears. As long as you make a little payment, the bank will continue to deal with you. It's very trusting.

"(c) Toward the end of the loan, the BM&D usually forgives the debt."

Liz, another BM&D borrower, said the bank canceled the last $1,000 on her car loan. Then it threw a party to celebrate.

Liz says the typical BM&D "has survived the Depression. They aren't rich, but they save their money. Now they want to save their children some grief.''

Their children are typical of their generation, too.

John said, "We grew up with rising expectations, and wound up with rising interest rates."

The BM&D is a conservative lending institution. "You never borrow for anything frivolous," John said. "You couldn't ask for a vacation loan. The bank would say if you can't afford a vacation, you can't go.

"The BM&D only makes loans for solid and substantial purchases: a house, major home repairs or a car. The car has to be something sensible with four doors."

If the bank approves a loan, "any work it finances must be inspected. I borrowed major money—more than $10,000—for an enclosed porch. No project has had such supervision since the pharaohs built the pyramids. The BM&D came out and personally checked every board. My porch will outlast my house. It has a 24-inch concrete foundation. It's so solid, I could land helicopters on the roof.

"The bank also chose the contractor. My cousin.

"Talk about a bank that cares. The BM&D not only lends you money, they make sure you come home at a reasonable hour and don't drink too much. They also encourage you to date nice girls who clean the oven."

Free advice is another bank service. And credit counseling. "When you have a loan with the BM&D, you must get approval for all major purchases—even if they don't give you the money for them. The bank said it was OK to buy a new refrigerator. The bank subscribes to Consumer Reports, so they even told me which brands were best.

"But I once bought a set of expensive china on sale. The bank disapproved. It said the food would taste just as good off my old plates. It took me several years to recover from this fiscal frivolity."

Some BM&D loans have strings attached. One bank requires the debtor to show up every Sunday for dinner.

John's loan has this condition: "I have to keep my oven clean," he said. "My mother can't stand a dirty oven. She drops by my house to inspect it."

John's bank also asks for regular check-in calls. "Three times a week. If I don't call, Mom calls me and says, 'Is your finger broken?'

"Once I told her the phone worked at both ends. She said, 'I'm your mother.' She said it with such gravity, I knew she stood for neglected mothers everywhere.

"You can resent an ordinary bank. But you can't rail against the BM&D. They're wonderful. They love you. And if you don't make a payment, the guilt is terrible. Especially since the bank is so nice about it.

"A BM&D loan," John said, "is guilt-edged security."

# (66) The Missouri Lottery: Don't Listen to This Ad

I love listening to that Missouri Lottery ad on the radio. I just hope it doesn't persuade someone to go out and buy a ticket.

Because that would be breaking the law.

You know the ad. It starts off with loud cheers and an exciting series of clicks. Then the announcer intones dramatically:

"It stands a mere one inch tall. Yet it has the power to change lives. To shape the future. And fulfill the fantasies.

"The power of millions of dollars.

"This week it could happen to someone.

"They could come from anywhere in Missouri and they could go home a millionaire.

"If that one-inch white ball lands in the space between two particular pegs. The space marked with seven letters. The ones that spell— JACKPOT!"

Then the cheers get even wilder. A man starts yelling: "It's in there! It stayed! . . . Holy Cow, do you believe it?"

The announcer intones again:

"The Missouri Lottery Jackpot spin. It could make one of your neighbors a millionaire this week.

"The Jackpot is now $2.5 million dollars. That's 2.5 million. And if no one wins this week, the next Missouri Lottery Jackpot will be worth even more. Prizes are 45 percent of sales."

I was so excited I wanted to run out and buy a ticket. Then I heard the end of the ad:

"This announcement is for informational and educational purposes only, and is not intended to induce any person to participate in the lottery or purchase a lottery ticket."

What was the matter with me? I'd been having a good time. I should have been learning something. I felt like one of those weirdos who goes to the Art Museum to look at the naked statues.

So I gave myself a test. What educational information was in that ad?

(a) The Missouri Lottery uses a one-inch white ball.

(b) The word Jackpot has seven letters.

(c) I could make my neighbor a millionaire.

Why would I want to make my neighbor a millionaire? His dog barks all night.

He'd probably win the lottery and turn his backyard into a kennel.

On the other hand, my neighbor doesn't like me any more than I like him. So why should he spend his money to make me rich?

Do you get along with all your neighbors? Be honest. For most of us, the Hatfields and the McCoys are what being neighborly is all about. So why is the Missouri Lottery telling me to make my neighbor a millionaire?

And what's wrong with trying to get me to buy a lottery ticket?

It's illegal, that's what.

Jana Hume, Missouri Lottery public information officer in Jefferson City, explained.

"The law is real vague and hard," Jana said. "It says we can educate people. But we are not allowed to induce people to play. The law says induce is 'false or fraudulent persuasion.' It's difficult to define exactly what that means. That's probably why the ad says it could make your neighbor a millionaire.

"The law spells out exactly what can be said in lottery ads," she said. "The ads can include only statistical information on the odds of winning and the average return on the dollar in prize money, and 'strictly factual statements.' "

Those include "the time, date and place of the lottery, the prize structure and the type of lottery game."

That weird disclaimer at the end of the ad is required by law. The wording comes straight from the law itself.

Take a look. The law says a lottery ad must say it's for "informational and educational purposes only, and that it is not intended to induce any person to participate in the lottery or purchase a lottery ticket."

This is the greatest disclaimer since that truck-stop classic: "For prevention of disease only."

But we can thank our Missouri lawmakers for that lottery disclaimer. And we can probably thank them for ads that promise to make someone a winner. Or make your neighbor a millionaire. But not you.

Missouri's lottery got off to one of the most successful starts anywhere in the nation. The first day, the lottery sold 5.6 million tickets. That's more than one ticket for every man, woman, and child in Missouri.

So I don't know how much more education we need.

But I bet you didn't know one thing: You were buying that ticket to make your neighbor rich.

## *(67) Foundations of Faith: Black Bras and Nuns*

I wasn't impressed by the scandal over Imelda Marcos' 500 black bras. It was overkill. We'd had a bigger flap over three black bras at the convent.

My parents were devout suburbanites. I grew up in North County, in a split-level with aluminum siding, a birdbath and a barbecue pit.

I was taught by sisters at the local Catholic grade school. This was some 25 years ago. Sisters were terrifying authority figures then. They wore black habits with long black veils. No cop ever inspired as much fear with a blue uniform as the sisters did with that black habit. And the nuns didn't carry guns.

The rosary beads at the waist were a sister's badge. The beads were also a blessing for us kids. They belled the cat. The beads clacked and rattled when sister walked. You knew when she was nearby. You stopped whatever you were doing, because it was probably wrong.

The sisters' message was as stern as their robes: We were here to know, love and serve God, and be happy with him in heaven. God could recall us at any moment—like defective cars.

One sister had us watch the classroom clock for 60 seconds. Then she announced, "You are now one minute closer to your death."

It made us pretty jumpy, but it also cured us of clock watching.

This sort of sister seems to have disappeared. The ones I know now are fairly cheerful. They wear business suits and crosses, and are versed in child psychology.

The black bra scandal would not be possible today. But you can see why it never occurred to us to ask what the sisters wore under those habits. You might as well wonder if angels wear underwear.

I only found out through extreme daring. One day, three grade school kids were delegated to carry textbooks to the convent: Linda, Kathy and me.

Visits to the convent were rare. The class was rife with rumors about what was actually in there.

The convent was an ordinary three-bedroom ranch house. But it didn't look like our homes. It was dim and cool inside, and smelled of furniture polish. There were no toys on the floor. No voices yelled to clean up your room NOW.

We stood in the hallway, and got a clear view of two rooms. One room had a blond oak dining table with a lace cloth. The other room had a pale 1950s living room suite.

Linda swore she could see into the kitchen, and there was a chrome kitchen set like hers at home. We didn't believe her.

I asked to use the bathroom. I hoped to get a look at the bedrooms. Sister showed me down the hall. She turned on the light and said, "I hope you don't mind my laundry hanging in the shower."

It wasn't laundry. It was three black bras.

In those days, black bras were wicked. Even our mothers, who were married and could do anything, only had one black bra. They saved it for New Year's Eve and their wedding anniversary.

I was stunned by this sight. But not so stunned I didn't look at the label. Sister wore a size 36B.

I could hardly wait to get outside with my news. The class was shaken. How could the sisters be holy, and wear black bras?

Our mothers refused to be shocked. They said things like, "Of course, sisters wear black bras. Otherwise, they would show under their clothes."

After two weeks, we concluded they must have a dispensation from the pope.

But the awe was gone. The habit could no longer terrorize, if we knew there was a black bra underneath.

But Linda had been thinking. She said, "If sister wore a 36B, she could have gotten married."

It was a tenet of our pre-teen faith that many women became sisters because they couldn't get married. We also believed that anyone with a real bosom would automatically get married.

We contemplated the immensity of sister's sacrifice.

Awe was restored.


## (68) The Bridal Shower

Any modern woman is pleased to see the embarrassing, sexist ceremony of the bridal shower replaced by something more mature—like an evening of drinks and male strippers.

Before the bridal shower disappears, we should know what we are throwing away. A bridal shower answers certain ancient needs. It is the first chance to meet the new in-laws. And hold them up for loot.

I have consulted my city etiquette expert, Janet Smith, on the art of the traditional shower.

Janet said, "The bridal shower needs these key elements:

"First, the shower must be a surprise. This is difficult. The modern bride is crafty. Often the family has to set up two or three events that look like surprise showers, before they spring the actual shower on her.

"One poor bride walked into what she thought was a Tupperware party. She'd wanted to return some defective Tupperware. The video camera caught her trying to stash old Tupperware behind her back."

A bridal shower needs the right food. "In the past, it was always cake and punch. Now, it's turning into a full meal: Ham. Tuna or chicken salad." The chicken salad is often landmined with grapes, pineapple or walnuts.

And mostaccioli?

"Certainly not," Janet said. "You have to save something for the wedding.

"The shower also has to have a decorated cake and a cute punch, which nobody drinks."

A proper punch contains one or more of the following: Lime sherbet, cheap champagne, Jell-O, pineapple juice.

"If you really want to get fancy," she said, "float some strawberries on top."

At the shower, "at least one member of the family will not be speaking to another. They will exchange curt nods, and pointedly avoid each other—provided you didn't spike the punch."

A shower is a chance for a new generation of feuds. Someone is sure to be offended when a bride's relative calls the groom "what's his name."

"Since this is the first meeting for most of the family, all the best clothes come out, complete with new earrings. Guests also bring out their best manners."

The veneer of civilization lasts until the games. Shower games have been blamed for the high number of unmarried women. The games are revolting. But no shower is complete without them.

"The dignified facade dissolves under the pressure of that shower favorite, Rob Your Neighbor. This is a charming game. Guests roll dice for wrapped presents. The presents keep changing hands until time runs out."

Sweet-faced grandmothers will kill for a pot holder. Top game presents include ring holders, terry tea towels and big plastic hangers. These earn the highest shower compliment: "a lovely gift."

Speaking of gifts, shower presents are used to judge the generosity of in-laws.

"The bride's mother gets high marks if she gives queen-sized sheets. This is a direct challenge to the groom's mother. There's also the traditional sniping between the relatives who give frivolous gifts and the ones who come up with Corning Ware.

"At the shower, you must keep a list of all the gifts."

So the bride can write the thank-you notes?

"No," Janet said. "You'll use that gift list for the rest of your life. That way, you'll know how much to spend on their gifts.

"You'll also have some gifts you can't return. You give them as presents to someone else. The list will save you from giving the cake plate to the person who sent it to you."

Gift returns are revealing. You'd be surprised how many people try to pass off a cheap gift in a box from a fancy store.

During the gift-giving, someone is sure to embarrass the bride with a "Honeymoon Pack." The pack includes a small bottle of champagne, a deck of cards, a bottle of aspirin, and a flimsy nightgown labeled "in case of fire."

One daughter has been delegated to smother the Aunt Who Will Say Anything—before she does.

You can spot this aunt. Her clothes are as loud as she is. She's often wearing rhinestones or gold lame.

The new in-laws would be shocked by what she blurts out. If they weren't trying to shut up their own aunt.

## (69) High Noon: The Day the Marshal Came Downtown

It was just past high noon when the marshal came into the building. Soon there would be a showdown.

"I am a federal marshal," she said, pulling out her badge. The gun she packed left little doubt.

"I've come to collect these documents," the marshal said, whipping out two very official letters.

It sure was a dramatic way to take a book out of the library.

For the federal marshal was in the downtown public library, flashing her badge at the documents librarian.

The official letters said the marshal was there to fetch back "highly sensitive material." The national security was at stake.

Check this out: The St. Louis public library is a federal depository library. That means it gets more than 50,000 federal documents every year. Somehow, sensitive information had slipped out. Now, government secrets were loose in the library.

Documents librarian Anne Watts read the official letters. Anne was ordered to surrender federal document J25.8:M 35/rev. 1, better known by its snappy title: "United States Marshals Service Manual, Revision 1 of Chapters 1 and 2."

The official letters warned: "The sensitivity of these documents for reasons of national security precludes making them publicly available. It is imperative, therefore, that they be recovered by the U.S. Government as soon as possible."

Anne said, "I went to get the documents. They were corrected pages of the federal marshals' manual. When there are mistakes, the government doesn't reprint the whole book. It just sends out the corrected pages. You know, Page 35, 57, 68."

(For security reasons, I have changed the page numbers.)

What was in the documents?

"Of course, I had to read them," said Anne. "To make sure I had the correct documents."

Of course.

"The sensitive pages were baby blue. I didn't understand a word. Something about stun guns. They didn't make much sense."

Fortunately for our nation, the reading public agreed. The library had the secret documents for six months. No one checked them out.

The feds sent marshals to every place in the nation that had the secret documents—more than 830 libraries.

Anne said, "We've never had a federal marshal here before. Usually, the government sends out correction notices, and asks us to throw the old stuff away."

Anne handed over the documents. The marshal headed for the door—and the showdown.

"The clerk checking books at the door wouldn't let her out," Anne said. "He thought she was stealing. She showed her badge and her letters. The clerk said she couldn't take the materials out of the building. It was against library rules.

"The marshal was really nice. She didn't make an issue out of it. She came back to the documents department, and said she couldn't get out."

So Anne escorted the armed marshal out the door. That was proper library procedure.

The secrets are now back in federal hands.

But I think they were safer in the library.

## (70) The Feds and the $5 Ticket

Consider this sad scene. It is morning at the Majestic restaurant in the city's West End. A man with a full mustache, and a full life ahead of him, is being served.

But it's not breakfast. It's a summons served by a federal marshal. Right in front of his wife, his silver-haired father, and his shrewd lawyer.

For a $5 parking ticket.

The mustachioed miscreant is Ron Igou. The feds set four marshals on Ron because he ignored a parking ticket.

Ron is a St. Louis contractor. "I was doing some work at the post office downtown," he said. "I parked in the loading dock, like I'd been doing for three years. Except this time, I got a ticket."

Ron treated the federal parking ticket like any other. He tossed it in his truck, and forgot about it.

That was in March. "At least, I think it was," Ron said. "I didn't worry about it. I wasn't aware that any notices were sent to me."

The notices went to his father's house. Clarence Igou said he threw them away. "They were addressed to I Gau. I didn't know anyone named that."

Then, on Thursday, June 12, "two armed federal marshals appeared at my parents' house." Here's what Ron said happened:

"The marshals showed their badges to my 74-year-old father. They said they wanted to serve me with a federal summons for a parking ticket.

"My father said, 'Leave it here, and I'll make sure he gets it.'

"The marshals said they had to serve me in person. My father said he'd have me call them.

"The marshals said, 'Where is he?'

"My father said, 'He's not here. You'll have to find him yourself.'

"They had a few more words. My father told the marshals to leave. The marshals went to the front yard, and started taking his license number. My father told them to get off the property. He said they had no right to be there."

Next morning, Ron called the U.S. marshal's office. "They knew my name. I'm now known to the federal government, because of my father."

Not to mention the parking ticket.

"I complained about the way they treated my father. They said they were doing their job, and my father was rather abusive to the marshals."

Besides, they still had a summons for Ron. "I said, 'Can you mail it?' They had to give it to me in person. They didn't want to come by my house. I said they could meet me at my job the next day. They said they had to be in federal court delivering prisoners. They said they had more important things to do than chase people with parking tickets. I was hurt.

"I said, 'How about Monday?' They said they were busy.

"I said, 'How about Tuesday?' I made an appointment for 9 o'clock at the Majestic restaurant."

Let me get this straight, Ron. You made an appointment with the federal marshals to serve you. Would Capone do that? Or Dillinger? Some fugitive from justice you are.

Ron said, "Do you know what this $5 parking ticket cost the taxpayers? It took four marshals, and several hours of federal time to track me down."

Ron invited his wife, Donna Igou, his father and his lawyer to watch him being served.

Just after 9 o'clock, a pair of federal marshals came into the Majestic.

One marshal showed her badge and asked, 'Is your name Ron Igou? I have a summons to appear in federal court for a parking violation. I must give it to you personally.' ''

She did. The restaurant applauded.

The summons looked fierce and official. It began, "Summons in a Criminal Court." It said Ron should appear in U.S. District Court at 2 p.m. on June 20. It also described his offense: "Parked at Dock 5-11. No Permit Displayed/Postal Vehicle Parking Only. Violation #170206."

One more thing. When the federal marshals served Ron, they parked in a No Parking zone.

The marshals didn't get a ticket. (There's never a meter maid around when you need one.) But the marshals' supervisor said federal marshals should obey city parking ordinances.

So think about this: To serve Ron a summons for his $5 federal ticket, the marshals committed a $10 city parking violation.

Maybe Ron should make a citizen's arrest.

## (71) Evelyn West, the Biggest and the Best

I must have been 11 years old when I asked my mother The Question. And it was all because of Evelyn West.

In 1961, Evelyn was getting a lot of exposure in St. Louis. She was a stripper.

Evelyn danced at the old Stardust Club on the DeBaliviere strip. Her ad ran in the Post-Dispatch. I can still quote it. It was almost a chant.

"Evelyn West, the biggest and the best, and her $50,000 Treasure Chest."

Here's the part that got me. Sometimes the ads would say: "Insured by Lloyd's of London."

At least, I think it was Lloyd's of London. It sure wasn't State Farm.

The Evelyn West ads fascinated me. The woman's legal name was actually "Evelyn $50,000 Treasure Chest West." She changed it to that from Patricia McQuillan.

Evelyn made $50,000 her middle name because, she told the judge, "People don't remember the name Evelyn West." (Evelyn spent a lot of time in front of judges for some of her activities, but that's another story.)

The Associated Press discreetly added, "She said her bosom is insured for $50,000."

Thanks to inflation, $50,000 is a barely respectable sum these days.

But in 1961, it was big money.

Every evening, I'd get the newspaper and go into my regular reading routine. First, the funnies. Next Ann Landers and Dr. Molden. Then I'd ponder Evelyn's mysterious ad.

Finally, I asked my mother The Question: "When can I get my chest insured like Evelyn West's?"

She said, "Huh?"

I said, "If that's not going to develop into a major asset, maybe State Farm can take out a policy on my legs. Or my hair."

There had to be something worth insuring.

I'm not exactly sure Evelyn was a role model, but she definitely encouraged sound business practices. I believed that insurance was one of the rites of puberty: As soon as you developed some assets, you got them protected.

And protected was the right word.

Evelyn sure didn't have them covered.


## (72) Life's No Picnic With the Aunts

I don't know if the Marines have found those few good men yet. But if they had any sense they'd give up and start looking for an army of aunts.

There's no greater peacekeeping force than a couple of aunts. And if you want fighters, I'd take one outraged aunt with a large black purse over a platoon of muscle men.

Most families have at least one of these aunts. Their actual title is usually Great Aunt, but they never use it. They don't need to. They know they're great.

These aunts have serious names like Adele, Sarah and Thelma. Aunts are never called Fifi, Sherri, or any other name that ends in i.

They are somewhere between 60 and 80 years old, although no one has to the nerve to ask.

Aunts can be thin or fat, handsome or ugly. Do not confuse them with grandmothers, who at the last minute may turn mushy, especially with grandchildren. True aunts have iron in their hair and steel in their spines.

What exactly do aunts do?

They keep the family conscience. They also keep all the records. Aunts are the official register of family births, deaths and marriages.

They know the pedigree of all 400 wedding and funeral relatives. (They're called that because that's the only time you see them.)

Aunts know exactly how you are related to your third cousin, whose mother used to date Uncle Mickey until she ran off with that drummer and it cost a fortune to get the marriage annulled.

They are the repository of old family secrets. An aunt still remembers that Roberta, now middle-aged, had a premature baby seven months after her wedding. The preemie weighted 9 pounds 8 ounces, but never mind. Roberta and Randall stayed married, and that's more than you can say for most couples these days.

An aunt remembers Harry's mid-life crisis, long after even Harry forgot it. Harry was seeing that no-good Maureen, who worked at the neighborhood beauty shop, Charles of Chippewa. Fortunately, the aunt had your grandfather talk some sense into Harry. He threatened to call in the house loan unless Harry straightened up and flew right.

An aunt is also the last word on new scandals. A simple question from an aunt: "Are you going to Jennie's wedding?" and you know a shaky alliance has official family approval.

Aunts also make periodic phone calls to check on wild nephews in college and young cousins living in sin. (Sorry, but aunts still use that phrase.)

Aunts have a sense of duty. They will shame you into attending the 50th wedding anniversary and the 79th birthday party. Aunts use a terrifying combination of guilt and logic.

"What do you mean, you're too busy for the birthday party?" an aunt will thunder. "Do you think Walter is going to live forever? You'll find time to go to his funeral, when it won't do Walter any good."

When life is no picnic, you can blame it on the aunts.

## (73) Linebacker in Lace

The worst line a woman hears is not from some man. It's from your best friend, just before her wedding. You're looking at chiffon bridesmaids dresses—doubtfully. Your best friend says, "Don't worry. You can wear it on New Year's Eve."

Like most lines, it makes sense at the time. You buy the chiffon. Only when New Year's Eve rolls around, do you wake up and realize you never wear peach chiffon with a built-in train.

I didn't realize there was more to this phenomenon, until I got two phone calls in one week. One was from a woman who said, "My sister got married and put me in lavender chiffon with ruffles. I looked like a Cabbage Patch doll. She did it to get even. When she was little, I told her she was adopted."

I'm sure all the other bridesmaids looked equally lousy in lavender, ma'am.

"They did not," she said. "I was the only one. Do you think my sister hates me?"

I did. Until Steve called. He said, "My wife was the One Bridesmaid." You mean maid of honor.

"No. Big church weddings have a maid of honor. But they also have the One Bridesmaid who stands out because she looks so bad.

"The dress makes her look horrible. It's designed for the majority. If all the other bridesmaids are thin, she's the one who's fat. If they're tall, she's short. If they're in scoop necks, she's concave and they're convex. Or vice versa.

"In my wife's case, it was the color. She wore a kind of turquoise you only see in redneck bedrooms. The other bridesmaids were brunettes. They looked great. My wife was a blonde and the color turned her skin a weird green. Every time I looked at her, I wanted to call an ambulance.

"The funny thing is, my wife is an attractive woman—the One Bridesmaid usually is. It's only when you put her in a group, she becomes the One Bridesmaid.

"This doesn't happen to men. We all look about the same in a tux. But the bridesmaids dress always looks ugly on one woman. Do you know why this happens?"

Sure. I was the One Bridesmaid once. I'm 6 feet tall. My friend was about 5 feet tall. So was the groom. They looked so cute together, I never stopped to think that short people come from short families—and they would all be in the wedding. It gave new meaning to the phrase "small wedding."

The trouble starts because bridesmaids dresses are chosen by a democratic process. We vote on the style we like best.

I knew I was in trouble when I showed up at the bridal shop. If you stacked the whole wedding party, they wouldn't reach the ceiling. Even worse, the other five women were wearing ruffles and lace. Like most tall people, I prefer straight, simple lines. Imagine Grace Jones in ruffles. Imagine me in misery.

I looked at all the bridesmaids dresses, and voted for the simplest long thing I saw—the dressing room curtains. They were a stylish gray.

I was outvoted. The other bridesmaids wanted pink ruffled chiffon with lace jackets that stopped under the armpits. They looked dainty. I looked like a linebacker in lace shoulder pads.

I told myself it was just a dress. It didn't look that bad. My escort was reassuring. He said I didn't look like a linebacker. I looked like a road company "La Cage aux Folles."

At least, he tried to tell me. He was laughing so hard, he cried. He told me he always cried at weddings.

By now, I knew a line when I heard one.


## (74) The Twinkie Lady: The Important Stuff

After 58 years, Margaret Branca of Brentwood has come forward and confessed. She may be the first Twinkie stuffer in the United States.

This means Margaret is in on one of the great secrets of the universe. She knows the inner workings of the Twinkie.

Margaret was 16 when she was initiated into the mysteries.

"It happened in 1930," she said. "It was during the Depression. I had to go to work. I started at the old Hostess bakery in north St.Louis, icing cakes."

Then, one day, she was tapped for her historic role. "The boss said they were making something new—Twinkies. They didn't know how Twinkies would go over. To think they didn't know if people would like them."

The new Twinkies needed a special machine. "The boss just told me what I had to do, and I did it."

In 1930, each Twinkie was hand-filled. "You took two sponge cakes— one in each hand—and you shoved them into these little pipes. Then you pumped a pedal with your foot, and filling squirted into the Twinkies. You had to pump the pedal just right, or too much filling would shoot out. If I over-squirted, the Twinkie would explode.

"Of course, that wasn't so bad. I got to eat the crippled ones."

Margaret said she never tired of Twinkies.

"All the Twinkies you can eat at 16! It was wonderful. I never lost my appetite for them. Not only that, I lost weight. I was a butter ball when I started working. I got thinner on Twinkies.

"They were delicious in those days. Boy, if I could get hold of one now. They were pure. Now the filling seems all synthetic. But I still eat them."

But don't get too lonesome for the old days. Look at Margaret's job.

"I worked six days a week. I made 2 bucks a day. You worked 8, 10, 12 hours, and you didn't make one extra nickel in overtime. We were on our feet the whole day. We had 20 minutes for lunch. We gobbled it down, and zoom, back we went. We couldn't be late. We had to punch the time clock, even though we didn't make any more money. I wanted the union, but the other women voted it down."

Margaret doesn't know how many Twinkies she filled each day.

"Being 16, I didn't keep count. I just grabbed two, and then two more, two more until the day was done. You make a rhythm for yourself. We could hardly keep up with the demand. You'd think people had nothing to do but eat Twinkies. They sold like hot cakes."

Margaret liked her job. She was the only Twinkie stuffer.

"Then the efficiency experts came along. They'd stand by you with a stopwatch, and see how fast you worked. Those stupid jerks. I couldn't take that. I told them, 'I quit.' I'd worked there not quite a year.

"I went to work for a toy factory. The first day, I wrapped a cowboy suit for Rogers Hornsby's little boy. Hornsby was a famous baseball player. My dad was so proud of me."

Twinkies did well, too. The cream-filled sponge cakes were quickly absorbed into American life. Twinkies were touted on the old Howdy Doody show in the '50s. Archie Bunker had Twinkies in his lunch box.

Twinkies even became a legal legend. In 1979, the man accused of killing the San Francisco mayor blamed his violent outbursts on his junk food diet. It became known as the "Twinkie Defense."

There is also a St. Louis connection. Twinkies are made by the Continental Baking Co., now a subsidiary of Ralston Purina.

A Ralston spokesman said Margaret's story made sense, according to the company histories. Twinkies were invented by James Dewar, a manager at Continental's Chicago plant, in 1930.

The spokesman said Margaret may be the first—or at least one of the first—Twinkie stuffers not only in St. Louis, but the whole United States.

The spokesman also answered a question Margaret has had for 56 years: Where did they get the name Twinkies?

"Right here in St. Louis," the spokesman said. "The inventor was on a business trip here when he saw a billboard for Twinkle Toe Shoes. He shortened the name to Twinkies."

## (75) Rich and Bruno Make Wine

I was about to taste one of the most expensive wines in St. Louis. Bruno Mazzotta poured me a glass. I sipped.

Er, it tastes thick, I said.

"It has body," Bruno said.

It's strong.

"No wimp wines here," said Rich Hinds, proudly.

Rich, Bruno and their friends didn't mean to produce the most expensive home-made wine in the city. It happened by trial and error. Mostly error.

This is how Rich tells the story:

"Six years ago, my friend Bruno said, 'Want to make a little wine?' I figured 10 or 15 gallons of home-made wine would be nice.

"Bruno said, 'I'll buy the grapes.' He bought 1,300 pounds. That's about 150 gallons of wine. Then Bruno invites me to dinner. Some dinner. I ate grapes for two nights. It's all he would feed me while I shucked the stems off 1,300 pounds.

"Bruno had got 10 friends to clean and wash all the grapes. Later, we learned you don't do that. But Bruno's background was science. We did everything but sterilize those suckers."

They also bought a shiny new crusher.

"But we stored the barrels free. Bruno knew this guy in the suburbs. He let us use his garage."

What barrels?

"We wanted to do the wine right. So we bought old whisky barrels and scraped them out. There was only one problem. Wooden barrels should be kept full of liquid. We'd let the barrels dry out, and now they were leaking wine all over the suburban garage. We lost 25 gallons.

"Even worse, the wife of the guy who owned the garage said the leaking wine was attracting rats. Drunken rats.

"She called an exterminator. He complained about the smell."

That's the wine smell, not the rat odor.

"After the barrels failed, we used 5-gallon glass bottles: 80 of them. Washing them was fun. I'd rank it with jumping up and down on a barbed-wire trampoline."

Rich and Bruno had to get the wine away from the drunken rats.

"We knew someone who knew someone at a warehouse. There was unused space, so we sort of used it."

And didn't pay.

"Then we noticed the wine levels were going down in the jugs. What an honor—somebody besides a rat wanted our wine. We added water and upped the sugar content to compensate. That made it pretty powerful, but it didn't have that real grape flavor.

"Then somebody stole 50 gallons on us. We didn't mind the wine, but those glass jugs were expensive."

After nine months, Rich and Bruno decided the wine had aged. If it hadn't—they had.

They had fancy wine labels printed, and divvied up the jugs among the grape cleaners. Since most of them worked at Firmin Desloge

Hospital, the labels said in fractured French: "Chateau Firmin Desloge, Vin Tres Ordinaire."

"It was very ordinary," Rich said. "We could have had the finest French wines for what that stuff cost us."

But Rich and Bruno learned their lesson.

"We made more wine," Rich said. "This time, we did it right. We thought it would taste better if we had our own grapes. So Bruno bought 500 vines. And I helped plant them. How can I quit? I had a masochistic interest in this wine.

"We just tried the newest batch. It needs work, but it's going to be good."

Rich and Bruno have plenty of the first vintage left for comparison.

"It's not bad enough to throw out, but it's not good enough to drink.

"The only way to get rid of it is to give it to unsuspecting people."

And he poured me another drink.


## (76) Getting Hooked on Books

Some barflies get thirsty at the whiff of an old-time bar. There's something about the smell of stale beer and Lysol.

But I lust for libraries. And for the same reason: I, too, heard temperance lectures. "Seven books at once is too much," they'd say. "Learn self-control."

Usually, I hang around city libraries. They smell dark, old and mellow. Sometimes, I'd sneak off to the county library, and drink in a different smell: sharper, lighter and newer.

I especially like the county libraries with blond book cases, big glass windows, and that peculiar greenish aquarium light.

If you want your kids to read more, try the tactics parents used when I was growing up: Ban books. Restrict library trips. Limit reading time. Soon your kid will be sneaking off to read "The Grapes of Wrath."

Thanks to these measures, I was addicted to books by the fifth grade. I read anything. I stashed novels under the couch cushions and biographies in the linen closet. Encyclopedias would fall out of the clothes hamper.

I graduated with a five-book-a-week habit.

But this reading program needs the cooperation of home and school. I grew up in the suburbs, and the '50s lasted a long time there. So did the doctrine of the Well-Rounded Person.

In those days, suburban parents had two goals: Get their daughters to wear shoes around the house (mothers believed running around barefoot encouraged your feet to grow) and make them into Well-Rounded Persons.

Well-Rounded Persons should be good—but not too good—at sports, school and social life. Parents watched carefully so kids didn't do too many things in one category. Reading had to be tempered with social activities and sports. Too many books would ruin your eyes.

Like any addict, I made deals: I did godawful stuff like play softball and basketball, so I could go back to the books. I even joined the Girl Scouts, where I coated strips of cardboard with paraffin, and rolled them into empty tuna cans, to make buddy burners. Those were home-made stoves.

If God wanted me to camp out and cook on a buddy burner, he would have never invented room service.

Clubs and sports didn't cure me of my addiction. Restricting books only made them more attractive. In my room, I rigged up a system of flashlights under the covers and rugs stuffed under the door, to indulge in late-night reading.

My school helped, too. It faithfully followed some bishop's list of banned books. We were warned these books could cause impure thoughts.

Naturally, we could hardly wait to get our mitts—not to mention our minds—on such racy stuff as Steinbeck and James Joyce's "A Portrait of the Artist as a Young Man."

No matter how many books we read on this list, our minds stayed distressingly pure. We finally had to grow up, and get corrupted on our own.

Some people think libraries are dull places. But the best drama in town took place every Saturday at the local bookmobile. We used to hang around and see if anyone would check out The Book.

The thrill we got depended on two '50s facts:

Folks didn't fling around so many four-letter words then. At least, not in public.

And libraries checked out books with the old Dictaphone system. The librarians read the titles out loud.

Once a month, someone would check out The Book, an Erskine Caldwell novel. We would watch the librarian hesitate a little, and then whisper the title in public: "The Bastard."

## (77) Save the Baby Polyesters

There are two reasons why I don't wear fur coats: Mamie Eisenhower

and the late Mrs. Mettermann.

Remember all those '50s photos of Mamie in her fur?

Me, too.

Mrs. Mettermann's fur was even worse. Mrs. Mettermann wore a couple of dead foxes—the kind where the heads bite the tails. She always wore them to church.

Every Sunday, I sat behind Mrs. Mettermann and watched the foxes chase each other around her neck. When she moved, the dead paws dangled pathetically. Mrs. Mettermann's foxes inspired more thoughts about mortality than any sermon.

It was in memory of Mrs. Mettermann's foxes that I bought a fake fur coat this winter.

It was white, with black splotches and squiggles. It didn't look like any animal, except maybe a polar bear with a leaky pen in its pocket.

But the wily coat has managed to fool any number of animal lovers. It really makes them hot under the collar.

The fiercest animal defender is 12 years old. She decorates her room with magazine pictures of koala bears, horses and baby seals.

She looked at my coat and said, "Did you kill any animals for that?"

No, it's fake fur.

"How do you get fake fur?"

You skin teddy bears, I said.

"You're lying," the kid said.

Yes, I am. Honest, I didn't kill any animals. Scientists made the coat from chemicals.

"Why would they make something that looks like it's been killed?" asked the kid, with terrifying logic.

The adult animal lovers are easier to deal with. Most are like the gentleman who stopped me and demanded righteously: "How many animals died so you could dress like that?"

Millions of baby polyesters, sir.

I grinned evilly and added, "I made sure they were clubbed to death."

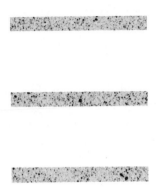

## (78) They Wanted Him for His Body

Frank Foley made his stage debut at age 68. They wanted him for his body.

Frank played a corpse in "Arsenic and Old Lace" at the American Theatre.

He didn't lie down on the job. Frank was one of a dozen dead men who walked up from the basement at the end of the play. He stepped on stage to enthusiastic applause—after the curtain came down.

Frank's entrance works like this: "At the end of the show, the cast comes on and makes their bow. The curtain comes down and goes up again. Then up come the 12 bodies from the basement. We always get a big laugh.

"We're only on stage two minutes, but it's an important thing. They talk about these 12 bodies all during the play."

Frank is also an usher at the American. He works "Arsenic and Old Lace" from the aisles and on stage. You could say he passes out programs at the start, and passes away at the end.

"I heard about the auditions, and showed up at the stage door at 7 o'clock. Wally, the stage manager, counted out the first 12 of us, and told the rest to go home. We had to pick out a coat and suit and try them on. They were pretty nice clothes. I pulled my tie off center, and my hat is pretty caved in. We're supposed to be down and out, but not seedy."

The deceased were elderly gentlemen "helped" to a peaceful death by the play's sweetly batty old aunts. They were done in with poisoned elderberry wine.

Frank says being a corpse is not a grim job. "We're supposed to smile, because we're on elderberry wine. They want a pleasant look. We died peacefully.

"We don't wear makeup. They also prefer we don't wear glasses. But some do. The corpses really can't see without them.

"People came from all over the city to audition. It's an honor," Frank said. "Some of those guys really fit the part."

Frank looks like a younger, handsomer George Burns, with very white hair and very blue eyes. He's a retired medical illustrator. Now he uses his talented hands to make exhibition quilts.

When Frank told his quilt group about his part, it sounded like a scene from the play. He announced deadpan, "I've got a part in a play. I'm a corpse."

"I got my other friends on the phone. They always break up. Then they want to know all about it."

No wonder. In his first part ever, Frank shares the stage with Jean "Edith Bunker" Stapleton and Larry "F Troop" Storch.

Jean Stapleton is nice, Frank said. She comforted a scared corpse the first night, and told him not to be nervous.

Frank successfully plays dead now. A few years ago, he couldn't even stand up in front of a crowd.

"I used to be so bad, even the thought of taking an evening class and standing up before my fellow students was too much."

Then Frank retired, and became a volunteer usher at the Fox Theatre. He loved it. "They were looking for tour guides, and I wanted to be one. I thought that's how I could get over my fright—giving tours.

"It worked. Then I volunteered for the Missouri Historical Society. I even got into a speakers bureau. My only regret is I waited so long."

But it was worth it. The stage is "a thrilling experience. I've always wanted to be backstage when a play is over. There's such energy. Our first night, the audience applauded us. Then the whole cast applauded us."

He's paid, like any other pro. "I make $15 a performance, but you don't do this for the money. I signed a two-page contract, too. The type was too small and it was too long to read. But I asked for a copy. I'd like to see what I signed.

"We rehearsed our part one time. I thought we could have used more. I think I had it, but I'm not so sure the others did. When you're on stage, you can't see anything but a blank space. The lights are in your eyes."

I watched the play. All 12 looked good. Frank was Corpse No. 3. He came out, cool as you please. He was dead right for the part. Frank looked so natural.

# (79) Should a $200,000 House Have a Bathroom Door?

What do you think is standard equipment for a new house? Ceilings? Walls? Floors? How about a bathroom? Or a bathroom door?

It's silly, I know. But Rachel assumed her $200,000 home came with a door on the master bathroom. After all, the bathroom had a marble tub, brass fixtures and a planter.

"We're building a new house in a subdivision near West Port," she said. "We bought our house before the display homes were built."

Rachel could hardly wait to see the new display homes—there was her dream house, in solid brick. It had everything: Fireplace, wet bar, three bedrooms, and a magnificent master bathroom with cultured marble tub, cultured sink, cultured planter. And no bathroom door.

To Rachel, this wasn't too cultured.

"They call it the new 'open look.' It is. You can see right into it.

"I called the sales office. They said the bathroom door was optional. They're going to charge me extra—$225. I was furious. A bathroom door is not a luxury. This is a room with marble and brass and no door.

"I called the builder and said, 'What a dirty trick! Do you like a bathroom with no door?'

"He said no.

"I said, 'Then why are you asking me to pay $225 for a bathroom door?'

"He said the plans didn't show a bathroom door. I admit, I didn't check for one. I just took it for granted that doors came with the place. I called two other subdivisions with different builders. You won't believe it. In about half their display homes, the master bathroom door is not standard. It's some kind of trend. My subdivision gave me coffered ceilings and crown molding, but they're charging me for a door.

"The builder said if I was upset, he'd give me back my $10,000 down payment. I don't want that. I just want my door."

She also doesn't want to spend another nickel. "I've already spent over $200,000. I'm not buying a door, too. I wouldn't have cared if they'd built it into the price of the house. They could have hidden the cost where it didn't show."

Rachel has a plan to beat the system. "I've got this tremendous walk-in closet in the bedroom," she said. "I'm going to have them put the closet door on the bathroom. Then I'll put my own mirrored door on the closet."

I had to see this radical new home improvement. I drove out to Rachel's subdivision. All the other baths in the house had doors. Except the master bath.

This was a dazzling expanse of white marble and green plants. The commode was partially hidden by one wall. Mirrors cleverly reflected most of the room.

The bath was downright Roman. In fact, anyone could roam on in. The only doors were the ones to the bedroom. The three words you'd hear most in this bedroom would be, "Don't come in."

The "open look" is not for me. I don't want an open life. What if I was caught playing with my rubber duckie in the marble tub?

What if I had a party and my guests wanted to use the master bath? They'd have to close the bedroom door. That causes ugly rumors.

Maybe I was missing something. I called Rachel's builder, and asked about this new trend.

"That's the design of the house today," he said. "It's the open look. We offer the bathroom door as an option, but it's not standard. It's like if you bought a house and assumed it had a door between the dining room and the living room."

Not quite. A bathroom door is a little more basic.

"We don't build all our bathrooms without doors. Some master bedrooms have them, some don't. That model doesn't. It's not on the plans. It's not in the display house. It was never falsely represented.

"Sure, if I lived there I'd want a door on my bathroom. I'm just like that. But this is not a bathroom as we know it."

I called Rachel with the momentous news.

The builder says this is not a bathroom as we know it.

"Does it have a toilet?" she said.

Yes.

"Then I'm familiar with it."

# (80) The Office Wedding

Talk about an office romance—and we all do, don't we? This bride and groom were married before the office high altar: the copying machine.

You can't duplicate the wedding of Chris Ederer and Brenda Kent. It was charming.

Chris works for Rug Doctor Inc. Brenda works at Weatherline Inc. in Bridgeton. That's a nationwide telephone weather-information service. Here's the wedding story from Brenda's boss, Nancy Friedman.

"Brenda asked her supervisor for three days off," Nancy said. "She said she was getting married at City Hall.

"My husband Dick said, 'City Hall is no place to start your life together. Brenda should get married here at Weatherline.' Besides, we like office parties."

The 35 employees went to work. On the wedding.

"We all volunteered to do something," Nancy said. "All Brenda had to bring was the minister and the groom."

On the wedding day, the staff got in early to get the office ready. They took down all the racy cartoons. They blew up helium balloons and tied white ribbons on them. The balloons bobbed festively along the ceiling.

Flowers and a guest book were placed on the reception desk. The wedding area was hung with white crepe paper and white bells. Brenda and Chris would stand together where she stood every day—at the office copying machine. It was decorated, too. So was a long table with a tiered wedding cake. Champagne stood ready for the bridal toast.

There were bows on the office plants. Even the office cat, an elegant gray named Bob (short for Roberta), wore a pearl necklace. Bob retired to a back room and tried to remove it.

There was also office work to get out of the way. "We got the Federal Express out before the wedding," Nancy said. "We put the phones on the answering machine during the ceremony."

Elizabeth Lagermann wrote a poem, "Ode to Brenda's Wedding." Here's my favorite stanza:

"Agreeing to share this important event
"With such an obnoxious crowd
"Will only help her remember the date
"That her love was so solemnly vowed."

The staff took care of every detail, even the garter. "We almost forgot that," Nancy said. "But one of the engineers found a garter in his car."

The engineer declined to say how it got there.

Chris looked like all grooms: poleaxed. Maybe he was trying to figure out how he wound up getting married in an office. He had proposed a simple ceremony.

"We don't have any family in St. Louis," Chris said. "And we're not religious, so we decided to get married at City Hall. Then Brenda came home from work and said, 'The office wants to give us a wedding. Do you mind?'

"I said, 'Mind? Do I have a choice?'

"Actually I was glad when I found out who was catering it. The food here is good."

The staff whipped up shrimp de Jonghe, chicken curry balls with coconut, artichoke dip, croissant sandwiches and that perennial office-party favorite, vegetable dip.

"Everyone brought a dish," Nancy said. "The whole thing was spread out in the conference room."

The bride got dressed in president Richard Friedman's office. Before the wedding, he paced like a nervous papa.

"This marriage has a good chance of lasting," he said. "The length of a marriage is in inverse proportion to the amount spent on it."

The staff stood around the desks, drinking punch and answering the ringing phones. The punch bowls were set up by the computer printer.

Shortly after 2 p.m., the Rev. Stanley C. Cadwallader said, "OK, here we go."

The groom and his best man, Timothy O'Riley Hart, solemnly marched over to the copying machine. The maid of honor, Robin Gaston, followed. She wore pink and carried a pink bouquet.

The bride, in traditional white lace, walked down the aisle from the president's office. She came to the main office area, stopped and said cheerfully, "Here I am, everyone."

Everyone cheered.

Then the minister began the ceremony. It was dignified. And appropriate. Especially the part about how a marriage is "working together."

The phone rang. The answering machine picked it up.

Brenda's supervisor, Joan Maniscalco, leaned forward on a computer terminal as the minister intoned:

"Brenda Elaine, do you take Christopher John. . . ."

She did.

Chris kissed the new Mrs. Ederer. The office applauded. The phone rang. Again.

That made it a double ring ceremony.

## (81) The Snitzy Survival Guide to West County

Buffy comes from a grand family. Her folks lived two blocks off Grand in south St. Louis.

Now she lives in the wealthy West County suburb of Town and Country. "West County is infiltrated with South Siders," she said. "One of my neighbors has a whole acre yard done in Zoysia."

Buffy keeps some South Side ways. "I still spring clean," she said.

"But I hire people to do it."

Buffy has palmed herself off as a West Countian for 20 years. This is her **Snitzy Survival Guide:**

**Dress:** "Never wear red, white and navy. Those are too middle class. You must wear lime green with hot pink. If you're daring, throw in a splash of buttercup yellow. Navy is only safe with lime green and spouting whales.

"Straub's is the West County 7-Eleven. It's the only supermarket with cocktail napkins right by the door. If you don't want to look like the maid when you go there, wear your oldest wrap-around skirt or A-line. Get a lady in Florida to sew cute things on them: Pelicans. Sand dollars. Marching ducks. Mushrooms are very cute."

**Grooming:** "You can wear sculptured nails, but no claws. They must be working length. Especially if you don't work.

"The only lipstick colors are Sphinx Pink and Red Red. No makeup is best.

"Hair is never teased. If you wore a pageboy in seventh grade, you'll wear it when your hair turns white. Perfume must be Chanel No. 5 or Estee Lauder Youth Dew."

**Kids clothes:** "Buy them at Chocolate Soup. When the kid outgrows them, sneak off to the resale shop."

**Cars:** "Cadillacs, Lincolns, Jaguars. If you're environmentally concerned, Hondas and Volvos. The older you are, the bigger your Cadillac."

**Food, grownups:** "You know Brennan's, the New Orleans' restaurant? The West County Hamburger Helper is Brennan's jambalaya mix. Buy a package, add a can of tomatoes and a half pound each of chicken and shrimp.

"Never serve red meat. It's seafood, no matter how bad. Fake crab sticks are big. So are swordfish steaks. If nothing else, burn the fish on the grill and claim it's blackened. One friend serves blackened tuna: A can of burnt tuna."

**Food, kids:** "If you don't have time to make dinner, don't give the kids soup and sandwiches. Make fajitas. I once gave the neighborhood kids macaroni and cheese. They loved my 'pasta.'

"These poor kids have never had pork and beans with little hot dogs. I get rave reviews on mine. Except from mothers. They whisper, 'She serves junk food. No wonder her little boy is so big.'

"Big is suspect. You could be a fashion model, an athlete or dumb. Small people are smart."

**Jewelry:** "Wear five gold bangle bracelets, from wrist to elbow. That shows you've got money. Neck chains are out."

**Tan:** You got it playing tennis. Even if you didn't.

**Evening dress:** "West County women have at least three ballgowns. But sequins are in. You need $1,200 for a new dress. You take your oldest gown and hang it in the sun. Then send it to a cheap cleaner and pray they ruin it. Then your husband will let you buy another one.

"Smart stores have no-return policies. Women have been known to buy an expensive gown on Friday and try to return it Monday. They don't know how the makeup got on the neck."

**Movies:** "It's fashionable not to see them. Typical conversation is: 'Did you see "Star Wars"?' 'No, was it good?' "

**Mail:** "Good mail is any medical or legal journal, *Smithsonian*, *Food & Wine* magazine and three pieces of alumni mail."

**Breeding:** "Excitement is low-rent. Death is embarrassing. You may get upset only for something serious. Here's the polite way to say it: 'The only thing that really bugs me, I mean really bugs me, is the girl in Better Dresses didn't hold that dress. This is carriage trade, isn't it?' "

**Tradition:** "Every summer, you must take the kids to Busch's Grove for dinner in their little log houses. Women must wear white pique dresses and eat barbecue."

## (82) Kids in the Doctor's Office

Sick of waiting at the doctor's office? Tired of sitting in the emergency room? Sometimes, the wait goes on forever.

A woman I'll call "Mrs. X" may have the answer for you. She discovered it by accident.

Mrs. X knows how to cut hours off her waiting room stays. Her discovery could work not only at hospitals and doctors' offices, but at any place that puts you through a long, unpleasant wait.

Mrs. X has three active kids, so she has logged her share of time in hospital emergency rooms. "Emergency" implies quick, urgent movement. That's only if you're deathly ill. If you have middling-serious lumps, bumps and thumps, you can wait for hours.

The last time I was in an emergency room, the hospital removed my wallet with lightning speed. Once they determined my insurance would pay the bill, they beached me in a wheelchair for four hours.

I handled this with mature restraint. I whined quietly in a corner.

Mrs. X isn't so lucky. When she's stuck in the emergency room, she has three kids to keep quiet. Recently, young Tanya had a medical emergency. Mrs. X called the family doctor. He said to take the child to the hospital. Right away. Mrs. X gathered up Tanya and little Timmy,

3, and headed for the emergency room.

"The hospital put the kids in a little examining room," she said. "Then we sat. For hours."

Mrs. X did her best to keep the children occupied. She read them books. She told them stories. She let them bounce a sponge ball off the ceiling. She told them if they shrieked again they were dead meat.

"The kids were behaving themselves. I was proud of them. They weren't acting like some kids there. These mothers let toddlers roam the halls. In dirty diapers, yet.

"These kids yelled and cried. They were tearing the place apart. They opened drawers, pulled out Band-Aids and threw them on the floor. They grabbed the expensive medical equipment hanging on the walls. Sometimes, they even chewed on it."

Mrs. X noticed these families weren't around long. She also noticed that she was.

"The nurse kept saying, 'Are you still here?' Finally, after six hours, she said: 'This is ridiculous. I'm going to check what's going on.' "

Mrs. X followed quietly behind. She used the stealthy walk perfected by mothers and Indian scouts.

"I heard the nurse ask the technician, 'Hey, how come you aren't taking these people? They've been patient for six hours.'

"The technician said, 'We're really busy.'

"The nurse said, 'Oh, come on.'

"The technician said, 'We've got to get those others through. They'll destroy the rooms. These kids are behaving themselves. Let them stay there.' "

Mrs. X stood there and said, "I heard that."

"The nurse said, 'You're next.' "

Mrs. X felt like a real chump. "I was outraged. My kids were being punished for being good. I thought I was taking care of them. I was nothing but a sucker. I started watching carefully. This wasn't the only place where it happened. But there's a knack to it.

"It doesn't make any difference if the kid screams. Nurses and receptionists turn a deaf ear to that. It has to be actual destruction. Breaking furniture is good. Breaking equipment is better."

Some emergency rooms are prompt, she said. And some doctors never make you wait more than 10 minutes. But they are rare. She suggests you wait 15 minutes before you unleash the young terrors.

"Unruly kids get the most action in crowded waiting rooms filled with professionals and old people. They hate children."

Tantrums are needlessly tiring. "If you want quick action, just give the kids a sucker or some chocolate. Then let them roam. They'll leave their sticky little hands on chair arms and window glass.''

Mrs. X has even figured out how to pay the medical bills not covered by insurance.

''I'm renting my kids out to childless couples.''

## (83) Emily Post Never Had This Problem

If you're a woman looking for a health club, they'll never tell you about one thing. Not until it's too late.

So I will. There are two kinds of clubs: the ones where you wear your skivvies in the locker room, and the ones that wimp it and have private dressing rooms.

We who belong to skivvies clubs feel vastly superior to the wimps. It means we are serious jocks. ''Girls'' have dressing rooms. Men have open locker rooms. Women should, too.

After all, we're adults and fully liberated and . . . flapping in the breeze in front of perfect strangers.

The open locker room is the perfect place for a dangerous experience: the surprise meeting. Usually, the person you haven't seen in years comes breezing into the locker room in 300 bucks worth of stone-washed denim. All you're wearing is a baggy birthday suit.

Surprise meetings take place between ex-wives and new loves. Old loves and current wives. Or worst of all, old friends.

I overheard this encounter. ''Maggie!'' squealed some character in a blue suit with a bow at the neck like a pussycat. ''I haven't seen you since high school.''

Loud pause. ''You've only changed a little,'' the pussycat said.

It was obvious Maggie had changed a lot. She'd put on more than a couple of pounds. Considering what she was wearing at the time, she couldn't blame it on bad tailoring.

I get my own variation of the close encounter. My photo runs in the paper three times a week. But I don't look like it, so I live in pleasant anonymity.

Except in the locker room. I can't figure out how these women know me. Sometimes, they don't even see my face.

It's unnerving when you're peeled like a boiled egg and a stranger says, ''I know you! You write for the *Post-Dispatch*.''

I grope for a towel and think about saying, ''You've got the wrong person. Elaine's much thinner.'' But it's difficult to lie with no clothes on. (Note to young persons: This is only true in locker rooms. Other-

wise it's easy. Ask your mother.)

So I say something like, "How nice to see you. I wish you weren't seeing so much of me."

Proper etiquette says you should never introduce yourself to a naked person. Wait until they are dressed. Better yet, ignore them till they're in the gym.

I do this very well. Sometimes, too well.

Last week a woman stopped by my desk at work. She said, "Don't you know me?"

I looked at her blankly. I was sure I'd never seen her before.

"I used to go to your gym."

Oh, I said. I didn't recognize you with your clothes on.

## (84) Borrowing a Man's Razor, and Other Close Shaves

The closest shave I ever had in my life was when I was 15. I was baby-sitting at home. I'd packed the kids off to bed, and settled in for a nice 3-hour talk on the phone.

I didn't know my father had been trying to call home—for 2½ hours. He didn't know I was using his razor.

It was a nasty shock when he stormed through the door and caught me talking on the phone and shaving with his razor. He was speechless. At least in the beginning. I was lucky to escape alive.

That's when I first learned that men freak out when women use their razors. Even worse, men can't explain why they don't like it. Ask the smartest man you know why a woman shouldn't use his razor and you'll get one of these dumb answers.

(1) It dulls the blade.

(2) It re-arranges the molecules.

(3) Women don't do it right.

(4) It's too personal.

That last remark comes from a man who'll let selected women share his life and his toothbrush. But no one gets her hands on his razor.

"It dulls the blade" doesn't cut much with me, either. All you have to do is put in a new one.

A shrink who won't let his wife use his razor said, "Some things are men's things."

What kind of answer is that?

"You want a rational explanation for the irrational," he said.

"We just don't like it," Charlie Conway said. And he's with Gilette safety razors in Boston.

Then Charlie tried to be rational. "A woman shaves a greater area," he said. "If you took the square feet of her legs—if I can say that—you'd see there's much more shaving area. It's the equivalent of two or three blade shaves. The blade gets much more damage.

"A man's face is so sensitive he knows just how many shaves are left on his blade," Charlie said. "He can tell. There's a slight pulling sensation. The razor is so personal, it becomes part of him. When his pattern is interrupted, it throws him off. That's why men don't like to share their razors."

Dwayne, a full-time shaver, had the most rational irrational argument. "There's an easy explanation," he said. "You know how poets rhapsodize about a woman's raven hair, but if they find one strand in the butter, they go crazy?

"Well, many men like women with smooth legs. But heaven help them if they use the guy's razor. Women think we'll never know if they clean it up and put it back in the cabinet. But we do. We're not that dumb.

"See, shaving is one the most basic rituals of manhood. It's morning, and you stumble in. You look in the mirror and make a few faces. You lather up. You start to shave. It's a wonderful feeling.

"But if a woman has used your razor, things happen you'll never believe," Dwayne said. "You draw that blade down your cheek, and it's as if the flesh is coming off the skull. The pain is immediate. You can feel your teeth coming through your cheek. You feel like every whisker has been torn out by hand.

"It's happened to us all at least once. After that, we never trust women again. At least, not with razors."

## (85) *The Difference Between Tourists and Travelers*

The worst thing you can call anyone on vacation is a "tourist." Say the word with a hissing sneer and you can see the flowered shirt and the camera dangling on the beer gut.

And some male tourists look even worse.

But if you're a "traveler," you're sophisticated. Of course, it's not easy. You have to know the right names to drop. You need to know how to brag. You need to read my travel guide—**How To Sound Like a Real World Traveler.**

**Bragging:** You're spending 10,000 bucks to stay in some godforsaken place where you can't get a cold beer. You'd like to impress your friends, but you don't know how.

You can't just tell them what the trip costs. That's crude.

Nobody's impressed by lavish accommodations. The local Holidome is fancier than most foreign palaces. So brag about the things people can't get at home: Hardship. Discomfort. Inconvenience.

Forget the palm-fringed beaches. For real romance, talk about the poisonous snake in your bed. And the rooms with four-legged guests.

One traveler told me her hotel in the Orient was infested with rats. I said it sounded horrible.

She promptly put me in my place. "Rats don't bother you," she said. "Just don't leave food out at night. Remember, you're still living better than 99 percent of the population."

There is one thing world travelers are afraid to find in their hotels—tourists. A serious infestation sends them shrieking off to another "undiscovered" place.

True travelers feel personally responsible for every American on vacation. They sigh with relief when the bozo in the Budweiser hat turns out to be from Australia.

**Destinations:** Tourists go to London, Paris and other places with good food and five-star hotels. World travelers want some place unspoiled. By any modern convenience.

If it takes more than 12 hours to fly to your destination, and you can't drink the water, you're probably in the right place.

**Fear:** Only tourists worry about terrorists and plane crashes. Travelers glory in slow, bumpy flights on Russian-made propeller planes.

But they also like speed. Especially bus trips on steep mountain roads. When the driver flies around hairpin curves at 70 miles an hour, scattering ox carts and chickens, only tourists remember those stories beginning: "Thirty-six persons, including six Americans, died in a bus crash in the province of . . . ."

**Water:** Travelers don't mind rickety planes, but they live in terror of a fresh tomato. It contains water. Dinner turns into a debate on what you can eat. Purists claim you can't eat any local produce with a high water content. Tomatoes and watermelon are said to be deadlier than a boa constrictor. The verdict is still out on cucumbers.

Travelers know all about not drinking the water. They'll even tell you to keep your mouth closed in the shower.

**Food:** You can spot the native people in the local restaurants. They're the ones pouring ketchup on their french fries. The world travelers are chewing on braised cow stomach.

**Restrooms:** World travelers do not compare hotels. They rate restrooms. They love to discuss unspeakable plumbing from Paris to

Japan.

**Sights:** It is not cool to be overwhelmed by tourist sights. If you go to China, say it's a Good Wall, but not a Great one.

Travelers spend a lot of time hanging around tombs. One told me she'd just bought a ticket to Tibet and maybe she'd be lucky enough to see a "sky burial."

"Sky burials are only for the very rich," she said.

I doubt if they'll make "Lifestyles of the Rich and Famous." In a sky burial, a priest chops you up with an ax and the birds pick up the pieces. At least, I think that's what she said. She was talking during dinner, while I looked at a plate of spiced pork tendons.

**Walking:** Americans are usually fatter than other travelers. There's also another way to spot us. Even if we usually drive to the corner store for cigarettes, we walk everywhere on vacations. You'll see us hiking to the tops of sacred mountains, castle walls and historic views. This way, we can prove we aren't fat Americans.

**The one question guaranteed to make you sound like a tourist:** "How much is that in real money?"

## (86) The Men's Shower

The wedding shower had all the traditional touches: punch with floating fruit, cake with sugar roses and ridiculous games.

There was just one difference.

The shower was for the groom.

The cake roses were blue. And it was his male friends who were roped into spending Sunday afternoon sitting on folding chairs.

This trend-setting event took place in south St. Louis. Janet Smith gave the shower. But she refuses to take credit for the idea.

"It's nothing new," she said. "There are lots of male showers these days. I think the brides' families push them to discourage bachelor parties. These take place at a dangerous time—the night before the wedding.

"The bride worries all night that the groom will get hurt. The bride's mother worries about his reputation. What if he does something stupid and gets his name in the papers? The father sweats it out, too. If anything goes wrong, this expensive affair will be canceled."

But invite the men to a shower and your worries are over. They're too embarrassed to face each other again.

Janet gave the shower for a young man who works with her husband.

"The hardest part was finding the right invitations. They're all so flowery.

I finally used generic ones with rainbows that said, 'It's a party.' I wanted to call it a 'groomal shower,' like a bridal shower. But I figured no one would know what that was.

"Naturally, none of the men RSVPed. I had to call them. Seven of the 14 I invited showed up. That's not bad."

Were any male relatives there?

"Both fathers were busy."

I bet.

"You have to be tricky to get men to a shower. I had plenty of beer. I explained it was also a barbecue, so they could eat. And men eat. Unlike women, they don't take a spoonful to be polite. The first guy in line cleans you out.

"It was a surprise shower, so I had to let the bride know, so she could get the groom there. At first she thought it was crazy. Then she thought it was funny. Then she decided it was only fair after all she had to go through.

"The groom thought he was coming to a barbecue. He was so surprised, he almost dropped his teeth. But I had a hard time making him know this was a shower. The men refused to yell 'Surprise!' like you're supposed to.

"I coached them before the groom showed up. I explained they had to yell it when he came in the door. They refused. So I said, 'Do you want to eat?'

"When the groom walked in they just sat there. He looked bewildered and said, 'What are you doing here?' I glared at the men. They got out a feeble 'Surprise.' But there was no enthusiasm."

Janet spared the groom the ritual of oohing and ahhing over bath towels and Corning Ware.

"I specified tasteful gag gifts. The groom opened one box. Inside was this lacy thing. He closed it. Finally, he got up the nerve to open it again. Inside was a nice manly coffee mug and a lace apron."

Just who would wear the apron was not specified.

The groom also got a candlelight dinner for two: a box of tapers, two champagne coolers, two glasses and candle holders. Someone else gave a gift certificate for dinner.

"Then we played shower games. I wasn't about to let them off the hook. When I brought out the games, several men said, 'Well, it's been a nice party,' and headed for the door. I said, 'You eat, you play.' They sat back down. We played Rob Your Neighbor."

In this charming game, guests roll dice for mysterious wrapped packages. These quickly run out. Then the guests start taking packages from each other.

Soon people are fighting viciously for some useless gift, like a tea towel. This game teaches you a lot about life.

"The guys got involved and really fought over this box. Inside was one piece of candy, but they didn't know that. They almost killed one another."

As at any shower, the prizes all went to the wrong people. "The bald guy won the men's hair spray. The oldest guy won the strip dart game."

Did you play any of the other dumb games women have to play?

"No," Janet said. "I was gentle with them. After all, it was their first time."


## (87) The Arabian Big Mac Attack

This may be the ultimate Big Mac attack.

A St. Louis couple was thrown out of a McDonald's in Saudi Arabia. At least they thought it was a McDonald's. It sure looked like one. And the Big Mac on the sesame bun tasted like the real thing.

But hold the pickle. This Saudi joint doesn't cut the mustard. McDonald's says the couple were booted out of a McRipoff. There are no McDonald's in Saudi Arabia.

I have been trying to get the McNuggets of truth. Here's the story as I heard it.

"I've been thrown out of some classy bars and some lousy bars," Don Sprengel said. "But this is the first time I've ever been thrown out of a McDonald's."

Just what did you do, sir?

"I brought my wife."

And what did she do?

"She's a woman."

It happened in Saudi Arabia. Don is married to Terry Dent. They were visiting a Saudi friend in Riyadh. "Our friend wanted to show us this was a modern city with everything—even a McDonald's," Don said.

"He said the McDonald's name would not go over in Saudi Arabia. Besides, Saudis needed to own at least 50 percent of a foreign business. So they were called Herfy's. I believe that's the name. But they imported everything from McDonald's.

"It was just like walking into a U.S. McDonald's. They had fries, shakes and Big Macs, except they called them Big Herfys. They were served in the same boxes. I even saw something like Chicken McNuggets. The signs were in English and Arabic. The prices were about what you'd pay here. You could get a Big Mac with or without cheese.

"We went in and sat by the door. Our friend went up to order. Then the manager told him we'd have to leave. He was polite. He said women weren't allowed in there. He said the police would padlock his place if they saw her. I'd have to leave my wife in the car. It was about 115 degrees.

"I went out with her. The manager brought our hamburgers to the car."

Why didn't you protest?

"This country doesn't fool around. They still cut off people's hands as punishment. Troublesome foreigners are simply escorted to the airport and put on the next plane."

Terry Dent said, "Our Saudi friend wanted to show us how much his country had progressed. He showed us superhighways and modern buildings. He drove us around in a white Mercedes.

"Of course, he did buy me a black robe and veil to wear in public. And I had to sit in the back seat of his car. But I didn't say anything. I wanted to absorb the culture.

"He took us to this Herfy's. He said it was really a McDonald's. It looked just like one. Except for the sign that said, 'No entry for women' in English and Arabic.

"I said to our friend, 'Are you sure I can go in here?'

"He said there was no problem. I was wearing the black robes, but it was obvious I was not a local woman.

"Once inside, I could see him talking with the manager. They kept looking at me. Finally, our friend came back and said we'd have to leave."

Terry thought this routine was eerily familiar. "They had a separate entrance and a separate area for women upstairs. But it was closed, so I had to sit in the car. It was also strange to hear that old argument for discrimination: 'I don't want to do this. But they'd close me down.' It made me see how much women are still oppressed."

But mostly, "I was amused. I thought, 'Wait till I tell my friends back home I've been kicked out of McDonald's, the most wholesome place in America.' "

A McScandal. A greedy corporation sold out women for a McBuck.

Except it's not true. At least, McDonald's says it's not. "We have no restaurants in Saudi Arabia," said Stephanie Skurdy at McDonald headquarters in Oak Brook, Ill.

"We have no deals with anyone to use our products under a different name. We zealously guard our trademarks. This is absolutely unauthorized. It has happened before in other countries.

"I would like to assure the couple this has been an illegal use of our products, and that we will investigate it.''

Maybe there's been some McStake.


## (88) Flying Steerage

My ancestors didn't come over on the Mayflower. They came steerage. A hundred years later, I travel the same way.

I fly coach.

When I'm in line with my boarding pass, I look like any other passenger. The flight attendants warmly welcome me aboard. But the smiles get thinner the farther back I go. By the time I'm in coach class, I'm wearing a shawl and a babushka.

Once I tried to hang a garment bag in the divider between business and coach.

"May I see your boarding pass?" said the attendant.

I showed her.

"This isn't for you," she said. "Go back where you belong."

But there's room here, I whimpered. It's between the two sections.

"You must stow your luggage in the rear of the plane," she said, firmly.

So I picked up my straw suitcase and my chicken, and headed for steerage.

Life is stern and simple back with the peasants. Another flight was delayed more than an hour. We sat at the gate, strapped in our seats. The captain announced another 10-minute delay. I asked if I could go back to the restroom. The flight attendant said yes.

I started down the aisle and a second attendant said sharply, "Where do you think you're going?" Rows of bored passengers pricked up their ears.

I told her—and everyone else. I also said I'd raised my hand and gotten permission.

"Well, OK," she said. "But hurry up."

Food is the great class divider. In steerage, you're served last. You see the trays covered with real cloth napkins going up the aisle to business and first. Their crystal clinks invitingly. The flight attendant draws the curtain between your section and theirs with a coy motion that promises orgies of whipped cream and champagne.

Finally, after the others are served, your food is shoveled out. I'd read that savvy travelers could get special meals, even in steerage, at no extra charge when you made reservations. I tried it once. I ordered the seafood plate. It looked beautiful: chunks of plump shrimp, crab and smoked salmon on fresh lettuce.

The other steerage passengers ate their gruel and looked hungrily at my meal. I lost my appetite. It was like feasting in front of 200 Tiny Tims.

Only 6 percent of the 418 million air travelers flew first class in 1986, the Air Transport Association estimates. They say officially there's no difference between business and coach.

But we know better.

Once, on a long flight to the Orient, we ran short of booze. Back in steerage, we were forced to survive on lemon-lime soda. The liquor was saved for business.

On the return flight, five of us got upgraded to business class. Better yet, we flew with the first-class passengers. We sat in the same extra wide seats. We scarfed up the same liquor and soft drinks, including exotica like Schweppes canned lemonade. It tasted terrible, but we knew steerage didn't get it.

At dinner time, the flight attendants closed our section and spread crisp white cloths on our trays. But the first-class passengers got hot appetizers. We got nothing.

Next, first class got a small green salad. We got nothing. Finally, the main course came. We got everything served at once on a tray. First class had chicken and steak on china plates.

Our meal would have tasted fine if we hadn't seen theirs.

Rumor said the only difference between business and the lower orders was an extra dish of pudding. Steerage got only cake.

Three children from steerage ran into our section. The business passengers threw the little blighters out.

Let them eat cake.


## (89) The Gas Station's Sacred Pact

There is a sacred bond between a driver and a gas station. You promise to buy their gas. The station promises to have a restroom.

After that, anything goes.

You can gouge us for Styrofoam thimbles of bitter coffee.

And not clean the windshields.

And make us ask for a key attached to a 5-pound slab of wood.

It's even all right to turn off the hot water tap and paint the restroom battleship gray.

But now the natural contract is being broken. Gas stations along interstate highways are abandoning their responsibilities.

I found out the hard way, on a recent trip to Chicago. I was driving. We made good time, fueled by premium gas and 32-ounce sodas.

About 40 miles outside Chicago, the car was almost empty and I was almost full. I stopped at an Amoco station. It was a new self-serve one, with a clerk in a bulletproof booth.

Fill 'er up, I said, and where's the restroom?

"We don't have one," said the clerk.

You what? I couldn't believe it.

"Sorry," the clerk said. "How much gas do you want?"

None, I said dramatically. It was a painful decision. But I refuse to patronize a place that breaks the sacred bond of the open road. I drove off in a huff. A 1986 Huff with white sidewalls.

"Oh, my gawd," said my passenger, sliding under the seat in embarrassment. "I can't believe you said that. Couldn't you just buy a couple of gallons of gas and look for another place?"

No. Some people still have standards.

"But it's an Amoco station," he said.

I pulled into the nearest truck stop. This place certainly provided service. It not only had restrooms, it had showers. And a lot of brightly painted women hanging around the lobby.

For the rest of the trip, I brooded. What if this became a trend? What if carloads of innocent families were lured into fraudulent gas stations? What if they bought gas before they found out?

If I were a powerful person, I could do something about this. Rep. Louis Ford, who has a seat in the Missouri House, once introduced a bill to require all gas stations to have public restrooms after he had a close encounter on the road. His efforts were not flushed with success.

But what can we do?

We could protest by turning a carload of cranky kids loose on the station, but that would only harass some underpaid clerk.

Or we could call Amoco and make them squirm. It's only fair. They did the same thing to me. I talked with Chuck Mason, an Amoco public relations director.

"We prefer to have full-service facilities," he said. "The problem is the world we live in. It's not perfect. If you have a public facility, you must watch and care for it, or terrible things can happen."

Chuck used so many euphemisms, I couldn't tell if the public facility was a monument or a gas station. And what were the terrible things?

You mean like muggings, rape and murder.

"Yes. We or the dealers are responsible. We could be sued. Aside from that, if we don't care for the facilities, they get dirty.

"In certain areas, we are building pumper stations—24-hour self-service facilities with bulletproof glass. It is company policy that those clerks not leave the glass booth during their shift. They cannot go out for anything. Holdup people attempt to lure them outside. A public restroom would give them another excuse.

"I understand your problem perfectly," he said. "I feel the same way you do. I wish all our stations could be full-service."

Understanding is no help, Chuck. What we need is some indication the station has no restroom. A sign, maybe. High on a pole, where we could see it from the highway.

"That's a good point," he said. He couldn't promise anything, but the suggestion was "reasonable. I'll ask about it."

I hope he does. Because they're going to have a good time making up a symbol for a "no restroom" sign.


## (90) A Suburban Bash

There was a real holiday bash in West County this Labor Day weekend. Similar ones took place in suburbs all over the nation.

But some of the participants aren't celebrating.

The bash was held on certain West County mailboxes. Someone beat the boxes with baseball bats.

Mailbox bashing is the favorite sport of rich kids. It's similar to polo. You play it with six to eight horses, except these are all under the hood.

You take the car Daddy bought you for your birthday, and load it up with your friends. Then drive slowly down the street, bashing boxes with a tire iron.

Bashers are gentlemen. They know it's not cricket to hit a poor person's mailbox. There's another reason to stick with your own kind— nobody's going to make too much trouble for good old Thurston's son. Not if you live on the same street. And if for some reason you do make trouble, Thurston can afford a good lawyer to get the kid off.

I heard about the latest attack from a man who lives on Conway Road. Actually, I heard it from his brother. Jim, the bashee, is out of town.

"My brother's been hit again," he said. "The mailbox bashers wiped out every mailbox on both sides of Conway Road for a one-mile stretch. Jim lost his fifth mailbox this year."

Jim is determined to beat the bashers. He's an engineer. After each attack, he designed a different mail box.

"After the first one, he went for durability. He bought an iron mailbox and attached it to a huge wooden stake. The bashers couldn't get the mailbox, but they broke the stake.

"Then he built a braced mailbox—a metal A-frame structure with the box inside. St. Louis County sent him a letter saying he'd have to get rid of it. They said it was an obstruction. But the mailbox got knocked down before the notice was delivered.

"Jim decided he was giving them too big a target. So he bought the smallest mailbox he could find. The bashers smashed that sucker flat in no time.

"Next he tried to make it a narrow target. He put the new mailbox on the slimmest possible stake. It was wiped out in the last bash."

Jim went off to buy his sixth mailbox and added up the score: The big one broke, the armored one crashed, the small one smashed, the thin one bent.

"He wanted to put the mailbox on a stone post, but his lawyer said no. If someone had an accident and drove into it, Jim could be sued.

"He talked about a putting a plastic bush in front of it for camouflage, but the county said no. It was another obstruction.

"One of his neighbors tried to devise a mailbox that would shoot red paint on anyone who moved it, but he was afraid of getting sued, too."

But Jim didn't give up. "He drove up and down Conway and examined the damage to see what he could learn. He found out white mailboxes get zapped more often. That gave him his latest inspiration.

"Now Jim's making the mailbox invisible. He's painting it dark green to match the grass. He's using a flat non-gloss paint so it won't pick up any reflection from headlights.

"But he's not stopping at camouflage. He's designed a break-apart mailbox, that flies cleanly and lightly when hit. Jim figures it will sail about 35 feet. That should make the bashers happy, and maybe save the mailbox."

## (91) Watch That Fancy New Car

You've just pulled into the parking lot, right next to a fancy car. You look at it and think, "Probably belongs to some rich creep. Bet he made his money cheating widows and orphans. I work as hard as he does—probably harder. But he's driving a car that costs as much as my house."

Do you open your car door as carefully as you should?

Tell the truth, now. Have you ever dinged the door of a Mercedes, a Cadillac, or some other expensive car—accidentally on purpose?

Because a lot of luxury car owners think you do.

A Jaguar owner says his car doors were nicked three times in nine months. Each time he had them repainted, somebody whacked the doors again. Then it's back to the shop for five coats of red and three coats of clear lacquer. He has to drive an inferior rental car for weeks.

And the cars that did in his Jag? He's pretty sure they included a camper with a "Buy American" bumper sticker, and a clunker. A blue clunker. The last gash had blue paint on it. But he can't prove anything.

"I always park way back in parking lots," he said. "I think the cars go looking for me. After the first gouge on the door, I started noticing other Jaguars. They all have chips, dings and dents along the door line. I think people enjoy hitting expensive cars."

Of course, a couple of dented car doors doesn't prove anything. But what about the people who deal with life's hard knocks professionally?

What about the shops that do body work?

I ran the question past Jack Reinwald, service manager at Moore Cadillac-Jaguar. Do people like whacking the doors on expensive cars?

"I can't prove it," he said. "But I'll be honest with you, that's my feeling, too. I think it's got something to do with somebody having more than you."

Greg Reininger at Classic Refinishers Ltd. said, "I don't think they pick on rich cars. I had an old Plymouth, and it got hit six times in a row in one year. Nobody left a note. They get everybody. I think people's attitude is just loose nowadays."

Valerie Cocos-Heath added another opinion to the body of evidence. She's at a St. Louis shop with the wonderful name of Wreck Masters. I asked her, Do people have more fun bashing fancy cars?

"Oh, yes," Valerie said. "They seem to delight in it. It's almost like they say, 'Look, there's another one. They're going to get it again.'

"They go after Mercedes, Volvos, Cadillacs. Caddies really get them. They like Lincolns and smaller sporty cars, too. We've never had a Rolls, so I don't know what happens to them."

You know what really makes people see red?

"They especially love to get red cars," Valerie said. "Stand out like sore thumbs. We're doing a red Ferrari right now. We just did an estimate on a red Jaguar.

"I think red cars are gorgeous, but I never realized how much people loved to hit them until I got in the business."

Valerie has statistics to back up her theory. "You know how many car colors there are available now," she said. "But one-third of the cars we repair are red. My boss likes red cars and he should know better."

The boss goes out of his way to save his doors. "He has a brand-new red Monte Carlo SS. One cold and snowy night he goes to the grocery store. He gives me a ride. He parked two blocks away from the store. I had to trudge after him in the snow, so he could save his car from getting dents on the doors.

"I said, 'Heck, if I knew you were going to do that, I would have brought my car. I can park it anywhere.' "

What do you drive?

"A nice, safe brown car," she said.

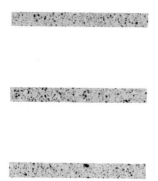

## (92) *Just Leave Your Mink in the Trash Bag*

If you had a full-length mink coat, would you leave it on a doorstep in a trash bag? Even if you were very rich? Even if you were giving the mink to charity?

I'm not making this up.

The mink coat was donated to a charity couture fashion sale. Someone dumped the mink-lined green plastic trash bag on chairwoman Kathy Kline's doorstep.

What's wrong with the coat?

"Nothing," Kathy said. "It's in good condition. It's still in style."

Then why is she giving it away?

"Who knows? It's 5 years old. I guess all her friends have seen it. The woman said she was going out of town, and she'd leave a package for the sale on my doorstep. Inside was this mink."

It looks like it costs more than a small car.

"The least she could do was put it in a designer trash bag," Kathy said.

"Listen, honey," said her co-chairwoman, Alice Ludmer. "You won't believe what goes on here. We can tell you some stories."

And so she did. Alice and Kathy are chairwomen of this year's National Council of Jewish Women's Couturier Fashion Sale.

"Shoppers line up at the door hours before," Alice said. "We open and they scream, 'Where's the furs?' They rush over, grab them and scream, 'Where's the jewelry?'"

Some of this year's furs arrived by even stranger ways than trash bags.

"One woman wanted to donate a sable shrug and a mink coat. But only if I'd meet her secretary at a big department store," Kathy said. "I said, 'How will I recognize you?' "

It was easy. She was the one handing out free furs.

"I think some people feel better about buying a new coat if they give the old one to charity," Kathy said.

"And if his girlfriend is wearing a new fur, his wife should, too," Alice said.

Do you have people who do that?

"We don't know and we don't ask," Alice said.

But they suspect.

Some rich not only giveth, they taketh away. "One woman gave away her blue-jean skirt—then wanted it back. She said it was back in style," Kathy said. "Can you believe it? Do you know how many jean skirts we have?"

Then there was the woman who thought she donated the wrong pair of Weejuns. She asked Alice, "Would you go and find them for me?"

"We have a mountain of shoes. I told her she was welcome to look for herself."

Most donations come from the richer suburbs, Clayton, Ladue and Frontenac. But the best clothes don't always come from the best addresses. For a certain type of rich person, the dowdier you dress, the older your money. Old money is better than new money. It puts some distance between you and the rascals who made it.

One woman donated a rather dull ball gown. But she said it had been to only the best parties. And she asked for a large tax credit. The dress was rotted out under the arms.

Ball gowns are always sensitive. The couturier sale has some real bargains on designer dresses. But it's embarrassing to show up wearing your hostess' castoff.

"We have a system," Alice said. "When we get something pretty nice, we put a donor number on it. It's a code. That way, we can look up the name and avoid embarrassment."

Nothing is more embarrassing than donating an outfit that's unwanted.

"I had this little spaghetti strap dress hanging in my closet," Alice said. "I didn't want to give it away. I really liked it. But I felt I should donate something nice. So I did. Nobody bought it. They wouldn't even try it on. And it was marked down 50 percent. Now I wonder about my other clothes."

Many sale customers are not rich. "The proceeds benefit the poor," Alice said. "But in a way, the sale is charity for the middle class—the people who want the best for themselves and their children but can't afford it."

They have some, uh, offbeat customers. "Undercover police officers are regular buyers of our men's wear," Kathy said. "They need so many suits."

Speaking of undercover, "One nice young officer was going on a cruise with his girlfriend. We found him a very good tux."

Then there are the men who shop in women's couture. "Some men pretend to shop for their girlfriends. But their voices are very high, they're never with girls, and they know exactly what they want.

"Some customers are very wealthy. One man came here in a Rolls-Royce—and he didn't even shop in the designer section.

"We have some smart shoppers," Alice said. "One year, a woman wanted a beautiful satin quilted robe. It was $12. She said it cost too much. We never change our prices. But I felt sorry for her. She looked so shabby I thought the poor thing would never own anything nice. The sale was ending in a few minutes. I let her have it for $10.

"Then I get out in the parking lot. I see her driving off in a new $20,000 Volvo."


## (93) Well-Read Drivers Are a Menace

One afternoon I was speeding down the highway when a man in a sporty little Mercedes two-seater passed me.

That was bad enough. But not only was the guy faster and richer—he was reading a newspaper while he whipped my car.

That's right. He must have been going 80, and he had the paper propped on the steering wheel. He was reading while he drove along. This wasn't some deserted road—it was a busy stretch of interstate highway.

The man looked like an executive. I caught a flash of white shirt and expensive silver hair.

Jeez. Talk about speed reading. It takes real ingenuity to make something as harmless as reading lethal.

It's not the first time I've seen people reading while they drove. Once I ran into a bookworm in the fast lane. It was during morning rush hour on Highway 40. There was an accident up ahead, and traffic slowed to a crawl. The car ahead of me was strangely out of sync with the rest of the traffic. It kept missing chances to move ahead. And it was shifted with a jerk.

I got a good look at the jerk, when I passed him. The guy was reading a book. His steering wheel made a great book rest. First he shifted, then he turned the page.

"Reading in the car is a real problem," said Sgt. Ron Beck. "And we're seeing it more and more." He ought to know. Sgt. Beck is in the safety education division of the Missouri Highway Patrol.

"Inattention is the No. 1 cause of fatal accidents in Missouri."

"Inattention" includes anything from taking your eyes off the road, to yelling at the kids fighting in the back seat, to putting on lipstick or straightening your tie.

"You won't believe the crazy stuff people do in cars," Sgt. Beck said. "We're seeing more and more reading while they drive. You'd expect it on the rural roads. But it's most common where there's traffic.

"You know what interstate highway traffic is like—you've got to be alert every minute. Well, we saw this guy driving along reading a newspaper. We couldn't believe it. We stopped him and asked what he was doing. He said he was looking for a job.

"They're just not reading newspapers—we see people reading novels, appointment books, note books—you name it."

Is it illegal to read while you drive?

"There's no actual law that states you cannot read in a car. But there are laws governing car movement and driving in a 'careful and prudent manner.' "

If you're a rolling reader, the police will probably nail you for the results of your inattention—speeding, crossing the center line or following too closely.

It's no accident that we Americans live out of our cars. They're part of our lives. But cars used to be an extension of our living rooms. The big plush seats were like sofas. The dashboard was the mantel, decorated with plastic statues. The rear-view mirror was festooned with fuzzy dice and lacy garters. We turned on the radio for entertainment.

But the mobile phone turned our cars into part of the office, complete with papers, briefcases and appointment books. Now we conduct business while we drive.

"You see people driving along, one hand on the phone, the other writing down notes," Sgt. Beck said. "I haven't seen any accident statistics yet, but those car phones have got to be dangerous.

"You know what I think it is? People are so rushed, they're doing all this work in their cars. They're running from one meeting to another, trying to catch up on notes and appointments and phone calls."

Ray the Cab Driver, the philosopher of the freeway, had the last word.

"Some people," Ray said, "are just driven."

## (94) An Emergency Sales Pitch

There's nothing more frightening than a phone ringing late at night. You wake up, run for the phone and wonder: What's wrong? Did something happen to the kids? Has there been a car accident?

Now here's a new midnight worry to add to your list. That call could be something really horrible—a telephone salesman.

Wait till you hear Betty's story.

Betty is a widow who lives in Swansea, Ill., north of Belleville. Her three children are grown up and moved away. So late-night phone calls can be scary.

"Lucky for me, I wasn't asleep when this happened," Betty said. "Otherwise, I would have had the daylights scared out of me.

"I was talking to a friend on the phone. When she calls we like to hash things over, and before I knew it, it was almost midnight. We heard this flickering on the phone. My friend wondered if someone was trying to get through. Suddenly we heard the operator.

"She cut into the middle of the conversation and said, 'Is this 237----? That's my phone number. I said it was. The operator said, 'I have a collect call for you from Bob. He says it's an emergency. Will you accept it?'

"Bob had a last name, too. But I don't remember it," Betty said. "I was too upset.

"I said I didn't know any Bob, but put him on. After all, the operator said it was an emergency. I was afraid it was one of the children. Maybe they'd been in an accident, and this Bob was calling from the hospital or something.

"My friend hung up, and the operator put the call through. Bob gave his name. Then the next thing I hear is, 'This is a recording.' It was a recorded sales pitch! I couldn't believe it.

"The operator was still on the line. The minute she heard the recording she disconnected it. She apologized and hung up. That's all I know. I was cut off after that."

What was Bob selling?

"I don't know. I was too stunned. It all happened so fast. I'm just glad the operator cut it off.

"A collect recording. I can't imagine anyone trying to sell anything that way. I don't know how he got my phone number. I just hope this isn't a trend."

Imagine getting out of the shower to answer the phone—and finding out it's a collect commercial. And what kind of bozo tries to sell something at midnight—something legal, anyway?

I asked Dick Hill, the Illinois Bell spokesman, if collect recorded calls were a trend. He sounded more outraged than Betty.

"I've never heard of anyone doing anything like this," Hill said. "And I've been in this business a long time. This is scary."

Hill checked up on Betty's story. He confirmed that the incident did take place.

It could have been worse, if it wasn't for a smart operator.

"I found out why the operator was still on the line," Hill said. "The practice in Illinois is if an emergency call comes in, the operator is required to stay on, to see if she can lend further assistance. When this operator heard the recording, she disconnected it immediately. That's not policy. She just used her common sense.

"I talked with people who handle odd-ball calls. They said this is a very rare case."

Automated recorded sales calls are big now. It is possible, just possible, that Bob was trying to get around an Illinois law that prohibits automatic calls dialed intra-state. (Out-of-state automatic calls are OK).

Illinois Bell does not know who made the collect emergency call. It was not traced. "We really don't know why he did it," Hill said. "It's almost like a prank.

"I can't imagine any reputable salesman making calls like this at midnight. It's a bad business practice. He's sure not going to be prosperous with those tactics."

Maybe that's what you call a hard sell. It would be hard to sell me, anyway.


## (95) The Bloom's Never Off Her Rose

The bush in Kathryn Bernstein's front yard stumps people.

"I can't tell you how many people knock on my door and ask what kind it is," she said. "Others stop their cars and get out just to see it."

That's what I did. At first, it looks like the stump of a large dead bush, with artificial flowers tied on it.

But it's really a South Side landmark.

For more than 12 years, Kathryn has been decorating that bush on the corner of Fyler and Brannon. And it still stops traffic.

Last time I looked, it was abloom with red silk roses, wired to the branches with green trash bag ties.

One neighbor says he has fantasies of sneaking over late at night and decorating it with plastic grapes and bananas, but so far he's restrained himself.

"Instead, I wait to see what the bush lady will do next," he said. "We all do."

The bush used to be an ordinary evergreen. "It got full of bag worms and died," Kathryn said. "I stripped them off and left the stump there. One neighbor offered to take the stump out for me, but I said, no, I had another idea. I was going to paint it white."

Instead, she left the wood natural, and put on artificial flowers.

If I had to review Kathryn's creation, I'd say it combines the starkness of a Japanese flower arrangement with South Side practicality and permanence.

"In the beginning I had it full of plastic rosebuds," she said. "Twenty-four red ones. I bought them for 10 cents apiece at a dime store. You can't get them at that price anymore."

How long do you keep the flowers on the branches?

"I leave them up till they strip them off. They disappear, sometimes overnight. I'll wake up and find my bush stripped. But I had some pink chrysanthemums up at Christmas that lasted till spring.

"Most people like it. They tell me it's a clever idea. Little kids come by and pull a flower off to see if it's real.

"But I know not everyone likes it. In fact, some hate it. Once a bunch of teen-agers passed by in a car and yelled, 'That's dumb!' I know it's different. I'm the talk of the neighborhood."

Kathryn gets by with a little help from her friends. "It's quite a chore, putting on those flowers. I'm 86 now, and I can't stand as long as I'd like anymore. My feet, you know. My neighbor who cuts the grass helps me out."

Other friends and neighbors—even strangers—give her flowers.

"I couldn't do it without them. Flowers are so expensive. My neighbor gets me used ones from the cemetery. Another lady who works in north St. Louis helps me out. Sometimes strangers leave them on the doorstep.

"Those are silk ones out there now. They're from some man who drove by my house in a big Lincoln. He saw the flowers were off again, and asked what happened. I said, 'Kids.'

"I didn't even know him, but he promised to bring more. He did. I found a whole bag of silk roses on my porch. Expensive ones, too. They must have cost $7.50 at Grandpa Pidgeon's discount store."

## (96) Saloon Etiquette

The true city saloon is not a place to get drunk. It's a social club. And an exclusive one. It's easier to get in to some country clubs than most city saloons. Especially now that the South Side has become fashionable.

To make it worse, the social rules are unwritten. So it's easy to make a faux pas. South Sider Patty Hofer says West Countians are wandering into Cherokee Street bars and calling the regulars "cute."

This behavior is likely to provoke that sign of severe social disapproval, the "cut direct"—someone knocks the top off his or her beer bottle, and goes for your throat.

To avoid these social embarrassments, Patty, the social secretary of the stein, has devised this Guide to Tavern Etiquette. Here are Patty's rules:

(1) Never walk into a joint and go straight to the bathroom. One always walks directly to the bar (table service is for food) and says, "Hello," and asks, "Who's ready for a drink?" orders a drink, then puts a bill on the bar as payment. Generally one's change remains on the bar so the barmaid may easily take the money for following rounds.

(2) Never ask for a running tab. That instantly marks you as an outsider.

(3) He who orders the drink pays for it.

(4) Customers are not required to listen to the house bore. Simply pick up your drink and change and move to the other end of the bar. This is especially effective if there are only two of you in the place.

(5) All gambling debts must be paid promptly, that is, before closing. The final authority on all bets is the head reference librarian at the downtown library.

(6) The house telephone is not to be used for placing or receiving bets. Get busted on your own phone.

(7) Pool tables and other games must be shared. If you want to play, reserve your spot by putting a coin on the machine.

(8) It's not polite to play the same record on the jukebox over and over. Even if you just got fired, divorced or dumped.

(9) If you're in a tavern talking about your speeding ticket, and someone offers to fix it for $50, don't give him the money. You'll never see it again—even if he's been drinking there for three years.

(10) Never stiff the house. Patty said, "We were having dinner in a neighborhood saloon one evening when the place caught on fire. One party left without paying. That was considered very bad form. The bar

owner had already lost money from the fire and some jerk beat him out of a measly dinner check."

(11) If the bartender takes a dislike to you, leave immediately. Nothing will fix it, not even big tips. You must look for a new home.

## (97) A South Side Christmas

As any hostess knows, planning a sparkling society event is no party. You can wear yourself to a frazzle. Especially during the holidays.

You need help. But party planning guides seem so out of touch. They talk about how to deal with the caterer, the florist and the servants, while you're bribing the kids to scrub the tub.

But this holiday season, four prominent South Side hostesses—Joann Brueckner, Kathy Moore, Betty Mitchell and Barb Hartman—compiled a practical Christmas party guide. Here is their:

### Guide To A Seasonal South Side Soiree

**Place:** "The party is always in the basement," Kathy said. "You must scrub the floor on your hands and knees. Get all the dryer fuzz off the pipes. And hang colored sheets to cover the tools and the furnace."

**Decorations:** The traditional red-and-green motif, set off with silver. That means crepe-paper streamers and silver garlands. You must have a silver Christmas tree on the dryer—one that's too ratty to go upstairs. A fake cardboard fireplace with glowing logs makes the room look warm and cozy.

"The home should have at least three nativity scenes. If there are kids under 5, there's always something bizarre around the crib: a zebra or a toy truck."

The bathroom will have a cute Santa commode cover and Christmas elf soap.

No one ever has the nerve to use the soap.

**Entertainment:** A Ping-Pong table. Plus you have the kids do what they did in the school Christmas pageant.

**Coat check:** "When guests arrive, boots must be left on the throw rug at the front door," Kathy said. "Then you put on the slippers in your purse. As the party warms up, the women will go barefoot."

Coats are left on the bed.

**Correct catering:** Call everyone and have them bring a covered dish. Food must include ham and mostaccioli.

The buffet is served in the dining room. Just follow the plastic runners. Serving suggestions: Stuffed celery. Stuffed eggs. Rye bread dip. "Countless creamed vegetables with soup." And Jell-O salads. One out of three dishes will have pineapple.

**Security:** "Use only the best," Kathy said. "St. Louis' finest are a phone call away, ready to remove the larger drunks from the front lawn."

Do delegate certain people to keep warring relatives apart. They'll make sure Uncle Mike, who likes to dip into the eggnog, will not ask divorced cousin Harold, who's dating a 21-year-old chickie, "Is that your daughter?"

**Dress:** Polyester is always proper. So is anything glittery and black. Women often wear a plastic Christmas flower, and enameled earrings with holly and reindeer.

**Music:** Perry Como singing "Ave Maria."

**Refreshments:** Eggnog served in an heirloom bowl from Target. The eggnog is from an old grocery store recipe, cut with milk and laced with plain-label bourbon.

For beer, Anheuser-Busch products are served exclusively. For other booze, stick with the off-brand bourbon and the 3-gallon jug of wine, on sale at the drug store.

"Name-brand liquor bottles are lined up along the bar, but those bottles are sealed," Kathy said. "Don't you dare crack one open.

"Like the Christmas soap, they're only for show."

## (98) *The Cat vs The Carpet*

I have this cat, see. And I have this carpet. Occasionally, the cat likes to use the carpet. Usually I keep the lawless animal in line with a water pistol. But even shooting her right between the eyes didn't work this time.

I tried all sorts of remedies: Red pepper. Mothballs. Patent cat sprays. I even covered the spot with a 4-foot sheet of Plexiglas.

Finally, I gave up. I offered anyone who could come up with an answer a free dinner at Tony's, one of the best restaurants in town.

Your response was amazing. I now have more than 100 different remedies. Readers told me about cat products, cat psychologists—even a cat psychic.

That came from Lisa. She and her husband are "young, conservative professionals. . . . We had a problem with our two cats when we tried introducing an abandoned cat into the family scene. After a 20-minute conversation with a California animal psychic, we learned how our two cats thought and felt about the third animal. . . . It really helped us cope.

"Like I said before, we're normal, really!"

Relax, ma'am. You're talking to someone who put red pepper and mothballs on her living room rug.

Leann Rolape didn't have much of a solution. But just reading about her cat, Kozmo, may make you feel better.

Kozmo not only sprayed "the TV set, stereo, closets, plants and bookshelves," she wrote. "Kozmo also sprayed my album collection and, yes, it was fun trying to deodorize the covers of one hundred records.

"He sprayed the curtains in the bedroom and the living room, so I took them down and washed them. Then I had a bright idea. The curtains in the bedroom didn't need to be floor-length, so I shortened them.

"I shortened the wrong curtains."

Kozmo now lives in a cage in the back yard.

Jean Iezzi keeps her cat in a playpen. "An old screen door and a fireplace screen are placed on top to keep her from escaping. We have to weight down the screens with two giant wrenches and a board."

She writes ominously: "The only permanent solution to rug pollution is death or the playpen."

Not for Julie Ganey. She just changed the brand of cat litter.

"I had been using a brand with a deodorant. When I changed to a plain, no-name, generic cat litter, my cat never used the living room carpet again."

Julie's suggestion was so practical and cheap, I tried it right away. It didn't work.

Then there's Janet Vanderplas' idea. She wrote: "Buy a cactus with spines about 1-inch long. . . ."

Jacob Schaefer had this four-step program:

(1) Take up old rug.

(2) Put down new rug.

(3) Roll up old rug and insert cat.

(4) Place old rug with cat in dumpster.

"NOTE: If dumpster is too practical for your tastes, substitute a friend or relative with whom you'd just as soon not exchange birthday and Christmas cards anyway."

Sorry, Jacob. After I blabbed about the cat's problems in the paper, I can't even give her away.

Ardith Mendes says I need to retrain my cat. "Place the litter box right on the rug. Then gradually, inch by inch, move the box back to where you want it. Sneaky? Yes. But it usually will work."

I believe you, Ardith. But we may never get to our dinner at Tony's. It's more than 60 feet from the living room to the cat box. By the time the box inches to the right spot, we could both be gumming mush in some rocking chair ranch.

Chris Ochen of Edwardsville says her solution works on dogs and cats. She cleans the spot with straight Pine-Sol.

"I reinforce the learning procedure by waving the Pine-Sol towel near the animal's nose before I clean the spot up."

It won't work for me, Chris. I grew up in South Side saloons. They reek of Pine-Sol. One snort, and I go off on a binge, swilling orange soda, eating pretzels and playing the same song over and over on the jukebox.

But maybe I can find something on James F. Bender's list. James has never been to Tony's so he really wants to win. Here's part of the list:

(1) "Blindfold the cat. If she wants to find the carpet, make her work for it. (Where is Tony's? I'll need directions.)

(2) "Blindfold yourself. If you can't find the living room, then there's no problem. (Can I get a brain sandwich at Tony's?)

(3) "Put a mirror over the spot where the cat goes. It may cause the cat to reflect on what she's doing. (Is Tony's near a bus stop?)

(4) "Take the cat to a tennis match and warn her if she doesn't quit with the rug bit, she'll wind up in the same racquet as her dad. (Can I get a draft beer at Tony's?)

(5) "Use the litter box yourself. It may make the cat jealous and, what the heck, it's only for 30 days. (Will Tony put the game on TV if we ask?)

(6) "Get a pet for your cat. Try a pit bull. (What is Tony's last name? One of the wife's in-laws used to work in a restaurant and she thinks. . .)"

I'll keep trying your ideas until I find one that works. And I'll report on any progress.

Linda Poor, a cat behaviorist at Kennelwood Village has an interesting retraining program.

But before I try it, she says I should have the cat checked for kidney problems.

I will. I'm leaving no stone unturned.


## (99) The Cat Cure

It was Friday night, and I was dangling a bunch of Christmas ribbons over my cat, Elsah. She was leaping into the air and taking swipes at them. Sure, there are better ways to spend Friday night, but this was doctor's orders.

It turned out to be a winner of a suggestion from Linda Poor. A yard of curly red Christmas ribbon and a couple of closed doors helped solve my cat problem.

Linda, our contest winner, is a cat behaviorist at Kennelwood Village, which boards and trains animals. She's sort of a cat shrink, except she doesn't put cats on the couch. She doesn't want cat hair all over, either.

I had a bigger problem than cat hair. I have two cats. The oldest, a 12-year-old calico named Elsah, liked to use the living room rug. I tried everything to stop her: red pepper, mothballs, anti-cat sprays. Finally, I asked for your help. More than 200 people wrote in with solutions, including Linda.

Linda's specialty is hopeless cases—cats who are on their way to the Humane Society for the Big Sleep. Consultations are $15 for a half-hour on the phone, $30 for an office visit.

"I think your cat is trying to communicate the only way she knows how," Linda said.

Could you teach her to use a Magic Slate?

Nope. Linda wanted to help me figure out what the animal was trying to say. She started asking questions. Did the vet check the cat for urinary-tract disease? Yes. She's healthy. Is the cat more attached to you or your husband? Me. Where does she sleep during the day? In my closet.

"Do you keep your shoes on the floor?" Linda asked.

Yes.

"That's where your scent is strongest."

I beg your pardon.

"Even when you're gone, the cat is trying to be close to you," Linda said. "The carpet problem got worse about two years ago. What changed in your life?"

I got a part-time job and began traveling more.

"So you were home less with your cat?" Linda asked. "How often do you play with her?"

I scratch her when she wanders by. But I don't really play with her. She's very dignified.

Linda made a partial diagnosis. I needed more Quality Time with my cat. At least 15 minutes a day.

Great. I didn't have kids because I couldn't give them Quality Time, and here I was fooling around with a cat. But I'd take the cat to dinner and a movie if it would work. All the cat wanted me to do was dangle a bunch of red ribbons over her head.

For two weeks, the rug was cat-free. Then Elsah started up again. Linda was back asking why.

The answer came the next day from Sarah Watts. Sarah is sixteen. She watched Hodge, the younger cat, tease and chase Elsah around our house. "Hodge is just like my little brother," Sarah said. "He won't leave Elsah alone for a minute. He's always teasing her."

Linda thought Elsah was trying to tell us that Hodge, the young, ram-
bunctious cat, got on her nerves. She needed time away from him. Linda
recommended a week of a "confinement cure." Many vets and readers
said confinement worked for their problem cats.

It goes this way. You keep the cat in a small, uncarpeted room for
seven days. A half-bath is ideal. Fix it up as comfortably as possible with
the cat's favorite toys, blanket, food, water and most important, a clean
litter box.

"This is not a punishment," Linda said. "You must take out your
cat frequently, pet it and play with it. During and after confinement,
you need to give the cat lots of attention. Just don't allow it to wander
anywhere unsupervised."

I felt terribly guilty when I chucked the cat into the little room. But
she seemed content. I'd been a big sister with three pesky younger
brothers, and I thought I recognized the look on her face.

At the end of the week, Elsah seemed better. The harried look was
gone from her eyes. Linda said we could let her out when we were home,
but we had to watch her. And, if we went out, the cat had to go back
to the closet for peace and quiet. We were to give her as much Hodge-
free time as possible—even if we occasionally "accidentally" shut a door
on Hodge.

After 21 days, the two cats divided up the house. Elsah had sole custody
of my study and the guest room. Hodge took the living room and dining
room. The bedroom and kitchen were neutral territory. Hodge got the
catnip mouse. Elsah took the Christmas ribbons. They had separate food
bowls and litter boxes.

Elsah not only quit using the carpet, she wouldn't go into the living
room. After 30 days, the living room was still untouched, and Linda
was a winner.

Linda has some warnings about cat confinement. "Do not try this
unless you take your cat to the vet first. Confinement is a behavior
modification method, but that alone is not the complete answer.

"You also need to find out what's causing the problem. Is it stress?
Is it a dirty cat, with poor litter habits? It may need to be retrained.
Is it a dirty owner who doesn't clean out the box often enough? Is it
hopeless—a senile cat losing its ability to function?

"Also, you must clean the spot with an enzyme-based cleaner, or the
cat may return to it. You can buy this cleaner at your vet's or a pet shop.
Make sure it does not have ammonia in it.

"These problems are often complex. Elsah was reacting to at least
two things: You were gone more and didn't play with her, and Hodge

teased and worried her."

Linda said Elsah "is not cured, but controlled. Your cat's response to getting upset is to use the carpet. She may do it again, and you'll have to find out what's causing the problem again."

One more warning: Confinement takes a lot of your own time and patience.

I think it's worth the extra effort. Just one thing bothers me: My family has started hanging around the living room, and they're circling the carpet.

## (100) Nailed by the Doctor

You've heard the story about the guy whose ears buzzed and his eyes popped. He went from doctor to doctor for relief. They took out his teeth, his appendix and his tonsils. Nothing worked. His ears still buzzed and his eyes popped.

Finally, one doctor said he had six months to live. The man decided to go out in style. He would cash in his savings, take a world cruise and get a custom-made wardrobe.

The tailor started measuring him for his new clothes. "Waist—36," he said. "Sleeve—35. Collar—16."

"No, wait," the guy says. "I wear a 15½ collar."

"No," said the tailor. "If you did that, your eyes would pop and your ears would buzz."

St. Louisan Don Perrin has heard that joke before, but he says his doctor story is funnier. He also says it's true.

"I wanted to improve my health, so I took up jogging," Don said. "My toenails turned black. It was scary. So I went to a podiatrist. He told me I had an incurable fungus. The only remedy was to remove my toenails. Permanently.

"The doctor said it could be done in the office with a local anesthetic. I got a quantity discount—eight toes for $1,360."

Don got a second opinion. "It was the same diagnosis, but a slightly lower price—eight toes for $1,250."

A third podiatrist was even cheaper. He would do it for $1,060. "He also said it was a simple procedure. It would heal completely in two weeks. He said I'd never miss them—toenails no longer served a useful purpose because man no longer climbs trees."

Don went with the lowest bidder. Just before the operation, there was a change in the simple procedure. "The podiatrist's secretary called. She said the doctor wanted to perform the procedure as an outpatient at a nearby clinic. She said it was more convenient than the office."

Don would be in by 9, out by noon. Just like a quickie dry cleaner.

The day of the operation "someone took my pulse and asked if I was allergic to anything. A nurse gave me a pill. I was zonked. I remember a voice giving instructions in the operating room. It wasn't my podiatrist. I asked for him. They said he was there. But I never saw him."

Two weeks later, Don's toes were "still swollen and painful. I couldn't wear shoes. The podiatrist saw no problem." He still didn't see a problem five, six, or even seven weeks later.

Now Don was getting bills from doctors he'd never heard of. One billed him for $60. "He said he took my pulse at the clinic.

"I got a $230 bill from an anesthesiologist. A third doctor sent me a $40 bill for a biopsy on the toenails. I got a $1,301.65 bill for the use of the operating room. And a $1,078 bill from the podiatrist.

"Plus an 'assistant's fee' of $270. I asked about that one. The podiatrist said he was just trying to get a little extra from the insurance company. If the company didn't pay it, forget it.

"It's now nine weeks later. My toes still hurt. I'm going to work in a business suit and running shoes.

"Finally, I went to my family doctor. He said the toes were infected. He gave me antibiotics. They worked.

"I made a final visit to the podiatrist. He was glad to see the toes had healed—to him, it confirmed his skill. I told him about the antibiotic cure. He was upset because I went to my family doctor."

Don's bargain operation cost him almost $3,000. He was exactly $1919.65 over budget.

"But here's the funny part," he said. "One day I'm reading this running magazine article. It says: Don't wear your running shoes too short, or your toenails will turn black. If you switch to the correct size, your toes will heal."

Don began to suspect he didn't need that operation.

"I told the podiatrist I'd pay him if the biopsy report showed signs of fungus. He sent me bills for a year or so. Then he stopped. I never saw the biopsy report. He never saw his money."

After all his doctor visits, Don's eyes don't pop and his ears don't buzz. But sometimes his toes hurt.

"Man hasn't evolved that far after all," he said. "When I drop something on my nail-less toes, it smarts."

## (101) Viets Tips for Travelling

When I went to China for two weeks, I took one carry-on bag. When I went to Chicago for the weekend, I brought two bulging suitcases and a shopping bag.

That's Viets' First Rule for Packing: The farther you go, the less you need.

More luggage doesn't mean you'll have more clothes to wear. It means you'll have to lug around two useless dresses and three sweaters you don't need. The raincoat you should have brought will still be at home.

That's just the start of my "10 Tips for Travelers." You won't find them in any guidebook. Here they are:

**Rule Two: Whatever the hotel gives you, you won't need.**

I'm talking about hotel freebies: bath gel, hand lotion, shampoo. The newer hotels seem to be outdoing one another with extravagant little extras. Too bad you can't use them.

If you forget your hair dryer, your hotel will have free bathrobes. If you forgot your bathrobe, your hotel will give you free shampoo.

Hotels leave chocolate on your pillow only if you're dieting.

**Rule Three: Whatever you left behind, you can't buy when you get there.**

A seasoned traveler once told me, "If you're going anywhere in America, don't worry. You can buy it when you get there."

Wrong. You'll be in meetings all day until the stores are closed. If they're still open, they won't have your size. If you can buy it, you won't be able to afford it. I once paid $4 for 2.5 ounces of shampoo at a New York hotel.

And it isn't even a controlled substance.

**Rule Four: The mini-bar is a cold-hearted seducer.**

If Satan staged that scene in the garden again, he wouldn't use an apple. He'd tempt Adam and Eve with the key to the mini-bar. How can those cute little airline-size bottles cause any trouble?

Even if you don't drink, the mini-bar is loaded with irresistible items 24 hours a day: imported chocolate bars, airplane peanuts and ice-cold $3 sodas.

But it isn't quite like sneaking out to the refrigerator at midnight. Wait till you see the bill.

This is the only refrigerator that raids you.

**Rule Five: Read the brochure carefully.**

Unless you understand travelese, you could be in big trouble. Here's how you translate these favorite travel phrases:

A hotel restaurant with "elegant dining" means it's overpriced.

"Regional American cuisine" means you pay $15 for meat loaf.

Watch out for those "simple islands." That means the god-forsaken hole has no nightlife. So does "spectacular scenery" or "unspoiled beaches." What spoils that spectacular scenery is luxury hotels, discos, casinos and five-star restaurants.

"Simple food"—you'd better like fish.

"Lively"—noisy.

"Live like the people"—the bathroom is down the hall.

"Sun-drenched"—hotter than blazes.

**Rule Six: Dirty clothes take up more room in a suitcase than clean ones.**

**Rule Seven: People who can summon a cab usually cannot summon a waiter.**

For some reason, the two skills are not the same. If you can summon a taxi with a finger snap, you probably have the sort of face that looks like it's already had a drink. Better latch onto someone who can flag down a waiter.

You'll need both these travel survival skills, especially in places where waiters and cab drivers don't speak English. Like New York.

That leads us to . . .

**Rule Eight: The Midwest is the last refuge of the native-born cab driver.**

**Rule Nine: Time goes faster on vacation, unless it rains.**

**Rule Ten: The postcards always arrive home after you do.**

## (102) The Vietnam Women's Memorial Goes to the Dogs

Bruno Mazzotta is a Vietnam veteran, and he gets fighting mad when other veterans are insulted. "You know about the Vietnam Women's Memorial?" he said.

Sure. It's a statue of a nurse. It's supposed to complete the Vietnam memorial in Washington, D.C.

"Well, some government guy said Vietnam nurses were no better than dogs. He said if the women veterans got a statue, they'd have to give one to the canine corps."

I don't believe it. Nobody is that dumb. Not even in the government. "I'll send you the proof," he said.

Bruno sent me a letter from the Vietnam Women's Memorial Project. It said project supporters went before the federal Fine Arts Commission in October to get the memorial plans approved. The commission turned them down.

The reasons included: "Mr. J. Carter Brown, fine arts commissioner, stated that if we allow a statue of a woman, we'll have to add other statues such as one for the canine corps."

That's not proof, Bruno. I need to see Carter's direct quote.

That was the end of it, I thought. But Bruno is tough and persistent. He sent away for the transcript of the hearing in Washington. He read 90 pages of bureaucratic twaddle. And he found the dog quote.

Along the way, he slogged through the sentences like this one. It's a whopping 70 words. I'll break in on the middle.

". . . I don't think the fear of being charged with making political decisions should obfuscate our objectivity in trying to analyze something of this sort. . . ."

Bruno deserves a combat medal for fighting his way to the historic pooch passage. Here it is:

Chairman J. Carter Brown is saying the women's statue does not complete the memorial. "I hope that they can recognize that it probably does the opposite," he said. "It dramatizes one more way the 'incompleteness,' if you are going to look for literal representations, as I would predict from many of the Americans who have already spoken up—the Park Service has even heard from Scout Dogs Associations— will never end."

That's a statement to sink your canines in, old J. Carter. His committee doggedly refused to allow the statue.

Frankly, I never saw what the big deal was. The women veterans want a single statue by the Vietnam memorial—not in smack dab in front, but in a nearby stand of trees. Technically, the woman in the statue is not a nurse. But she has a stethoscope on her, so most call her that.

The memorial already has a statue of three men. The commission says they represent everyone, men and women.

I always thought the two were quite different. I suspect if J. Carter Brown couldn't get a female date to the prom, he wouldn't find a male a satisfying substitute.

Washington has 38 statues of American soldiers. And not a single one of an American military woman. Not even after 300,000 women served in World War II. Ten thousand women served in Vietnam. And not one was drafted. They all volunteered.

That's another thing that makes them different from J. Carter Brown. Bruno's transcript says J. Carter never served in the armed forces.

But Bruno was there, under fire. I asked what he thought about the women's memorial.

"Those three guys don't represent everybody," Bruno said. "A man is not a woman. If they had left the memorial a wall of names, with no statues, I'd say it was fair.

"But they put in the statue of three men. So the women deserve some recognition. They were there. They were under fire. Give them their statue and let them get on with their lives."

Instead, they get compared to dogs. But maybe J. Carter changed his mind since October. Maybe he apologized. I checked with Suzanne Mills-Rittmann, executive director of the Vietnam Women's Memorial Project.

"There's been no apology and no change," said Suzanne. "Mr. Brown holds firm. He insists that women are a minority group, and our statue would encourage other minorities.

"I was there when he made the dog remark. I just about dropped my teeth.

"After we were rejected by the committee, we needed to regroup and make new plans. We decided to go the congressional route."

Congressional friends are sponsoring bills to require that the women's statue be added to the Vietnam memorial.

And if that fails, maybe the government can give the women veterans a nice bag of Purina Nurse Chow.

## (103) An Old Love Affair

Eddie said, "I heard that Americans have a love affair with cars. But I never understood what that meant until I saw the Buick. Everyone stared when she went down the street."

She was an old beauty—a 1932 Buick. "She was black and gray with white gangster tires."

This love affair was no one-night stand, but a real romance, rekindled after 56 years.

"I saw it all," Eddie said. "This company was making a commercial in St. Louis, and they used the Buick. I was on the set when it happened.

"Let me tell you how big and roomy that old car was. The commercial used a model who was 6 feet 1. He wore a top hat and tails—and he didn't have to take off his hat when he drove.

"The commercial was shot in front of a dignified old building. The crew was taking a break. We'd blocked off part of the street. We didn't have to block it, but we did.

"Along comes this stretch limo, about 4 miles long, with black glass. Out gets this chauffeur. He opens a door. Out steps this handsome old guy with a suit that says M-O-N-E-Y. You know the kind. Costs about

$900, all hand-tailored and made from wool woven by specially trained sheep.

"We think, 'Oh, oh, this looks like trouble.'

"The guy walks up to the Buick and says, 'What are you doing with this car?'

"We told him we were making a commercial.

" 'Look at that,' he said, in a soft, awed voice. He starts patting it. This is a man who could buy a dozen Buicks with his lunch money. But he had the good sense not to ruin it. He knew he had stepped into a dream.

"He said, 'Can I look inside?'

"We said, 'Sure.' He pushes down on an honest-to-God door handle, opens a door about 4 inches thick and sees the inside. It's immaculate. He starts stroking the car. Then he says, 'I'm riding in a piece of junk.'

"He turns to the chauffeur and says, 'I want to show my wife.'

"The chauffeur opens the door, and out steps this beautiful older woman. She says, 'Oh! Our first car.' The couple explained that they bought one just like it, when they finally made it. That was 1932, in the Depression.

"They get in the car. The back seat has a foot rest and two small crystal flower vases on the door posts. She says, 'Look at the vah-ses'—that's how she pronounces it.

"I can't resist. I whip out my Polaroid and take their picture.

"The old man says, 'Can I pay you?'

"I said, 'No, just enjoy it.'

"Finally, they walked back toward their car. He's holding her hand. Then the most romantic thing happened.

"He looked around. He thought none of us were watching. And he patted her on the bottom. Then they drove away, back into the memory mists.''

# STUDY SKILLS

### Exercise One: Classification

Outlining is a method of classifying and organizing ideas. In order to outline, you must understand how facts or ideas are related to one another. Study the two lists of information below.

To create better maps

To find fresh water

To find oil

To watch crops growing

To warn of natural disasters

To find large schools of fish

I. Uses for Landsats

   A. To create better maps
   B. To find fresh water
   C. To find oil
   D. To watch crops growing
   E. To warn of natural disasters
   F. To find large schools of fish

(Notice that the grammatical form of each topic is parallel.)

The list at the left contains the same information as the list at the right. But the list at the right is organized in a more meaningful way. The outlined list shows us the relationship of the topic to the lecture as a whole.

**Practice:** Organize the list on the left into outline form.

Chile

Water is black.

Canada

Rock is brown.

Brazil

Diseased plants are green.

Healthy plants are red.

Italy

Iran

I. A Landsat photo is printed through color filters to produce a false-color picture.

   A. _____

   B. _____

   C. _____

   D. _____

II. Other countries will receive Landsat data.

   A. _____

Name: _____   Date: _____   7

B. _____

C. _____

D. _____

E. _____

## Exercise Two: Classification

In order to classify ideas together correctly, you need to know which ideas are related and which are not. In the following exercise, three words in each line are related and one is not. Decide what the related words have in common. Circle the one word that is not related to the others.

| | | | |
|---|---|---|---|
| 1. photograph | picture | print | (variety) |
| 2. pattern | blue-green | black | brown |
| 3. accurate | observation | correct | exact |
| 4. Cape Cod | Cape Hatteras | Cape Kennedy | South Dakota |
| 5. provide | rotate | circle | orbit |
| 6. crops | disaster | plants | trees |
| 7. wheat | soybeans | acres | corn |
| 8. fires | earthquakes | concentration | storms |
| 9. recognize | launch | observe | identify |

## Exercise Three: Recognizing Main Topics and Subtopics

Below is a list of sentences in random order about Landsat satellites. First, read all the sentences. Look for the best way they can be organized into an outline. Then copy each sentence on the appropriate line in the blank outline.

The Landsats are two butterfly-shaped spacecraft.
The second use is to find oil and minerals.
Scientists base their interpretations on the patterns of the colors.

How do Landsats work?

The first important use is to create better maps.

They were sent into orbit in 1972 and 1975.

How can Landsats be used?

A photo is printed from a black-and-white negative through color filters to produce a false-color picture.

What are Landsats?

Another use is to find fresh water.

I. _____

    A. _____

    B. _____

II. _____

    A. _____

    B. _____

III. _____

    A. _____

    B. _____

    C. _____

## Exercise Four: Main Ideas and Supporting Details

Factual writing in English is usually organized in a series of main ideas and supporting details. Notice the organization of the following paragraph from the lecture:

> Another use for Landsat is to find fresh water. In dry areas such as deserts, Landsat photos may show black areas that indicate water or they may show red areas that indicate healthy plants.

I. Another use for Landsat is to find fresh
water. (main idea)

    A. In Landsat photos, black areas show
water. (supporting idea)

    B. Red areas show healthy plants. (supporting idea)

Here is another sample paragraph. Find the main idea and supporting details.

The fifth use is to warn us of natural disasters, such as the damage done by large forest fires, melting ice near the North and South Poles, and lines in the earth where earthquakes might happen.

I. _____ (main idea)

    _____

    A. _____ (supporting idea)

      _____

    B. _____ (supporting idea)

      _____

    C. _____ (supporting idea)

      _____

## INCOMPLETE OUTLINE

**Directions:** *Read the outline before you listen to the lecture for the first time, so you will know what you need to listen for. While you are listening, find the missing dates and phrases to complete the outline. Mark your paper while you listen.*

    I. Introduction
    II. What are Landsats?

A. Two butterfly-shaped spacecraft sent into orbit in

_____ and _____ .

B. They circle the earth _____ times every

_____ hours.
C. They photograph every part of the earth every

_____ days.

D. Each picture covers an area of about _____ square
miles.

III. How do Landsats work?

A. A photo is printed from black-and-white negatives
through color filters to produce a false-color picture.

1. Water is _____ .

2. _____ is brown.

3. Healthy plants are _____ .

4. Diseased plants are _____ .

B. Scientists base their interpretation on the patterns of the
colors.

IV. How can Landsats be used?

A. The first important use is to create better _____ .

B. The second use is to find _____ .

C. Another use is to find _____ .

D. The fourth use is to _____ .

E. The fifth use is to _____ .

F. Some other uses are:

    1. To find _____

    2. To show where _____

    3. To provide a record of _____

V. What are the future plans for Landsats?

    A. Another Landsat will measure _____.

    B. Other Landsats may be equipped with _____.
    C. Other countries that will receive Landsat data are:

        1. Canada
        2. Brazil
        3. Italy

        4. _____
        5. Zaire

        6. _____

## WORD RECOGNITION EXERCISE

**Directions:** *Fill the blanks in each word family by finding the missing parts of speech in your dictionary. Divide each word into syllables and mark the syllable that takes the primary stress, as shown.*

*Word Families*

| Noun | Verb | Adjective | Adverb |
|---|---|---|---|
| 1. pos si bil´i ty | XXXXXXX | _____ | _____ |
| 2. _____ | e volve´ | XXXXXXX | XXXXXXX |
| 3. _____ | _____ | ob serv´a ble | _____ |

4. cre á tion _____ _____ _____

5. _____ _____ pop´u la ted XXXXXXX

6. _____ XXXXXXX _____ ac´cu rate ly

7. _____ con´cen trate _____ XXXXXXX

8. _____ _____ _____ i den ti fi´a bly

9. _____ _____ for´ma tive XXXXXXX

10. in for má tion _____ _____ XXXXXXX

11. _____ rep re sent´ _____ _____

12. de vel´op ment _____ _____ XXXXXXX

13. _____ _____ in ter´pret a ble XXXXXXX

14. _____ in´di cate _____ XXXXXXX

## TRUE-FALSE EXERCISE

**Directions:** *Read these sentences before you listen to the lecture for the second time. While you are listening, decide whether each item is true or false. Mark your paper with a T for true or an F for false while you listen.*

_____ 1. Landsats take pictures of every part of the earth.

_____ 2. The colors in Landsat photos do not look like colors in ordinary photos.

_____ 3. Maps made from pictures taken from airplanes are better than maps made from Landsat photos.

Name: _____ Date: _____

_____ 4. Landsat photos can show the kinds of rocks that indicate underground oil sources.

_____ 5. Fresh water is blue-green on Landsat maps.

_____ 6. In Landsat pictures you can tell the difference between corn and wheat growing in fields.

_____ 7. In these photos scientists can see lines in the earth where earthquakes might happen.

_____ 8. The Landsats, by counting people, show how the population of the world is growing.

_____ 9. Future Landsats will photograph larger areas.

_____ 10. You can buy a Landsat picture.


## TOPICS FOR DISCUSSION AND WRITING

1. Do you think the Landsat spacecraft should be allowed to photograph other countries? How do you feel about the Landsats photographing your country?

2. How could your country use Landsat pictures? Which particular use of Landsat photos would be most important?

3. James C. Fletcher of NASA said that the Landsats are likely to save the world. Why do you think he said this?

4. Suppose Landsat photos show that the area of ice at the North and South Poles is becoming smaller. What might it mean? How could you use this information?

5. The lecturer states that people may purchase a variety of pictures for their own use. Do you think that the average person would have any trouble interpreting these pictures?

6. Imagine a situation like this: The Seasat satellite sends back information that there are waves 50 to 60 feet high in an area of the Pacific Ocean between Hawaii and Japan. How might this information be used?

7. Find these places on a map of the United States: Cape Cod, Long Island, New York City, Delaware Bay, Chesapeake Bay, Cape Hatteras, Cape Kennedy, Lake Okeechobee, Miami, the

Great Lakes, the Mississippi River, the Missouri River, the Great Salt Lake. Point the places out to your classmates.

## MULTIPLE CHOICE EXERCISE

**Directions:** *Choose the one answer that best completes each sentence. Write the letter of the correct answer in the blank.*

_____ 1. A Landsat photo is printed from
      a. black-and-white negatives.
      b. color negatives.
      c. false-color negatives.
      d. none of the above.

_____ 2. In false-color pictures, water is
      a. red.
      b. black.
      c. white.
      d. blue-green.

_____ 3. From a height of 570 miles, _____ can be seen.
      a. automobiles
      b. people
      c. patches of color
      d. trees

_____ 4. If you wanted to look for water in the desert, you might look in Landsat photos for
      a. black areas.
      b. red areas.
      c. white areas.
      d. both black areas and red areas.

_____ 5. Which of the following could *not* be seen in a Landsat picture?
      a. damage done by large forest fires
      b. schools of fish
      c. pollution
      d. the number of animals in an area

6. Which of the following may not be a feature of future Landsats?
   a. heat measurement
   b. radar
   c. X-ray
   d. photographs of smaller areas

7. Which will receive Landsat information in the future?
   a. Zaire
   b. China
   c. Argentina
   d. Germany

8. Which is not a natural disaster?
   a. a large forest fire
   b. crops growing
   c. melting ice near the North and South Poles
   d. lines in the earth where earthquakes might happen

9. One advantage of Landsat is
   a. it can produce more accurate maps than have been possible before.
   b. it can save time and money in the search for oil.
   c. it can predict the size of food crops.
   d. all the above.

10. Reading Landsat photos requires special training because
   a. the United States does not give out Landsat information.
   b. only patches of color can be seen.
   c. the system has many problems to be solved.
   d. only colorblind people can do it because the pictures are in false colors.

## FINAL LISTENING ASSIGNMENT: NOTE-TAKING

**Directions:** *Read these questions before you listen to the lecture for the third time. While you are listening, write the answers.*

1. What are Landsats?

2. How do Landsats work?

3. If Landsat photos don't show things as small as people or cars, how can they show how population is growing?

# Landsat System Update

Although there have been some problems with the Landsat system, in many ways the satellites have worked even better and longer than scientists had expected.

Landsats 1 and 2 were sent into space in 1972 and 1975. They were expected to work for about two years each, but they surprised scientists by sending back information for more than five and a half years. During that unusually long time, there were some changes in their performance.

The first change involved the Landsats' tape-recording *capabilities*. Originally each Landsat had two tape recorders which *enabled* them to take pictures of areas where there are no ground stations. The tape recorders held the pictures until the Landsat passed near a ground station. The pictures were then sent down. By the end of 1977, only one tape recorder of the four was working, and it was working only part of the time. During the times it was not working, Landsat pictures could only be sent to earth when the satellite was within *range* of a ground station.

Second, the orbit of Landsat 1 changed. At the time Landsat 2 was *launched* in 1975, it was placed so that together the two Landsats would pass over the same spot on earth every nine days. But by the time Landsat 1 had been in orbit four to five years, its orbit had begun to change due to the pull of earth's gravity. Therefore, it was necessary to fire Landsat 1 rockets for a very short time to correct its orbit. With the new orbit, the two satellites no longer followed each other every nine days. Instead, Landsat 1 followed Landsat 2 six days behind it, and Landsat 2 followed Landsat 1 twelve days behind it.

A third change concerned the *complex* machine that measured colors in order to send pictures back to earth. The machine was intended to measure four colors, but the part of the machine that *indicated* the color green in Landsat 1 stopped working, and for a time the spacecraft continued to operate with three color bands. Landsat 1 was finally shut down in early 1978 after five and a half years of operation.

Landsat 3 was launched to take the place of Landsat 1. Landsat 3 had the same uses as Landsat 1, and in addition, it was equipped with an *infrared* system to measure heat. This system failed after about two months. Landsat 4 is scheduled to be launched in 1981. It may also be equipped to measure heat if scientists can solve the

**Figure 2.** Seasat satellite.

Photograph courtesy of National Aeronautics and Space Administration.

problems that they had with Landsat 3. Landsat 5 (Stereosat) will be next. It will provide *three-dimensional* pictures of geological formations to help gas and oil companies find new sources of oil.

Seasat A was another satellite added to the Landsat system (see Figure 2). It was specifically created to gather information about the seas. *Microwave* instruments on the spacecraft were so accurate that they were supposed to be able to measure the height of the waves in the ocean to within 20 cm. (7.8 in.). Other uses for the Seasat were to watch the weather over the seas, to *forecast* storms and *floods*, and to provide information on *surface* temperatures, *currents*, and ice. Unfortunately, after operating for only 105 days, Seasat failed in October 1978 because of a loss of power.

The Landsat satellite system has sent back more data than has ever been completely and fully used. The system will continue to change. New ideas will be tried; some will fail and some will succeed. People who are interested in Landsats may read and listen for news about the Landsats in the future. At this point, nobody knows whether the program will be supported and expanded by the government, whether data will be sent to many other countries, and how data will be more fully used.

---

**capability**  capacity; ability

**enable**  make something possible

**range**  the area of activity

**launch**  to send; to set in motion

**complex**  consisting of interconnected parts

**indicate**  show

**infrared**  wavelengths greater than light, but shorter than microwaves

**three-dimensional**  showing length, width, and height

**microwave**  an electromagnetic radiation with a wavelength of from 1 millimeter to 1 meter

**forecast**  to predict, to tell what is going to happen in the future

**flood**  an overflowing of water onto land that is normally dry

**surface**  on the top

**current**  the steady, smooth onward movement of flowing water

## Comprehension Questions

1. In what ways have Landsat satellites performed even better than they were supposed to?

2. What was the purpose of the tape recorders aboard the Landsats? How did Landsats operate differently without them?

3. Why was it necessary to change the orbit of Landsat 1?

4. What was the Landsats' new schedule?

5. Why do you think it was necessary for Landsats 1 and 2 to follow the same route?

6. What was the purpose of the Seasat A satellite?

7. Give an example to show that the Seasat A instruments were supposed to be very accurate.

8. How could information from the Seasat be used?

9. How much time do you think has passed between the Landsat lecture and this reading? From what sources can you find out about future changes?

10. Do you think the results from Landsats are worth all the work and expense?

11. This supplementary reading contains a numbered listing similar to that in the lecture. Practice your skills by outlining the reading.

    I. Introduction: Unusual length of operation has caused some changes in the two satellites' performance.

       A. The first change

    _____

    _____

B.  The second change

_____

_____

_____

_____

_____

C.  The third change

_____

_____

_____

_____

_____

II.  Additional satellites

A.  _____

B.  _____

C.  _____
D.  Seasat: Uses

    1.  _____

    2.  _____

    3.  _____

    4.  _____

III. The future of the Landsat system

_____

_____

_____

_____

# LISTENING TEST: COMMUNICATIONS SATELLITES

## Incomplete Outline

I. Introduction

    A. Russia sent the first satellite into space in _____ .

    B. _____ man-made objects have been launched into

        space; _____ are still in space.

    C. The smallest objects weigh _____ ;

        the largest ones weigh _____ .

II. One very useful kind of working satellite is the communica-

    tions satellite. Communication means _____ .

III. How are communications satellites used?

    A. The first use is to _____ .

    B. Another use is to _____ .

C.  The third use is to _____.

      1.  Examples

          a.  International Olympic Games
          b.
          c.

IV.  Who owns satellites?

    A.  Russia
    B.  The United States

    C.  _____

    D.  _____
    E.  Canada

    F.  _____

    G.  _____

V.  What can a country that doesn't have a communications satellite do?

    A.  It can buy information from a private company called

    _____.

    B.  More than _____ countries are members of this company.

## True-False Questions

| | |
|---|---|
| 1. | 6. |
| 2. | 7. |
| 3. | 8. |
| 4. | 9. |
| 5. | 10. |

# UNIT 2

# SoLAR ENERGy:
# An ENERGy
# AlTERNATiVE

## INTRODUCTION TO THE LECTURE

### Topic: How Solar Heating of Buildings Works

The most widely used types of energy in the United States up to the present have been natural gas, oil, and coal; all three are fuels that exist in limited quantities in the earth. New energy sources which do not depend as much on the earth's resources are nuclear power and solar energy. This lecture explores the possibilities of using energy from the sun, solar energy.

### Thesis: Solar Energy May Solve the Energy Problems of the Future

Because the supply of oil is very limited, we need to develop new sources of energy as quickly as possible. Solar energy may be a good solution to our energy needs.

### Organizational Strategy: Generalizations and Supporting Examples and Steps in a Process

First the lecturer lists various sources of energy, describing their advantages and disadvantages. Then she explains the process for heating buildings with solar energy.

**Figure 3.** Solar-heated three-bedroom house.

Photograph by Patricia Wilcox Peterson.

     I. Introduction: The need for new energy sources
    II. Other sources of energy available to us
   III. The solar heating of buildings

## BASIC SENTENCES

**Directions:** *Together the basic sentences provide a short summary of the main ideas in the lecture. Read and study these sentences before you listen to the lecture for the first time.*

1. In the United States today we are using more and more oil every day, and the future supply is very limited.

2. There are three other sources of energy available to us: coal, nuclear energy, and solar energy.

**Figure 4.** Solar-heated apartment building.

**Figure 5.** Solar-heated condominiums.

Photographs by Patricia Wilcox Peterson.

**Figure 6.** Diagram of the hot-air solar heating system.

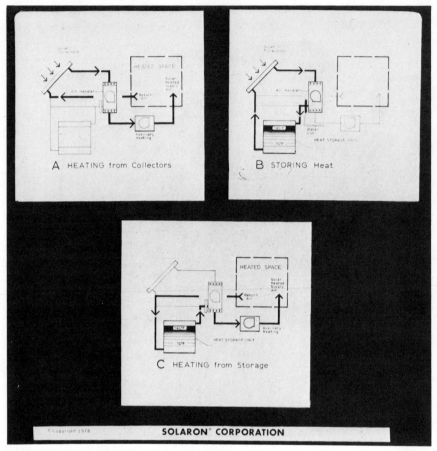

Photograph courtesy of Solaron Corporation, Denver, Colorado.

3. The federal government is spending millions of dollars to find ways to convert, or change, sunshine into economical energy.

4. There is no need to purchase fuel to operate a solar heating system because sunshine is free to everyone.

5. Once the system is installed, or put in, little or no maintenance is necessary.

6. The second advantage of solar heat is that it can be used almost anywhere.

7. In practice, the major expense involved in a solar heating system is the purchase cost of all the parts of the system and the cost of their installation.

8. An additional expense is the cost of an alternate heating system.

9. There are two main types of solar heating systems: hot-air and hot-liquid systems.
10. The parts of each system are: a collector, a storage unit, a thermostat, and an auxiliary heating unit.
11. New designs and mass production may lower the cost of solar heating systems in a few years.


## ADDITIONAL VOCABULARY

**Directions:** *Below are some additional words that may be new to you. Look up the ones you don't know before listening to the lecture.*

| | | |
|---|---|---|
| estimate | mine | uranium |
| inadequate | switched on | |

### Listening Cues: Vocabulary of Numerical Order

| | | |
|---|---|---|
| first | third | then |
| second | | |

**Exercise One: Classification**

Below is a list of information. Organize the list into outline form.

A storage unit

Hot-air systems

A collector

An auxiliary heating unit

Hot-liquid systems

A thermostat

I. Main types of solar heating systems

A. _____

B. _____

II. Parts of each system

A. _____

B. _____

C. _____

D. _____

Solar comes from the Latin word *sol*, meaning sun.

There are problems with mining it.

Production of new nuclear power plants has slowed down because of public concern over their safety.

There are problems with developing a way to burn it without polluting the air.

The amount of solar energy falling on the continental United States is 700 times our total consumption.

There are problems with transporting it.

The government once thought we would be getting 20% of our electric-

I. Other sources of energy available to us

A. Coal

1. _____

_____

2. _____

_____

3. _____

_____

Name: _____  Date: _____  **33**

ity from nuclear energy by the 1970s, but it produces only about 12% as of 1979.

B. Nuclear energy

1. _____

_____

2. _____

_____

C. Solar energy

1. _____

_____

2. _____

_____

## Exercise Two: Classification

In order to classify ideas together correctly, you need to know which ideas are related and which are not. In the following exercise, three words or terms in each line are related and one is not. Decide what the related words have in common. Circle the one word that is not related to the others.

| | | | |
|---|---|---|---|
| 1. endless | (inadequate) | unlimited | infinite |
| 2. auxiliary | practical | supplementary | alternate |
| 3. obvious | current | modern | present |
| 4. fuel | power | consumption | energy |
| 5. install | produce | develop | invent |
| 6. coal | oil | uranium | furnace |
| 7. expense | cost | finance charge | source |
| 8. solar | maintenance | sunshine | sol |
| 9. run out | estimate | guess | figure |

## Exercise Three: Recognizing Main Topics and Subtopics

Below is a list of sentences in random order about solar energy. First, read all the sentences. Look for the best way they might be organized into an outline. Then copy each sentence on the appropriate lines in the blank outline.

The second advantage is that it can be used almost anywhere.

This is a one-time cost that can be financed over many years.

What are the advantages of solar heating for buildings?

The major disadvantage of a solar heating system is the cost of the parts of the system and the cost of their installation.

The first is that it is cheaper to operate than gas or oil.

The approximate cost to buy and install a solar system in a three-bedroom house is $7,000 to $12,000.

I. _____

    A. _____

    B. _____

II. _____

    A. _____

    B. _____

## Exercise Four: Main Ideas and Supporting Details

Practice finding main ideas and supporting ideas. Notice the organization of the following material from the lecture. Find and write the main idea and supporting ideas in the outlines below.

Many experts believe that we must turn to the sun to solve our energy needs. Solar energy is clean and unlimited. It is estimated that the amount of solar energy falling on the continental United States is 700 times our total energy consumption. By the year 2000, solar technology could be supplying about 25 percent of the United States' energy needs.

Name: _____  Date: _____  **35**

I. _____ (main idea)

_____

A. _____ (supporting idea)

_____

B. _____ (supporting idea)

_____

C. _____ (supporting idea)

_____

The major expense involved in a solar heating system is the purchase cost of all the parts of the system and the cost of their installation. The approximate cost to buy and put a solar heating system into a three-bedroom house at the present is $7,000 to $12,000. This is a one-time cost that can be financed over many years. This finance charge may be more expensive than heating with oil at the present prices.

I. _____ (main idea)

_____

A. _____ (supporting idea)

_____

B. _____ (supporting idea)

_____

C. _____ (supporting idea)

_____

# INCOMPLETE OUTLINE

**Directions:** *Read the outline before you listen to the lecture for the first time, so you will know what kinds of things you need to listen for. While you are listening, find the missing dates and phrases to complete the outline. Mark your paper while you listen. You have been given the answers to part III. C-2 so you can look at the diagram as you listen.*

I. Introduction: The need for new energy sources

    A. For the last _____ years, oil has been an inexpensive source of energy.

    B. Oil may be a major source of energy for only _____ more years.

II. Other sources of energy available to us

    A. Coal

        1. Advantage: We have a lot.
        2. Disadvantages: There may be problems with

        _____ it, _____ it, and developing a way to _____ it without polluting the air.

    B. Nuclear energy

        1. Advantage: We have enough uranium for a long time.

        2. Disadvantages: Public concern over the _____ of nuclear energy. The government once thought we

        would be getting _____% of our electricity

        from nuclear energy by the _____, but nuclear

        energy produced only about _____% as of 1979.

C. Solar energy (from Latin *sol*, meaning _____)

    1. Advantages

        a. It is clean and unlimited.

        b. The amount falling on the U.S. is _____ times our total energy consumption.

        c. By 2000, it could supply _____% of U.S. energy needs.

    2. Disadvantage: The cost of converting sunshine to solar energy is high.

III. The solar heating of buildings

    A. Advantages

        1. It is cheaper than gas or oil.

            a. There is no need to purchase _____ .

            b. Little or no _____ is necessary.

        2. It can be used almost anywhere.

    B. Disadvantages

        1. Purchase cost

            a. The cost for a three-bedroom house is

            $_____ .

            b. This is a _____ cost that can be financed over many years.

        2. Additional cost—alternative heating system

            a. Solar systems can't always provide _____% of your heat.

            b. You must have a _____ , _____ , or _____ furnace.

C.  How solar heating works (hot-air and hot-liquid)

   1. Parts

       a. _____

       b. _____

       c. _____

       d. _____

   2. Hot-air system

       a. The collector catches _the sun's rays_.

       b. The sun heats _the panels_.

       c. The panels heat _the air inside_.
       d. On sunny days when heat is needed, hot air flows to

          the thermostat, into the _the building_,
          and back to the collector.
       e. On sunny days when heat is not needed, hot
          air flows to the thermostat, then into

          _the storage unit_.
       f. At night, the thermostat sends air from the

          _storage unit_ into the building.

   3. Hot-liquid system

       a. It contains _____ instead of air.

       b. The storage unit is _____ .

# WORD RECOGNITION EXERCISE

**Directions:** *Fill the blanks in each word family by finding the missing parts of speech in your dictionary. Divide each word into syllables and mark the syllable that takes primary stress, as shown.*

*Word Families*

| Noun | Verb | Adjective | Adverb |
|------|------|-----------|--------|
| 1. _____ | _____ | pro duc′ tive | _____ |
| 2. _____ | de scribé | _____ | _____ |
| 3. _____ | _____ | es′ ti ma ted | XXXXXXX |
| 4. _____ | con vert′ | _____ | XXXXXXX |
| 5. _____ | _____ | _____ | ec o nom′ i cal ly |
| 6. _____ | in stall′ | XXXXXXX | XXXXXXX |
| 7. _____ | _____ | _____ | al′ ter nate ly |
| 8. _____ | _____ | stored | XXXXXXX |
| 9. _____ | _____ | con tained′ | XXXXXXX |
| 10. _____ | _____ | _____ | ba′ si cal ly |
| 11. _____ | _____ | prac′ ti cal | _____ |
| 12. prof′ it | _____ | _____ | _____ |
| 13. _____ | _____ | min′ er al | XXXXXXX |
| 14. _____ | XXXXXXX | sys tem at′ ic | _____ |

40

# TRUE-FALSE EXERCISE

**Directions:** *Read these sentences before you listen to the lecture for the second time. While you are listening, decide whether each item is true or false. Mark your paper with a T for true or an F for false while you listen.*

_____ 1. Burning coal causes pollution.

_____ 2. Many more new nuclear power plants are being built every year.

_____ 3. Solar heating systems are cheaper to operate than gas or oil systems.

_____ 4. Solar systems provide 100% of your heat.

_____ 5. Solar heat cannot be used in colder areas of the world.

_____ 6. In a collector, the sun heats the black panels, which heat the air inside.

_____ 7. The auxiliary heating unit is a container of small, round rocks.

_____ 8. On cloudy days, hot air from the collector flows to the thermostat, through the building's heating system, and out into the house.

_____ 9. Hot-liquid systems operate in basically the same way as hot-air systems except that they contain liquid instead of air.

_____ 10. You can buy a solar heating system in most large stores.

# TOPICS FOR DISCUSSION AND WRITING

1. Many other products besides fuel can be made from oil. Some examples are plastics, dyes, fertilizers, cosmetics, and synthetic fibers such as polyester. Tell or write about some possible problems, besides those that are energy-related, that may arise when the supply of oil runs out.

2. Even countries (such as Saudi Arabia) that are rich in oil are concerned about what may happen when there is no more oil left. For this reason, Saudi Arabia has given millions of dollars to help support solar energy research in the United States. What characteristics does Saudi Arabia have that would make it a good location for solar energy stations?

3. Discuss some methods of fuel conservation that would help the world's supply of oil last longer.

4. Look at the diagram of the solar heating system in this unit. Present an oral description or write about the process, telling how solar heating works

   a. on sunny days when heat is needed
   b. on sunny days when heat is not needed
   c. on cloudy days or at night when heat is needed

5. Why do you think the collector panels must cover such a large area of the roof? Will houses need to be designed in new ways to accommodate solar collectors?

6. Do you think the houses in the pictures accompanying the lecture are attractive, or do the collectors spoil the appearance of the houses? What do you think houses of the future will look like?

7. Some people think the thermostat may be the most important part of a solar heating system. Why would this be true?

## MULTIPLE CHOICE EXERCISE

**Directions:** *Choose the one answer that best completes each sentence. Write the letter of the correct answer in the blank.*

_____ 1. Oil may not be a major source of energy after only _____ more years.
   a. 50
   b. 75
   c. 25
   d. none of the above

_____ 2. Which is *not* a problem related to coal?
   a. mining it
   b. purchasing it
   c. transporting it
   d. developing a way to burn it without polluting the air

_____ 3. Which is a problem related to nuclear energy?
   a. lack of uranium to fuel nuclear power plants
   b. converting nuclear energy to electricity
   c. the safety of nuclear energy
   d. none of the above

_____ 4. Which is *not* true about solar energy?
   a. It is clean.
   b. It is unlimited.
   c. It is cheaper than gas or oil.
   d. It can always provide enough heat for your house.

_____ 5. Solar heating is most practical in areas of the United States where
   a. there is a lot of winter sunshine.
   b. heat is necessary.
   c. fuel is expensive.
   d. all of the above.

_____ 6. The part of the solar heating system which directs the air into the house or into the storage unit is
   a. the collector.
   b. the thermostat.
   c. the auxiliary heating unit.
   d. the panels.

_____ 7. What contains metal panels coated with black paint to absorb the heat?
   a. thermostat
   b. storage unit
   c. auxiliary heating unit
   d. collector

_____ 8. On sunny days when heat is needed, the thermostat
   a. sends the hot air to a storage unit.
   b. sends the air directly into the building's heating system.
   c. sends the air through an auxiliary heating unit and then throughout the building.
   d. sends the air directly back to the collector.

_____ 9. On cloudy days or at night the thermostat takes air from the storage unit and then
   a. sends the hot air to a storage unit.

Name: _____    Date: _____    **43**

b. sends the air directly into the building's heating system.
c. sends the air through an auxiliary heating unit and then through-out the building.
d. sends the air directly back to the collector.


_____ 10. Which of the following ideas is implied but not stated in the lecture?
a. We have not been careful about our use of energy in the past.
b. Some people think that nuclear energy is not safe.
c. The only use of solar energy is for heating buildings.
d. The federal government is not encouraging the development of solar energy.


## FINAL LISTENING ASSIGNMENT: NOTE-TAKING

**Directions:**  *Read these questions before you listen to the lecture for the third time. While you are listening, write the answers.*

1. What are the problems with coal, oil, and nuclear energy?


2. Describe the characteristics of the areas in the United States where solar heating is most practical.


3. Using Figure 6 at the beginning of this chapter, tell how a hot-air solar heating system works.

# Energy Possibilities for the Future

Two imaginative ideas would supply people on earth with energy from space. One idea *proposes* a solar power station that would orbit the earth and send energy back by microwaves. The other proposes a power-relay satellite. The satellite would *transmit* power from a solar or nuclear power station located in an isolated place on earth to a receiving station serving a populated area on earth.

## The Orbiting Solar Power Station

This idea calls for a very large solar collector in orbit around the earth. The one shown in Figure 7 would be 7 miles or 12 kilometers long. The design in Figure 8 calls for the use of *solar cells* to collect electricity. The electricity would be sent to earth by microwaves.

**Figure 7.** Orbiting solar collector.

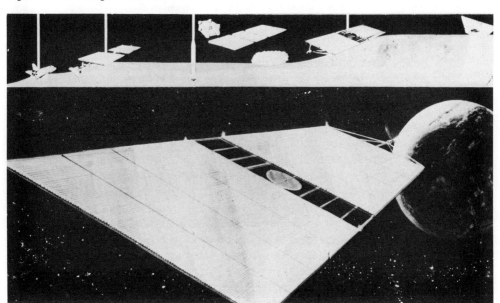

Photograph courtesy of National Aeronautics and Space Administration.

**Figure 8.** Solar power system.

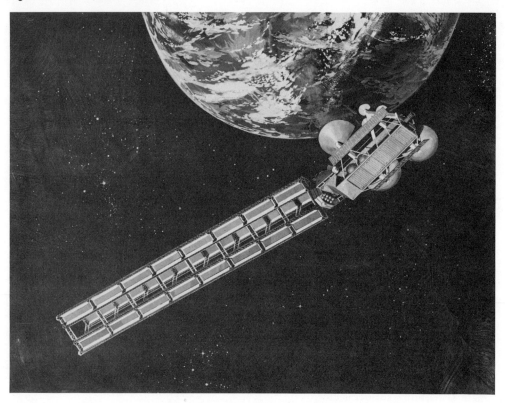

Photograph courtesy of National Aeronautics and Space Administration.

The microwaves would be collected by a very large receiving *antenna* and converted back to electricity.

An orbiting solar power station has several advantages. There are no clouds to block the sunlight from a solar receiver high in space. The sun is always shining in space; there are no day-and-night cycles. One orbiting station of 15 million *kilowatts* could supply all the electric needs of a city the size of New York City in the year 2000.

There are several disadvantages to an orbiting solar power system. First, the extremely large solar collector would have to be carried into space piece by piece in rockets and then put together in space by astronauts. This would be very expensive and difficult; some new technological advances will be necessary before this can be done. Second, the solar cells that will be used to collect the solar energy are very expensive at present. Finally, further experiments will be necessary to determine whether it will be possible or even safe to send the electricity back to earth by microwaves. There are still some important problems to be solved, but the designers of outer-space solar power stations think they can be ready for use within twenty years.

## The Power-Relay Satellite

This plan calls for a large solar or nuclear power station to operate in an isolated place on earth, perhaps in the desert. A power-relay satellite would be placed in orbit to relay the energy to cities in much the same way that a communications satellite relays TV and telephone calls now. The largest and heaviest parts of the system would stay on the ground; this would reduce the cost and difficulty. Because this idea also calls for relaying the energy by microwave, much more experimentation needs to be done before this idea can become a reality.

---

**propose** suggest

**transmit** send

**solar cell** a device, about the size of a large button, made of silicon crystal. As light strikes the cell, it causes positive and negative charges and starts an electric current flowing.

**antenna** metallic device for sending or receiving electromagnetic waves

**kilowatt** measurement of electricity